Black Manhood
on the Silent Screen

CULTURE AMERICA
Karal Ann Marling & Erika Doss,
series editors

BLACK MANHOOD
ON THE SILENT SCREEN

Gerald R. Butters, Jr.

University Press of Kansas

Published by the University Press of Kansas (Lawrence, Kansas 66049), which was
organized by the Kansas Board of Regents and is operated and funded by Emporia State
University, Fort Hays State University, Kansas State University, Pittsburg State University,
the University of Kansas, and Wichita State University

Library of Congress Cataloging-in-Publication Data

Butters, Gerald R., 1961–
  Black manhood on the silent screen / Gerald R. Butters, Jr.
    p. cm. — (Cultureamerica)
Includes bibliographical references (p.) and index.
  ISBN 0-7006-1197-5 (alk. paper)
  1. African American men in motion pictures. 2. Men in motion
pictures. 3. Silent films—United States—History and criticism.
I. Title. II. Culture America
  PN1995.9.N4 B88 2002
  791.43'6529286'08996073—dc21
                        2002001205

British Library Cataloguing in Publication Data is available.

Printed in the United States of America

10 9 8 7 6 5 4 3 2 1

The paper used in this publication meets the minimum requirements of the American
National Standard for Permanence of Paper for Printed Library Materials Z39.48-1984.

For my father,
who never forgot to tell his sons he loved them.

The myth is mystified. It is not the myth that must be destroyed; it is the mystification. It is not the hero who must be belittled; it is the struggle that must be magnified.

—Auguste Boal
Theatre of the Oppressed

CONTENTS

ACKNOWLEDGMENTS

This book has been ten years in the making. There are many people to thank for their assistance and support. First, I would like to acknowledge my three mentors. Early in my career, Gregory Black (University of Missouri–Kansas City) was a model of the historian I wanted to be. William Tuttle (University of Kansas), my graduate director, was the ideal adviser. He may not realize how much I appreciate our discussions around his kitchen table. Finally, Angel Kwolek-Folland (University of Florida) provided invaluable professional and emotional support during the production of this book.

I have been able to work out many of my ideas through teaching. Several of these educational experiences have proven to be particularly valuable. I would like to thank Margaret Wye and the graduate students at Rockhurst University, Delia Cook and her film classes at the University of Missouri–Kansas City, Dotty Hamilton and the Communication Studies Department at Avila College, and Charles Coleman and his staff at Facets Multimedia in Chicago. The opportunity to teach in each of these unique settings was a privilege.

I have been fortunate to meet some wonderful people at institutions where I did research. I would like to thank the staff of the Black Film Center at Indiana University, Rosemary Hayes and Madeline Matz of the Motion Picture, Broadcasting, and Recorded Sound Division of the Library of Congress, the staff of the Chicago Historical Society, the staff of the Art Institute of Chicago, Charles Silver and the staff at the Museum of Modern Art, the British Film Institute staff, the British Library staff, the staff at the Schomburg Center for Research in Black Culture, and the staff of the Department of Special Collections at the Charles E. Young Research Library at UCLA.

I have received invaluable financial assistance in the production of this book. I would like to thank President Rebecca Sherrick and Provost Andrew

Manion at Aurora University; the state of Kansas, which awarded me a Pearson Fellowship that allowed me to spend one glorious summer studying at the British Film Institute in London; the University of Kansas, for a Lila Atkins Creighton Scholarship for Graduate Research; and the administration at Donnelly College.

I would like to specially thank Gladstone Yearwood and the staff of the Summer Institute in Black Film Studies at the University of Central Florida. His National Endowment for the Humanities seminar, for which I was awarded a fellowship, has proven to be a landmark event in my intellectual development.

Three scholars in the field of film studies, all of whom I have enormous respect for, were significant to writing this book. I wish to thank Thomas Cripps for valuable advice he gave me early in my career; Richard Dyer, whose hospitality and encouragement were remarkable; and Mark Reid for his support and inspiration.

During my research, a number of individuals provided me with shelter, food, and comfort, and they must be acknowledged. They include William Jackson, Kelly Etter, Jeff Lodermeier, Kem Winston, and Richard Reno.

I would also like to thank friends and colleagues who have provided me with emotional support and academic feedback. They include Matthew Henry, Kimberly Brown, Joel Morton, Rusty Monhollen, Elijah Ward, Craig Prentiss, Charles Wilson, Genevieve Robinson, and Michael McDonald. A very special thanks goes to Paula Massood.

Portions of this manuscript have been presented at the following forums: St. Lawrence University in Canton, New York (at which I was a visiting scholar); the National Association for Ethnic Studies Conference in New Orleans, Louisiana; the Society for Cinema Studies National Meeting in West Palm Beach, Florida; the Mid-America American Studies Association Meeting in Minneapolis, Minnesota; the Midwest History Conference in Omaha, Nebraska; and the Conference of Literature and Film in Tallahassee, Florida.

Last but not least, I want to thank Zeinabu irene Davis, whose filmmaking awes and inspires me; Nancy Scott Jackson, my editor and heroine, who made this process a positive, enriching experience; my parents, who did not understand why it took so long, but never stopped encouraging me; and Boo, without whose love, support, and reassurance this final leg would not have been possible.

INTRODUCTION

This book examines portrayals of black masculinity in American silent film. The cinematic depiction of African-American masculinity, both gendered and given a racial hue, has a cultural history. Far from being eternally fixed in some type of historical past, the black male image has been formed and shaped by larger events in Western society (World Wars I and II) and events unique to the black experience (the Diaspora and the Great Migration). Building on the scholarship of Thomas Cripps (*Slow Fade to Black: The Negro in American Film, 1900–1942*: *Making Movies Black: The Hollywood Message Movie from World War II to the Civil Rights Era*), Mark A. Reid (*Redefining Black Film*), Jane M. Gaines (*Fire and Desire: Mixed-Race Movies in the Silent Era*), J. Ronald Green (*Straight Lick: The Cinema of Oscar Micheaux*), and Pearl Bowser and Louise Spence (*Writing Himself into History: Oscar Micheaux, His Silent Films, and His Audiences*), this book focuses on the black male identity in silent film.[1]

Black men have been the quintessential "Others" in American society. The positioning of African-American male Otherness has played out on the motion picture screen. Political and racial ideologies regarding the "place" of African-American men in American society have been incorporated into motion pictures narratives, illustrating a diversity of opinions and beliefs.

On a personal note, I first became fascinated with this topic during the mid- to late 1980s. At the time, I was teaching in a predominantly African-American Catholic junior high school and became keenly aware of the impact popular culture had on my students. Music, television, and particularly film significantly influenced their attitudes, behavior, and values. The eighties also proved to be a bizarre transitional time in popular representations of African-American men. Perhaps influenced by the burgeoning crack epidemic that tore apart black communities, African-American male images went from "comfortable" and "safe" (Bill Cosby, Michael Jackson, the De-barges) to threatening and violent (Ice T, Easy E, Dr. Dre, Ice Cube, Tupac Shakur). As gangsta rap influenced every major form of popular entertain-ment, my students were increasingly taught that African-American men were thought to be cold-blooded, nonemotional, misogynistic, homophobic "gangstas" who did not abide by anyone's rules other than their own. "Keepin' it Real" was a catch phrase for accepting only a narrow, limited def-inition of African-American masculinity. Education, work, family, and parent-ing responsibility took a backseat to the iconography of hardened black men who packed semiautomatics, sold drugs, and abused black women. These were not the African-American men I knew—the men who coached sports, financially and spiritually supported their families, and hugged their children. And then I wondered, what led to these negative images of black men that the white community accepted far too easily? What caused this sudden explo-sion of violent images? And what was the history of African-American male imagery on the screen? I felt it was important to start at the beginning. As I researched for the next ten years, I became dramatically aware that African-American men had used the motion picture as a tool to combat negative black male imagery on the screen that the dominant white mainstream media sold as entertainment. I realized that African-American men did not suddenly begin making films in the blaxploitation era of the early 1970s but that African-American film had a rich, full history. I also learned that the defense and redefinition of black manhood was the predominant theme in such films. This was important history; this was a story that needed to be told.

This project demonstrates the difference between cinematic myth and his-torical reality and the myth of the Euro-American–controlled cinematic por-trayal of black men and the actual black male experience. Expanding the discussion of race and representation beyond the debate about "good" and "bad" imagery, this book explores the construction of masculine identity and the use of race as device in the context of Western popular culture. It is my con-tention that for the last century both Euro-American and black men have de-fined their own sense of manhood through the cinematic medium. The era of American silent film, from 1896 through 1931, clearly illustrated that larger is-sues of racial and gender identification were prominent themes on the screen.[2]

The literature on portrayals of African Americans in film has been produced in three major waves. The first comprehensive study of the history of African-Americans on the screen was Peter Noble's *The Negro in Films* (1948). The volume remained the seminal work on the subject until the 1970s. The still from Mervyn Le Roy's film *They Won't Forget* (1937) on the dust jacket of *The*

Negro in Films was a telling thesis statement. Actor Clinton Rosemond looks on in fear as white hands viciously tug on his clothing. Noble wrote: "Cinema audiences regard the coloured man as a clown, a buffoon, an idiot, and a superstitious fool; and their feeling of contempt for him is a result of the manner in which he is invariably portrayed on the screen. The ordinary filmgoer has his whole outlook formulated by the film, politically, socially, intellectually."[3]

Noble argued that the popular screen image of African Americans caused sociological damage to both black and white audiences. He believed this was particularly damaging because of the international popularity of American motion pictures. Noble set a pattern for two generations of film scholars; in his chapter on the African-American presence in silent film he focused exclusively on mainstream Hollywood material.[4]

Throughout the 1940s and 1950s, African-American film critics and historians (few in number) focused their attention on contemporary cinematic portrayals of African Americans. Albert Johnson's "Beige, Brown or Black," which appeared in *Film Quarterly* in the fall of 1959, was a landmark piece. Johnson focused his article on mainstream films of the 1950s. One of his basic premises was critical for future scholarship—he argued that the African-American experience was not unvaried, static, or universal. Instead, the African-American experience was "beige, brown, or black," and if Hollywood filmmakers were going to transfer reality into celluloid then this meant breaking down age-old stereotypes. Johnson argued that African Americans were diversified by background, color, and regional dialect and that this had to be displayed on the screen if the "mysteriousness" of black Americans was to be eradicated by the short-sighted American public.[5]

During the second wave of scholarship in the 1970s and 1980s, the two most prominent scholars of the depiction of African Americans in film were Thomas Cripps and Donald Bogle. Cripps's *Slow Fade to Black: The Negro in American Film, 1900–1942* was the seminal work on African Americans in silent films for years. Cripps illustrated the complex relationship between economics, racial ideology, popular entertainment, and political activity. There were several critical ways in which *Slow Fade to Black* was "lacking," though, and I will address these issues.

Cripps titled his first chapter "The Unformed Image: The Afro-American in Early American Movies." I strongly disagree with the basic premise underlying this title. The early silent era (1896–1905) was one of the most virulently racist periods in American filmmaking. As I will illustrate, African-American cinematic depictions were anything but unformed—they were rabid racist attacks on black Americans—particularly black men. Cripps argued that "they [African Americans] portrayed a range of roles far more varied than American society would grant them in everyday life."[6] This was seldom the case. Instead, these "ruptures" in cinematic depictions of African Americans illustrated that reality was catching up with the fictional racist narratives woven by white American filmmakers that often espoused the worst of southern fears.[7] Charles Musser, in *Before the Nickelodeon*, agrees with my premise. He argues that "it is difficult to agree with claims that the first ten years of American cinema offered a kind of primitive, nonracist innocence."[8]

Cripps's second chapter, on *The Birth of a Nation*, is a breathtaking summary of the political and artistic maneuverings regarding the film but lacks a cohesive, descriptive film analysis. Contemporary scholars are well aware of the racist content of the film but have begun only recently to explore how director D. W. Griffith deliberately constructed such a model.[9]

More than any other scholar working in the 1970s, Cripps devoted a great deal of time and attention to African-American independent filmmaking in the silent era. Since Cripps's pioneering work in the field, a number of films by and about people of color have been unearthed and discovered in historical and archival circles. This body of work, which includes Oscar Micheaux's *Within Our Gates* (1919) and *Symbol of the Unconquered* (1920), has raised new questions regarding African-American visual production. Black filmmakers have perceived the world through the cinematic lens in ways that were both similar to yet different from the dominant culture, and this forces a reevaluation in interpretation.[10]

Donald Bogle, in *Toms, Coons, Mulattoes, Mammies, and Bucks* (1973), also contributed an important organizational tool to representations of African Americans in American film. Using five common racial stereotypes, he discussed the silent origins of each and demonstrated how it was transformed yet continued through the sound era.[11]

Other key works of the 1970s include James P. Murray's *To Find an Image: Black Films from Uncle Tom to Super Fly* (1973), Jim Pines's *Blacks in Film: A Survey of Racial Themes and Images in the American Film* (1975), and James Nesteby's *Black Images in American Films, 1896–1954* (1982).[12]

The last decade of the twentieth century has witnessed an outpouring of important scholarly works on African-American filmmaking and African-American imagery in motion pictures. In 1993 Manthia Diawara edited *Black American Cinema*, a compilation of essays that dealt with both black aesthetics and black spectatorship. J. Ronald Green's impressive *Straight Lick: The Cinema of Oscar Micheaux* (2000) discusses the filmmaker's concern for African-American uplift in his artistic productions. Pearl Bowser and

Louise Spence's *Writing Himself into History: Oscar Micheaux, His Silent Films, and His Audience* (2000) discusses the auteur's biographical legend and firmly places his work within his cultural and racial milieu. Jane M. Gaines's *Fire and Desire: Mixed-Race Movies in the Silent Era* (2001) is an important study of film theory and African-American filmmaking. Green, Bowser, Spence, and Gaines are prominent scholars currently working in the field, and their recent contributions have clearly demonstrated the real need for further exploration and development in African-American film theory and history.

This book is unique in that it takes contemporary and original film theory, applies it to a larger body of Euro-American and African-American–produced films in the silent era, and relates the meaning of these films to larger political, social, and intellectual events in American society. Although most of the current literature in the field stresses race, this work will examine the intersection of race and gender in African-American representation in silent film. As Mark Reid has argued, traditional theoretical approaches to film studies (such as Marxist, feminist, or psychoanalytic) cannot be simply applied to African-American film.[13] What has remained lacking is a comprehensive study of the African-American cinematic presence in silent film, one that incorporates both white- and black-produced films and goes beyond studies of positive and negative imagery.

The primary source material used in this book is also unique. The vast majority of literature written on the portrayal of African Americans in film focuses on mainstream, white-produced Hollywood films. This literature also largely ignores the silent era. I will focus exclusively on portrayals of African Americans in the silent era and will concentrate on films that have been largely ignored by most contemporary film scholars—films produced and directed by African Americans and white independent film productions of all-black features. These are also known as "race movies." These films have been largely ignored because the vast majority of them no longer exist. Most American silent films have aged beyond repair or have been destroyed. This is particularly true of race movies because they were considered culturally insignificant. I have reconstructed the narratives of these films through ten years of research and investigation.[14] There are three primary repositories of African-American films and archival source material related to African-American film production in the United States: the George P. Johnson Collection at the University of California in Los Angeles, the Motion Picture, Broadcasting, and Recorded Sound Division of the Library of Congress, and the Black Film Archives at

Indiana University in Bloomington, Indiana. George P. Johnson was one of the earliest black film producers. From the 1910s through the 1960s he collected a wide range of materials on African-American entertainment. These materials include studio documents, personal correspondence, press releases, and an enormous clipping file. Unfortunately, many of the newspaper clippings do not supply the date or the newspaper's name, making research cumbersome. The Motion Picture, Broadcasting, and Recorded Sound Division of the Library of Congress has one of the largest collections of early silent films (1896–1907) with African-American portrayals. The Library of Congress also has films from a number of white independent companies of the 1910s and mainstream Hollywood releases of the 1910s and 1920s. The Black Film Archives in Bloomington has a number of early silent all-black releases and primary source documentation on the Norman Film Manufacturing Company, one of the most prolific white independent producers of all-black features.

One of the most important sources for material on black cinematic self-representation are black newspapers from the 1910s and 1920s. Since these newspapers did not print motion picture reviews, I spent hundreds of hours combing through individual issues of important black newspapers such as the *Chicago Defender.* I used archives at the Library of Congress, the Schomburg Center for Research in Black Culture in New York City, the Chicago Historical Society, and the Kansas State Historical Society in Topeka, Kansas, to find these black newspapers. I am also indebted to Henry T. Sampson, whose *Blacks in Black and White* provided an invaluable compendium of source materials related to all-black and independent race features.[15]

Once the material was collected it was necessary to distinguish between mainstream Hollywood releases, racially collaborative independent productions, and black independent productions. Separate files were made for material on each film and each film company. The economic vulnerability of black and white independent film companies in the silent era meant that most companies only had one or two films to their credit.

It was then necessary to figure out what these films "meant." It is difficult for contemporary viewers not to be shocked by the overt racism contained in many of the shorts produced by all-white sources in the early silent era (1896–1905). Definite patterns and themes in white representation of African Americans appeared. The majority of cinematic representations of African Americans were of African-American men, who were targets for the most overtly racist activities, including stereotyped behavior, ridicule, violence, and lynching.

In 1912 William Foster became the first African American to produce and direct a film.[16] But the major catalyst for African-American film production was D. W. Griffith's notorious *The Birth of a Nation* (1915). From 1915 through the early 1920s, African-American men directed over one hundred films. The primary theme in most of these films was a defining (or redefining) of African-American manhood.

Historian Joel Williamson, in *The Crucible of Race,* helped me understand racial patterns of the era. Williamson identifies three dominant mentalities among white southerners from 1830 to 1980. He argues that at the crux of these mentalities was a "judgment" regarding the future of African Americans in the United States. The Liberal view, strongest in the decade of the 1880s, argued that "the capacity of negroes to absorb white culture . . . had not yet been fully tested."[17] Although clearly based on the ideology of Anglo-Saxon superiority, this white southern minority view was optimistic toward black absorption of white ideals. The Conservative mentality was based on African-American inferiority. It was centered on "defining and fixing his [African Americans] place in American society."[18] Williamson argued that this ideology was the dominant worldview of white southerners. The Radical view was the most pessimistic regarding the future of African Americans in American society. While the Conservatives attempted to fix African Americans' place in southern society, Radicals argued that they had no place and that their demise was imminent. A strong force from 1889 to 1915, Radicals argued that African Americans were bestial, savage, and doomed.[19] As Clyde Taylor has argued, "One contribution of Williamson's analysis is the restoration of variety, dynamism, and historical mobility to racialist representations."[20]

Williamson provided a basic framework of the concentric circles of turn-of-the-century white racism but also probed the links between race, gender, and violence. The beginnings of motion picture production in the United States coincided with a sharp increase in lynching, particularly in the South. The working class was the primary audience for early short silent films. Williamson argues that working-class white men were trapped by economic depression and propelled by psychosexual tensions. White men not only lynched and tortured African-American men in real life but they lived out these fantasies through violent cinematic attacks on black men.[21]

The major theme in films produced and directed by African Americans, spurred on by the phenomenal success of *The Birth of a Nation,* was a defense of black manhood. This was part of a larger organizational impulse within the African-American community that was attempting to combat Jim Crow, lynching, disenfranchisement, and a multitude of legal and social abuses. Motion pictures were a tool that African-American men used for uplift, instruction, and moral indoctrination.

I will combine film theory, American history, and film history and will demonstrate that both Euro-American and African-American men used motion pictures as gendering and racializing devices in the era of silent films (1896–1931) as a way to construct their own identity and collective identities of nationhood, racial group, and "maleness."

Chapter 1 summarizes race relations at the turn of the twentieth century and demonstrates the heightened level of white male anxiety during the era. It also discusses how popular entertainment of the era propagandized the politics of difference, particularly through the theatrical and cinematic use of blackface. Chapter 2 uses contemporary film theory to examine the depictions of African Americans in major studio productions from 1896 to 1915. Chapter 3 explores ruptures in African-American male presentation on the screen, particularly when real life contradicted white studio-produced typology of African-American male characters. Issues of black male sexuality on film will be addressed as well as the development of the Uncle Tom/loyal slave type. Chapter 4 focuses on D. W. Griffith's *The Birth of a Nation*. The film was a milestone in the history of cinema and in the history of African-American portrayals on the screen. The film was one of the major catalysts to African-American production of motion pictures. Chapter 4 discusses the thematics and development of black independent silent cinema and contrasts black male self-representation with that of Euro-American imagery. This chapter deals with films that have been ignored by most contemporary film scholars. Chapter 5 discusses the filmmaking of Oscar Micheaux, the most prolific and controversial of all silent African-American directors. A reinterpretation of Micheaux's work pays tribute to the filmmaker's daring ability to develop thought-provoking entertainment. Chapter 6 focuses on Micheaux's most infamous film, *Within Our Gates*. Released shortly after the devastating Chicago race riots of 1919, the film exposed the range of Euro-American abuses toward African Americans. Widely censored and highly influential, *Within Our Gates* was a forgotten part of African-American screen history until the film's rediscovery in the 1990s. Chapter 7 examines mainstream Hollywood studio, racially collaborative, and African-American depictions of black masculinity in the late silent era (1915–1931). This chapter discusses the groundbreaking role that sound played in black male representation. Initially devastating to African-American cinematic self-representation, sound eventually gave African-American actors a tool to redefine their characterization and to encourage their abilities.

1

RACIALIZED MASCULINITY
AND THE POLITICS OF DIFFERENCE

In 1896 two events dramatically affected the role and place of the African American in American society: first, the Supreme Court decision in *Plessy v. Ferguson* and, second, the first public screening and popularization of the motion picture. Both events projected the position of the African American as one of inferiority and degradation, and constitutional decision-making relegated the African American to a position of judicial separation through legal segregation. African-American men were stripped of their legal rights, and the new entertainment form of motion pictures portrayed them as subhuman.[1] This chapter examines the structure of racism and its dissemination through popular culture at the turn of the twentieth century and African-American organizational attempts to combat this negative imagery and inspire racial self-dignity. The portrayal of African-American men on the screen was not created in a vacuum. Larger cultural issues of race, gender, and self-definition played influential roles in this view of African-American men.

The case of *Plessy v. Ferguson* was a watershed in the history of American society. By upholding a Louisiana statute that required "separate but equal" facilities for white and African-American passengers in public transportation, the U.S. Supreme Court authorized legalized segregation in all aspects of American life. For the next forty years, southern states (and quite frequently midwestern and northern states) segregated restaurants, prisons, rest rooms, schools, streetcars, hotels, beaches, recreation centers, swimming pools, and drinking fountains.[2] In the *Plessy* decision, the Court also constitutionally protected the segregation of public schools. Through the passage of municipal segregation ordinances and the use of restrictive covenants, African Americans often were forced to live in sections of town characterized by substandard housing and inadequate services and where a brutal or negligent police force reigned.[3]

1

A persistent movement to disenfranchise African-American men occurred in the same years that Jim Crow enveloped the South. Beginning in Mississippi in 1890 and culminating in Oklahoma in 1910, the constitutional right to vote was stripped away by Democratic politicians, ready to exclude the Republican Party from any influence in their region.[4]

The late nineteenth and early twentieth centuries also witnessed some of the worst racial violence in U.S. history. Wilmington, North Carolina (1898), Statesboro, Georgia (1904), Atlanta (1906), Brownsville, Texas (1906), and Springfield, Illinois (1908), all experienced brutal race riots.[5]

Lynching, a vigilante form of white community punishment and control over African Americans, increased exponentially during the late nineteenth and early twentieth centuries. Between 1900 and 1914 more than 1,100 African-American men were lynched.[6] This barbaric form of torture was reserved almost exclusively for African-American men. The ferocity of these lynchings and the almost exclusive gendered and racialized quality of them (African-American men were the primary victims, castration was common, white men were generally the lynchers) demonstrated a communal reminder of white male dominance in the South.[7]

Race riots, lynchings, disenfranchisement, Jim Crow segregation—all represented civil, social, moral, judicial, and political assaults upon African-American men. What were the justifications for this racial brutality? What were the motivations and rationales for white supremacy?

White supremacy is the theory that the white race is biologically and intellectually superior to the darker-skinned races of the world. Populism, a political movement of rural America in the late nineteenth century, was a threat to the dogma of white supremacy. As C. Vann Woodward explained in *Tom Watson*, "The Populist program called for a united front between Negro and white farmers. . . . this bold program called for a reversal of deeply rooted racial prejudices and firmly fixed traditions."[8] Southern landowners, who controlled the political apparatus of the region through the Democratic Party, feared a combined electorate of poor white and black male voters. Populism called for an end to "race hatred, political proscription, lynch law and tension" and pleaded for tolerance and racial cooperation.[9] Conservative Democrats cried, "White Supremacy," and attempted to have African-American men disenfranchised when their power base was threatened. There was a ferocious attack on black men in the late nineteenth century. As George Frederickson argued, "The Negro became the scapegoat for the political and economic tensions of the period."[10]

Thus, "Southern Negrophobia" permeated the region and eventually enveloped the rest of the nation. Certainly, the South did not have a monopoly on racism toward African Americans. But the popularization of stereotypical portrayals of African Americans was widely influenced by southern artists, authors, and businessmen.[11] According to Thomas Gossett, the North made little attempt to challenge the extreme racism of the early-twentieth-century South. The dominant southern ideology of black inferiority became the popular national perception.[12]

In *The Crucible of Race*, Joel Williamson argues that in the late 1880s and through the 1890s, white men lost a sense of power in what they deemed a new and frightening way. They were seemingly powerless in the economic depression of the 1890s when outside forces seemed to control their financial destinies. African-American men were directly competing with them for jobs. Southern white men, therefore, could not adequately fill the role of breadwinner, a dominant masculine role in Victorian society. They began to emphasize their role as protector, as defender of white womanhood. Williamson argues, "Lynching and rioting, total disenfranchisement, and blatant segregation formed satisfying displays of power in one area of their lives when they could no longer display power in another."[13]

Southern white men were aided by scientific, scholarly, and popular tracts that attempted to prove that the African American was innately inferior to the white man. Many of these tracts were based on ideas of social Darwinism that placed African Americans at the primitive end of the scale of evolution.

Political and scholarly defenses of racism were not relegated to the American intelligentsia. The consideration of the "Negro question," or more frequently the "Negro problem," was a recurring theme in articles in popular publications of the day. Magazines and newspapers attempted to "understand," if not justify, vigilante violence against African Americans. In the *North American Review,* Marion L. Dawson explained, "It is unnecessary to shock the sensibilities of the public by calling attention to the repulsive details of those crimes [of which a young lynching victim is guilty]. They have always been, however, of a nature so brutal and so savage that no pen can describe and no imagination picture them."[14]

The African-American community did not silently submit to this all-out assault. African-American leaders who had emerged in academia, churches, and in political life struggled to figure out what to do against the tidal wave of intolerance and racism. As southern racial Radicalism and social Darwinism castigated both their race and their manhood, African-American male leaders looked for both immediate and long-term solutions to their survival.

African-American journalist John E. Bruce issued a challenge to the racists: "Wherever and whenever the Negro shows himself to be a man, he can always command the respect of even a cutthroat. Organized resistance to organized resistance is the best remedy for [this] vexed problem."[15]

As evidence that African Americans recognized the need for organization, black churches, fraternal orders, clubs, schools, and conventions were founded throughout the late nineteenth century.[16] It is clear that the grievous assault on African-American political and social rights in the 1890s demanded new forms of organization to combat the violence and economic disparity. In 1900 the vast majority of African Americans (85 percent) lived in the South. The newly founded organizational impetus mainly did not come from this segment of the population, kept under close supervision by southern whites, but from urban African Americans in the North. The explanation for this is twofold: the relative freedom of urban northern African Americans to organize and the urgent social problems that urbanization bestowed on the African-American population.[17]

Between 1890 and 1910 around 200,000 southern blacks moved to the North. African Americans faced a number of problems in urban northern cities including unstable employment, low salaries, a lack of adequate child care, segregation, and substandard housing. The most critical struggle African Americans faced was in the economic sphere. Denied equal opportunities to provide for their families, large numbers of African-American men turned to entrepreneurship and self-help. In this age of "heroic business enterprise," African-American men increasingly became their own employers as they attempted to provide essential services for the African-American community.[18] The systemization of Jim Crow segregated every aspect of life, so African Americans began "buying black."[19]

In August 1900 Booker T. Washington held a meeting of African-American businessmen in an attempt to form a permanent trade organization. Holding fast to the belief that white men would respect only African-American men who were hardworking, industrious, and economically successful, Washington believed that his National Negro Business League would transform black and white economic and social relations. The National Negro Business League was a self-help support group through which African-American men could create networks and encourage each other.[20]

Another such self-help organization was led by W. E. B. DuBois and others but on far different terms. In July 1905 a national conference of black political activists was convened in Fort Erie, Canada. Delegates at the conference demanded "freedom of speech and criticism, manhood suffrage, the

abolition of all distinctions based on race, the recognition of the basic principles of human brotherhood and respect for the working person."[21] The
"Niagara Movement" met for several more years. Within the Niagara Movement's program was a gendered subtext. In the Niagara Movement's Declaration of Principles the delegates boldly claimed, "Persistent *manly*
agitation is the way to liberty and toward this goal the Niagara Movement
has started and asks the cooperation of all *men* of all races."[22] Masculinity
and race were linked in the struggle for African-American social and economic rights.

Some of the leaders of the Niagara Movement later became founders of
the National Association for the Advancement of Colored People (NAACP).
Established in 1909 by a group of black and white progressives, the organization attracted the attention of African Americans nationwide. By 1912
there were eleven branches with 1,100 members. The *Crisis,* the journal of
the organization, had a circulation of 24,000 by 1912. Within two years it
had become the largest circulating magazine devoted to African Americans.[23] The widespread distribution of the journal, coupled with the creation of new black newspapers, made "literate African-Americans aware of
their national responsibilities and what the nation owed them."[24]

A wide variety of organizations geared toward black self-help and racial
solidarity originated between 1900 and 1915. The National Urban League,
another interracial organization, was created in 1912 to address urban and
industrial problems of African Americans. Charitable and religious organizations attempted to aid new black migrants to the cities. Several cities had
YMCA and YWCAs specifically for African Americans. Black social and fraternal clubs also proliferated in the era.[25] As one black newspaper editor proclaimed, "In unity there is strength. Get together Negroes."[26]

In the last few years of the nineteenth century and the first decade of the
twentieth century, the African-American man was under constant attack because of Jim Crow legislation, disenfranchisement, lynching, and popularized
racist diatribes. African-American organizational efforts were motivated by
white racial hatred and violence. Cinematic representations of African-American male buffoonery and the widespread dissemination of racial stereotypes
contributed to the popular mainstream ideology that black men were inferior. For the first sixteen years of American filmmaking, the institutional apparatus of cinematic depiction was controlled by Euro-American men.
Beginning in 1910, a group of African-American men would turn to the motion picture camera to combat racial prejudice. In this year, African-American William Foster formed the Foster Photoplay Company in Chicago. From

this point on, African-American men were able to create cinematic visions of themselves and their people. Along with the founding of organizations like the National Negro Business League and the NAACP, the beginning of black filmmaking represented an attempt by African-American men to create a defense against constant racial attack, develop racial self-help, and reclaim manhood.

Black filmmakers were obviously interested in the economic opportunities that motion pictures were bringing producers and distributors in the United States. But a definite racialized and gendered element lay behind the films of early black directors like William Foster; he was the first African American to counterattack overtly racist depictions on the screen by demonstrating new forms of cinematic black manhood. It is necessary to examine the institutional, artistic, and aesthetic cinematic base to which Foster and other African-American filmmakers were responding. African-American cinema was creative and independent, yet it also was a reaction against the dominant cinema's representation of black people. The vaudevillian roots of early American cinema are critical to an understanding of early racial and gender standards on the screen.

Motion pictures were first publicly exhibited in the United States in New York City at Koster and Bial's Music Hall in April 1896. Koster and Bial's was the leading vaudeville theater in New York at the time. Within two months the Vitascope (Thomas Edison's motion picture machine) had debuted in dozens of cities across the nation, primarily in vaudeville theaters. The immense popularity of these devices and managers' recognition that the new invention was a hit soon became evident. By 1908 over five thousand nickelodeons in the United States were selling over eighty million film tickets each week. This is a remarkable statistic, considering that there were only one hundred million Americans at the time.[27]

The majority of early films were extremely short, running from fifteen seconds to one minute. Because of the primitiveness of the motion picture camera and photographic process, it was difficult to film more than simple subjects.[28] Movies were only one segment of a vaudeville program but their brevity made them ideal as an added attraction. Although some storefronts also began exhibiting motion pictures, they were often surrounded by other forms of entertainment. Before 1900 it would have been unthinkable to offer an entire evening's entertainment made up exclusively of motion pictures.

Many films made in the years between 1896 and 1901 were "realistic" in nature. Audiences knew them as "Living Pictures" and were treated to films of world monuments, coronations of royalty, and exotic foreign locales, as well as simple depictions of everyday life: crowds on a boardwalk, children swimming in the ocean, acrobats contorting their bodies, and twirling dancers. These were nonnarrative, realistic shots of everyday life or filmed vaudeville acts. They did not attempt to tell a story as much as entertain audiences with moving pictures. It was not until 1902–1903 that filmmakers explored the theatricality of filmmaking as they began staging events and developing narrative stories. Included in these "familiar shots" were degrading portrayals of African Americans.[29]

The "realism" of these portrayals was influenced less by how actual African Americans lived and more by the dominant white culture's perception of them. In fact, the mythic quality of film was evident almost from the inception of the medium. Nonrealistic portrayals of ethnic and racial life and the aesthetic quality of film contributed to this mythmaking, the make-believe world of American movies. As film scholar Robert Sklar points out, film audiences may have thought they were seeing actual shots of real life when in fact they were watching life in a black-and-white silence, far removed from everyday life.[30]

Euro-American directors' sense of the realistic tradition evolved from vaudeville and popular theater. Stereotypical portrayals of African Americans were displayed in a wide range of media; variety shows, carnival midways, and popular literature all perpetuated such images. As Miriam Hansen has argued, "Early films, although they lacked the mechanisms to create a spectator in the classic sense, did solicit their viewer through a variety of appeals and attractions and through particular strategies of exhibition."[31] These "appeals and attractions" were existing forms of popular entertainment that presented a wide variety of insulting stereotypes of African-American culture and life. The "particular strategy of exhibition" was a segregated vaudeville house or storefront. In a segregated theater, members of the dominant culture could freely share in ridicule of the African-American cinematic character because African-American spectators were not present.[32] The *Washington Bee* reported in 1910: "There are separate motion picture theaters among the whites and blacks in this country."[33]

The influence of blackface on early American film is key. With the exception of some true-life footage shot in the experimental years between 1896 and 1903, the vast preponderance of African-American male portrayals before 1915 were actually of white men in blackface. I have viewed nearly one hundred films made between 1903 and 1915 with African-American male portrayals. Of these films, less than 5 percent have African-American men playing themselves on the screen. This is significant for several reasons. First, it demonstrates the influence that vaudeville, and blackface in particular, had on the early cinema. Second, it demonstrates the reluctance that white producers and directors had about allowing African-American men to portray themselves on the screen. Third, it meant actual African-American men on the screen were virtually nonexistent. Finally, it meant that all portrayals of African-American men were distortions, misrepresentations of reality, even when those in blackface attempted to portray African-American men in a sympathetic manner.

Blackface entertainment was one of the mainstays of the vaudevillian world in the 1890s and in the early twentieth century. With roots in minstrelsy, blackface entertainment arguably has been considered the most popular form of public entertainment of the nineteenth century. Blackface minstrelsy was essentially a white imitation of black culture. Its origins are a point of controversy for American academics. Some argue that the true roots of minstrelsy were that of the slave entertainer who performed, to his master's delight, at the plantation or other white venues. The demand for black entertainment stressed the concept of "difference," illustrating the supposedly frivolous nature of African-American manhood. It also fed the white desire to believe that African Americans were content under slavery. Others argue that the "explicit borrowing of black cultural materials for white dissemination" had little to do with actual African-American life and more to do with the white construction of supposedly African-American character traits and personality.[34] Thus, the blackface minstrel stage became the prime arena for white appropriation and misrepresentation of black culture. Prior to the Civil War, blackface entertainment was often used as a defense of slavery by portraying the inferiority of African-American men. The vaudeville stage served as an arena where the dissemination of southern ideology regarding race could be nationalized. By portraying African-American men in terms that supported slavery (by stressing the primitiveness and irresponsibility of African-American men), antiabolitionists used entertainment to popularize their views.[35] One such example of black male degradation was the pre–Civil War Bonja Song. The chorus sang:

> Me sing all day, me sleep all night
> Me have no care, me sleep is light
> Me tink, no matter what tomorrow bring
> Me happy, so me sing.[36]

Some scholars ascribe the beginnings of blackface minstrelsy to Daddy Rice and Dan Emmett. Both men blackened their faces with burnt cork, dressed in ragged clothes, and sang songs from traditional African-American culture. According to traditional folklore, Rice, a well-known actor and singer, borrowed both the clothes and song of a young/old man/black vagrant that he found outside the theater where he did his first blackface performance. Rice's success was instantaneous, yet he refused to give the black man back his clothes or pay him for his song. Thus, cultural appropriation became disguised theft as Rice went on to fame and riches. His tremendous financial success as the first full-time antebellum minstrel man guaranteed a host of imitators.[37]

The blackface minstrel performer was usually male. Even though the staging of minstrel entertainment changed after its emergence in the 1830s, the unique gendered order of blackface remained in place.[38] Although some white men played black women and some white women appropriated blackface, the primary stage parameter was of white men blacking up to portray black men. Blackface minstrelsy, as a form of popular entertainment, historically evolved over a one-hundred-year period. In the pre–Civil War period blackface remained a staged entertainment for the lower classes.[39] In the post–Civil War period, however, blackface spread and influenced other forms of media. The influence of blackface on motion pictures was monumental. Despite the relative scholarly neglect this subject has suffered, blackface portrayals of African Americans were the first mainstream depictions of black men in the early silent film era.

Four academics have recently influenced the literature on blackface minstrelsy and its meaning and influence on American culture—Robert Toll, Eric Lott, David Roediger, and Michael Rogin. All four authors support my argument that African-American independent cinema was primarily a reaction to the racist images of African-American men portrayed on the motion picture screen.[40]

Blackface was an attempt by white men to exert control and domination over American society. Robert Toll argues that in the late nineteenth century the blackface minstrel served as a kind of social commentator or Greek chorus. Blackface minstrelsy ridiculed not only African-American men; such entertainment demonstrated that white men had intellectual and social dominance over women, Asians, and Native Americans by also portraying these groups in inferior ways. Late-nineteenth-century blackface divided American culture along racial lines rather than ethnic lines. Michael Rogin points out that the two ethnic groups that predominated in blackface minstrelsy were Irish immigrants in the mid–nineteenth century and Jewish immigrants in the late nineteenth and early twentieth centuries. Both of these ethnic groups were discriminated against and harassed in American society in a period in which members of their ethnic group were performing in blackface. Minstrelsy, therefore, became a tool of assimilation. Blackface became a way to unite people along one set of cultural lines and divide them along another. Richard Dyer has argued that "the category of whiteness is clear and unstable yet this has proved its strength. Because whiteness carries such rewards and privileges, the sense of a border that might be crossed and a hierarchy that might be climbed has produced a dynamic that has enthralled people who had any chance of participating in it."[41] Michael Rogin acknowledges that "the importance of a common whiteness under blackface gave the minstrel stage the ability to foster astonishing ethnic diversity even during periods of anti-immigrant hysteria."[42] The "normalcy" of black/white divisions appeared as a given in the late twentieth century. This seemed much less the case in the late nineteenth century when Irish Americans were just gaining admittance to the white American mainstream and Jewish Americans were largely regarded as racialized Others.

Eric Lott's *Love and Theft* analyzes the origins and meanings of blackface. Lott claims that minstrelsy had less to do with white hegemony and more to do with "a cross-racial desire that coupled a nearly insupportable fascination and a self-protective derision with respect to black people and their cultural practices that made blackface minstrelsy less a sign of absolute white power and control than of panic, anxiety, terror and pleasure."[43] As white men in blackface, American minstrels could sing, dance, speak, move, and act in ways that were considered inappropriate for white men. In a one-sided discourse on power, minstrelsy created a dichotomy that constructed an abnormal performance (inferiority) versus a white standard of being (superiority). This "colonization of the discourse of normal" produced a wildly exotic, unnatural entertainment form that operated and commented on a wide variety of subjects.[44] The blackface minstrel addressed issues of race, gender roles, sexuality, employment, and immigration. Thus, much like ventriloquists, blackface minstrels focused on subjects that may have been considered uncouth for white entertainers. Rather than having a wooden dummy, the minstrel man could express what the white man "really" thought.[45] Historian Kevin Gaines claims that "minstrel performance rituals, both in public and at home, freed whites to entertain otherwise forbidden and dangerous ideas about sexuality, assuaged their guilt, and enabled them to maintain a sense of moral and racial superiority."[46]

Blackface, therefore, became a mask. Whiteness disappeared behind the minstrel facade. Clearly, a white man was addressing the audience. Spectators rarely assumed that this was truly a black man on stage. Thus, the minstrel show became a Kabuki-like ritualistic exercise in which the audience observed the theater as performance, not as a re-creation of reality. Through this ritualistic performance white Americans mirrored the Other at the same time as they distanced the Other. The black male image on the minstrel stage was both a figure to mock and ridicule and a mouthpiece for deep-seated obsessions and fears. Lott addresses the double bind of the minstrel show as a societal mouthpiece and an object of ridicule. He argues that the "primary purpose of the mask . . . may have been as much to maintain control over a potentially subversive act as to ridicule."[47] This was, in fact, "white involvement with black culture under control."[48]

At the center of blackface entertainment was a fascination with the black male body.[49] The dancing and singing of African Americans so entranced white Americans and were deemed such a matter of "difference" that the commodification of this entertainment in a capitalistic nation seemed only natural. But African-American men could not portray *themselves* to whites; indeed, they were usually barred from theaters and performance areas where such activity took place. Thus, the freedom of movement, the grace, and the emotionality of African-American entertainment became a negotiable commodity but one that derided and did not supply economic funds to the original producers. The body of the Other was on display without the body actually being present.[50]

Part of the fascination with the black male body was its association with primitiveness. Through gross stereotypes, the body was dehumanized, yet there remained an element of obsessive desire regarding this body. Fantasies about the "freedom" of the black man (not to follow the dictates of white masculinity) allowed white individuals to observe the racial Other. But as Lott points out, "because the Other personifies their inner divisions, hatred of their own excess of enjoyment necessitates hatred of the Other."[51] The Other, therefore, is ridiculed.

Blackface minstrelsy is therefore a complicated matter. The problem is not recognition of this form of entertainment, but the meaning, symbolism, purpose, rationale, and widespread popularity of it in American culture. A further complication is that some African-American entertainers put on blackface. Often this was because it was one of the few opportunities African Americans had in American entertainment. But the spectacle of African-American male entertainers putting on burnt cork and impersonating white minstrels impersonating African Americans demonstrates the excessiveness of the entertainment form and the contribution to exclusion that it made to

American society.[52] Accordingly, African-American entertainers could be considered "experts" on the appropriation of such material into creative performances. But the widespread popularity of "authentic" blackface and the inheritance of white-created stereotypes limited the creative freedom of African Americans.[53] As Robert Toll argues, "Black minstrels in effect added credibility to these images by making it seem that Negroes actually behaved like minstrelsy's black caricatures."[54]

In one sense, African-American minstrels could be considered to be playing "themselves" on stage. But the reality was that African-American men were negotiating performances within a burgeoning entertainment industry whose stories and performances frequently relied on and reproduced white supremacist structures of domination.

Two stereotypes predominated in male blackface entertainment: first, Sambo, the rural southern plantation figure, and second, Zip Coon, the urban dandy.[55] The plantation "darkie" and the city "dandy" became flip sides of the racial coin. Sambo was a lazy, dim-witted, slow-moving, and slow-talking yet good-natured man who meant right but always seemed to do wrong. He was always hungry and eager to find the easiest way out of a complicated situation. Sambo had big lips, gleaming white teeth, short nappy hair, and a body that moved like a primate. Zip Coon was a post–Civil War Negro—a black man who moved to the city and attempted to assimilate into white culture, usually with laughable results. Zip Coon wore flashy, multicolored clothing and spoke in a flowery language he did not understand.[56] In fact, the use of multisyllabic words became a staple of the vaudevillian routine.[57] Eager to get a dollar without any work, Zip Coon was always on the make. He carried a switchblade and was all too willing to take advantage of Sambo, his slower cousin.[58]

Zip Coon was the more dangerous of the two black male stereotypes. Although he was lazy and cowardly like his cousin Sambo, Zip Coon was more likely to have dangerous vices that were threatening to whites. According to Sam Dennison, Zip Coon's "longing to be white was expressed as a sort of covetousness of white values and standards."[59] This meant having all of the material trappings of the white man. This, of course, was dangerous because it placed the Coon figure on the same economic plane as the working-class white man. Therefore, whites had to ridicule the dreams and ambitions of the Zip Coon figure in order to guarantee the "natural" inferiority of the black man.[60]

The dichotomy of southern rural Sambo/northern urban Zip Coon was purposeful. Many of the songs and skits associated with blackface minstrelsy expressed a longing for the antebellum South.[61] Since blackface entertainment was multifaceted, involving song and comedy, this nostalgia for the past could be expressed in a variety of ways. The positive portrayal of the plantation validated working-class racism. In this view, slavery was natural and right. No matter how stupid Sambo may have been, he was usually happy. Zip Coon, on the other hand, was a product of the post–Civil War generation. Unhappy with freedom and not knowing his place, Zip Coon aspired to be what he clearly could not be—equal. Within the context of most vaudeville acts, Zip Coon ended up losing to his ignorant cousin Sambo.[62] The major plot device of the blackface act was to have Sambo mock and degrade the haughty, unrealistic pretensions of Zip Coon.

This form of popular culture was created in an era when divisions of class and race were unstable. Michel Foucault's work on the reprogramming of popular memory helps us to understand the sensibility behind this entertainment. Foucault argues that history is used as a systematic disassociation of identity. It is a "weak identity" and one that "we attempt to support and unify under a mask." Through popular forms of entertainment, the cultural plurality of the American population is homogenized under the guise of American melting-pot assimilation. Thus, in the cultural text there is the American—rather, the American male and the American female, the white American and the black American. Although Foucault argues that "it is a sign of superior culture to maintain, in a fully conscious way, certain phases of its evolution which lesser men can pass through," the system remains one that is "completely determined."[63] Accessibility to positions of power and influence (social mobility) remains a pivotal part of the American creed, yet the capitalist and racist hierarchy regulated this too. Actual opportunity and the myth of equal opportunity for all were contradictions in American ideology. In the traumatic period of Reconstruction, this cultural practice of guaranteed Negro inferiority was soothing and controlling. The social drama of blackface minstrelsy created order out of a chaotic world. Its repeated cultural performance pacified the anxieties of working-class white Americans. It assimilated European ethnic minorities into the superiority of white inclusion and created such an iconography of racial difference that this very "difference" implied, if not demanded, inferiority. Zip Coon and Sambo would transfer to the motion picture screen as representations of African-American male "normality." For the first sixteen years of American filmmaking, there were few cinematic visions that challenged these stereotypes.

2

THE PREFORMED IMAGE: WATERMELON, RAZORS, AND CHICKEN THIEVERY, 1896–1915

The African-American male image in film did not originate with the beginning of cinema in 1896. Its roots lay deep in the consciousness of the white American public, visibly displayed through various forms of popular entertainment. Vaudeville, blackface minstrelsy, popular songs, journals, and magazines all contributed to a cinematic vision of African-American male inferiority. Through the motion picture medium, the attack on black manhood became more acute. Derogatory depictions of African-American men could reach millions of Americans at their local nickelodeon or vaudeville theater through a seemingly innocent yet wildly popular new form of entertainment. This chapter will set up a theoretical model in which to examine the predominant images of African-American manhood available to viewing audiences from 1896 to 1915. These images help explain why African-American men would feel it was necessary to create alternative cinematic self-representations.

In 1914, Vitagraph, a leading motion picture company of its age, produced *Florida Enchantment,* a romantic comedy.[1] The story focuses on the relationship between Dr. Fred Cassadine, a young doctor for a Florida resort hotel, and Miss Lillian Travers, a young northern heiress. After receiving her inheritance, Lillian decides there is nothing left to delay her impending marriage to Cassadine. She goes to Florida, only to find her fiancé attracted to Mrs. Stella Lovejoy, a fashionable New York widow. This situation forces Lillian to take drastic measures to save her relationship. She swallows magical seeds, obtained from an ancient relative who had been shipwrecked off the coast of Africa. These seeds allow her to change her gender (apparently for the purpose of disrupting the growing relationship between Cassadine and Mrs. Lovejoy). After taking the seeds, Lillian still appears physically female although she begins to take on "masculine" characteristics. She flirts with

Bessie Horton, "a Florida flower who does not wish to blush." Insisting that she needs a valet, Lillian forces her mulatto maid, Jane, to take one of the seeds. Upon taking the seeds, Jane immediately becomes violent, hitting and pushing any man or woman in her way. She even hits her master with a pillow. In reality, Jane is a white actress, Ethel Lloyd. The irony of a white actress playing a mulatto maid and imitating and taking on the "characteristics" of an African-American man is based on early-twentieth-century assumptions of racialized and gendered behavior. This is an exercise in reflexivity, dependent on the premise that the spectator "knows" how African-American men and women "act."

Both Lillian and Jane are now respective embodiments of white and black masculinity. Thus, they begin their course as men. Lillian begins smoking, barks directions to her male valet, and pursues Bessie in a more aggressive manner. Lillian presents Bessie with an engagement ring and erotically caresses her arm. Jane openly pursues Cassadine's black maid Malvina. Upon seeing her beauty, Jane is mesmerized and begins doing a cakewalk. When Jane catches Malvina with Gus Duncan, a black delivery man, she flexes her manly bicep and beats him as Malvina calls for help. She even knocks down a white delivery boy to have her way with the maid.

The sex-changed pair further their progression to manhood. They adopt a masculine style of dress, cut off their hair, and change their names. Lillian Travers becomes Mr. Lawrence Talbot, who walks, talks, moves, and acts like a man. Eventually Lawrence/Lillian confesses her sex change to young Dr. Cassadine, who responds in disbelief. He takes a seed to prove him/her wrong, dresses in drag, and immediately begins to act feminine.

As with many other films that distort the parameters of reality, Lillian wakes up, realizing that she has dreamed the entire scenario. Obviously, this Vitagraph production was a send-up of gender roles and romantic triangles. But *Florida Enchantment* is also a fascinating depiction of gender stereotyping and gender expectations in the World War I era. Moreover, this film explores racialized conceptualizations of masculinity and femininity. At no point in the film does the viewer assume that a true sex change has taken place. In fact, one is in disbelief that the African-American characters were truly African American. Thus, the concepts of gender and race become social constructs that can be applied to the body of an individual who may not truly hold such characteristics. A white woman can play an African-American man. A white man can depict a white woman. What is important is not the physical attributes of the individual doing the depicting but the gendered and racialized behavior of these depictions.[2]

It is in this sense that *Florida Enchantment* is truly revealing. Strongly formed ideologies of racialized gender roles are pertinent to the reading of the film. The viewer clearly knows the race and gender of the actors but the viewer also "knows" of the racialized and gendered characteristics the actor is attempting to portray. *Florida Enchantment* encapsulates a litany of gender and racial stereotypes that assumes a viewer's recognition of these social patterns. This is so evident that the physical attributes of the stereotypes being performed are not necessary for the actor who is embodying these characteristics. *Florida Enchantment* is both a comic opera and an exercise in early-twentieth-century gender expectations. Moreover, it aptly demonstrates the racial differentiation in gender expectations in American society.

Throughout the first hundred years of American cinema, motion pictures have presented gendered and racialized norms for the screen. The male gender has traditionally held much of the power in Western society, including access to the mass media. Thus, as Bill Nichols has observed, mass media and other key institutions in society "reflect back on images of man that assures him of his rightful place within society, his status as subject, independent of the needs of others."[3] The mass media often simplifies the identification process by using messages of male superiority and gender conformity.

Visual production, in the form of motion pictures or other artistic renderings, has historically been a male-dominated enterprise. Men have traditionally controlled this process and have been considered the prime consumers of these images by the producers of the visual product. Within the world of visual production, culturally determined archetypes have been created that have attempted to explain the characteristics, behaviors, and attitudes of what it means to be a man or woman in society. These archetypes have become social constructs, demonstrating to the viewer how to adapt their masculine or feminine selves to their environment.

The institutionalization of the patriarchal ideal within the mainstream cinematic medium reinforces patriarchy through all aspects of society. Classical Hollywood filmmakers painted romance and love, family, the workplace, religion, and education with a patriarchal brush. Gender, however, is only the starting point in this analysis. Sexual orientation and racial differentiation are also key categories of difference built into the cinematic patriarchy. Man and woman, heterosexual and homosexual, white and racial Other, are all binary categories of acceptance and disavowal within the cinematic establishment.

Understanding the importance of motion pictures as structuring agents is essential in allowing us to acknowledge how people participate in the production of their own social consciousness. Since filmmaking and film watching is a reflexive exercise, both people involved in the productive process and those involved in spectatorship negotiate how they fit within the dominant structure and within the contradictions of these structures. Uncovering meanings in a given film is not based solely on the text but also on the forces at work in a given text's production and reception. Popular cinematic texts have meaning only when people apply and relate them to their everyday lives. Because popular cinema borrows from so many discourses—literature, fashion, politics, and music—it remains a collective of deep-seated ideological "understandings." Cinema is a dense system of meaning; it both reflects and shapes the culture around it.

The ritualistic behavior between film producers and the film audience, with the motion picture serving as agent, is based on a well-developed semiological understanding. A rhetoric of characterization, musical cues, wardrobe, and language exists between the filmmaker and the filmgoer. The multiplicity of motion picture screenings by the filmgoer over the course of his or her lifetime allows this symbolic basis of understanding to develop. The structured symbolism of race and gender also fits into this ritualistic exercise. As filmgoers make the weekly pilgrimage to the local theater, they also perceive or expect certain formulaic conventions or generic attributes in a given film.

The ongoing relationship between the cinematic spectator and the film medium also reflects the contentious relationship between the real and the ideal in society. As viewers are balancing real/nonreal and desired/undesired social conditions within the cinematic exercise they are also reflecting these conditions based on their own lives and experiences. I argue that silent Hollywood films often created a cinematic mythology that reflected the removal or dilution of conflict in the visual depiction of American society. Racial conflict, frustration, and agitation were largely absent from the American silent screen; in fact, they were often replaced with false, fabricated relationships or pleasing stereotypes.[4]

The fascinating element in this fabrication of American society is the reaction of spectators to what they are seeing on the screen. French psychiatrist Octave Mannoni has pointed out that mythic "illusions always rest on a delicate balance of faith and disavowal."[5] Thus, neither the studio heads nor the audience truly "believed" the American society they were seeing on the screen in this period, yet such films continued to be made and attended.

Richard Dyer, in a groundbreaking article, "Entertainment and Utopia," helps to explain this contradiction. He proposes that "entertainment offers the image of 'something better' to escape into, or something we want deeply that our day-to-day lives don't provide."[6] Dyer argues that popular cinematic entertainment offers utopian ideals but not a utopian world. These ideals include a world of abundance, energy, intensity, and community. Film offers "alternatives, hopes, and wishes" for the spectator.[7] But this is problematic when considering the lack of racial conflict and the supposed contentedness of African Americans in silent mainstream film. When considering these "utopian ideals," does the pacification and marginalization of African Americans represent a wish that they would go away? Is this a utopian dream that the two races could get along, that racial harmony could exist? Is this a self-imposed lie that African Americans were happy with the American dream and that what is being shown on the screen is reality, or a possible attempt at reality?

There is a need to modify Dyer's assumptions for this work. The silent Hollywood film often presented a model of a utopian world. Dyer claims that what really matters in this depiction of utopianism are the "feelings it embodies."[8] I argue that it means much more. By denying the existence of racial problems in American society, by fabricating a society in which all problems are resolved, and by giving a happy ending to each film, the filmmaking establishment was constructing a utopian world, a world of representation and symbolism, passivity and acceptance, benign approval and justification. One can trace this argument back to Jane Addams and her concern that American youth were formulating a false sense of the world in this "house of dreams."[9] In terms of resolution of conflict, the physical appearance of the stars, and societal acceptance and minority acquiescence, the silent Hollywood film depicted a false, hollow, mythological, nonreal world that had far more to do with cinematic wish fulfillment than it did with reality.

Dyer later acknowledges that "class, race and sexual caste are denied validity as problems by the dominant [bourgeois, white, male] ideology of society. We should not expect show business to be markedly different."[10] Assimilation into American society implied the creation of a utopian American landscape. Dyer argues that "this utopian sensibility has to be taken off the real experience of the audience."[11] This sensibility did not include the racial, gender, and ethnic contradictions in American society. Rather than depicting a mirror image of American society, mainstream silent film delivered a utopian extravaganza of the American dream.

Categories of construction within the cinematic world such as gender and race are types of cultural construction. Issues of domination and hegemony as related to gender and race are pivotal in this form of construction. Motion pictures "link symbols, formulas, plots and character in a pattern that is conventional, appealing and gratifying . . . in tales of redemption that show how order is restored."[12] This, of course, demonstrates dutiful submission to traditional authority in the context of gender and racial relationships. The narrative of motion pictures supports the maintenance of social order since the spectator learns his or her place in the world through viewing film. Although the language of film theory is often based on the premise of control and domination, poststructuralist theorists such as Michel Foucault have demonstrated that the structure of power is often precarious and unstable, allowing alternative readings of cinematic discourse.

The trope of race has been a powerful form of difference in American film. Racial differentiation creates societal Others. The Other is an alien to the dominant American cinematic landscape. It is a psychological tool used by filmmakers to stress difference. Terry Eagleton has described the Other as "that which . . . is always interior to us and will always escape us, that which brought us into being subjects in the first place but which is always outside our grasp."[13] The Other is often depicted along racial and ethnic lines. The Other often symbolizes the forbidden. Whether it is a lusty dance by Dorothy Dandridge in *Carmen Jones* or the romantic yet sexual Gus in *The Birth of a Nation*, the Other symbolizes what does not fit in respectable society. There is an implication of desire within this theoretical concept. Although the spectator may be visually or aurally entranced by the actions of the Other, this "different" individual is often degraded, humiliated, or forced to be punished within the narrative framework.[14] The black man has been the quintessential Other in the first one hundred years of American film. Whether he was marginalized by studio productions or portrayed by white men in blackface, "difference" remained the primary attribute of African-American masculinity.[15]

Between 1903 and 1913, when many of the films I will discuss were produced, the nickelodeon was the primary setting for the exhibition of motion pictures. In this early silent era, nickelodeons catered to the working class. Thomas Cripps claims that audiences were almost entirely white in some neighborhoods. He argues that "there were rows of [nickelodeons] with gaudy fronts and shrill barkers—all largely unavailable to Negroes."[16] Lewis Jacobs argues that the middle class and well-to-do looked down upon such theaters. As a "poor man's entertainment," therefore, these films need to be considered in relationship to issues of class. Appearing in a decade in which millions of first- and second-generation immigrants were attempting to climb the American ladder of social mobility, films with African-American portrayals tended to solidify "whiteness," stretching the boundaries to include the masses of newcomers who were attempting to be "American" (therefore, white and not "Other").[17] As Daniel Bernardi has argued, "Whiteness found its way into film at the hands of a number of studios and filmmakers . . . racial caricatures were one of the more popular attractions in a disturbingly 'primitive' cinema."[18]

Some of the earliest snippets of American film are shots of actors in blackface. The Edison Company, one of the first film companies, used the blackface/vaudeville theme for a number of its early shorts. In *Minstrels Battling in a Room* (circa 1897–1900), two white men in blackface impersonate an African-American man and woman dancing. "She" has a cigar in her mouth, an indication of her lack of true femininity. Another blackface entertainer accompanies them on a guitar. The "black" men are in tuxedos, an obvious sign of their attempt to be respectable. A white manager appears and seems horrified that any of them are there in the first place and attempts to kick them out. The cigar-smoking "woman" blows smoke in his face and the entire crowd of entertainers in blackface push around the white manager. The primitive technique of this early short makes it difficult to get a complete reading of the film but the premise is clear—when African Americans gather in numbers they will be belligerent and uppity with white authority figures. There are numerous instances of the direct incorporation of blackface vaudeville acts into early silent film.[19] Among such films were *The Edison Minstrels* (Edison, 1897) and *The Minstrel's Sacrifice* (unknown, 1908).[20]

Older African-American male images were also used in a number of shorts produced in the first few years of cinema. In *Laughing Ben* (Biograph, 1902) an older black man, who is missing most of his teeth, laughs out loud with his mouth wide open.[21] This close-up of Ben is a demonstration of the "congenial happy negro" stereotype. *A Good Joke* (Lubin, 1901) explores a similar theme. The summary in the Lubin catalog describes "three typical southern darkies each of which is over 90 years of age. One is engaged in telling a funny story and the facial expression of the three men will be enjoyed by everybody who witnesses it. We might say that these are members of an exhibit of the Pan American Exposition at Buffalo. You can not make a mistake if you buy this film."[22] This subgenre of early film stressed the satisfied, gleeful nature of the older black man (ex-slave). These early shorts were among the first close-ups in screen history. They were deliberately shot in an attempt to contrast the "old happy darkie" with the unsatisfied, ungrateful, post–Civil War black man. Both early blackface films and happy darkie shorts were attempts to restore order. Radical southerners were convinced that the "New Negro" (African Americans born after the Civil War) were retrogressing into savagery and primitive bestiality. The "New Negro" was often contrasted with the "happy darkie" who had experienced slavery and knew his place.[23] Early blackface films often restricted the "uncivilized" behavior of African Americans, whereas happy darkie films stressed the gleeful nature of African Americans who had been born under slavery, stressing the black desire and need to be restrained and controlled by white men.

Film is a communicative form that interacts with other artistic and aesthetic mediums. The stereotyping of certain practices or objects with African-American men was, therefore, a multimedia affair. Advertising, postcards, songbooks, porcelains, piano sheet music, vaudeville, and literature all contributed to the symbolic propagandizing of racism toward the African American.[24] The imagery of the cinema, particularly in the early silent period, was based on easily recognizable symbols and codes. As a strongly representational art, the codes "at work in cinema seem to refer to the conditions at work in everyday reality."[25] The early cinema simply reproduced many of the ethnic and racial codes that were already evident in popular culture. Stereotypes operate in the wake of preexisting ideologies that define and then appropriate the subject. The text of early silent film presupposed that the spectator already had some association with the material object or physical practice being depicted. The cinema ingrained these easily recognizable racialized symbols into the spectator's conscience through the viewing of a multitude of films. These codes appeared to embody the physical reality of everyday life and became a simplistic means to perceive racialized beings in the real world.[26] Between 1896 and 1903, African-American actors were "captured" on film involved in activities that conformed to these preconceived stereotypes.[27]

A number of physical activities or material objects were associated with the African-American man. Among these objects was the watermelon. Watermelon, as a visual symbol, appeared in countless numbers of early shorts featuring African Americans that were made between 1896 and 1905.[28] Watermelon was a strong visual symbol of the "appetites" of black men. The sexual imagery associated with the consumption of watermelon is apparent in contemporary film catalog descriptions. These descriptions were written for vaudeville theater or penny arcade owners in clear, simple language that was accessible to an ordinary individual. Catalog descriptions also appealed to preconceived racial familiarity. The uncontrollable desire that African Americans have for watermelons in early films is laden with sexual innuendo. Black men have a watermelon "appetite."[29] They are often in contests to see "who can eat the most."[30] The fruit is "luscious" and the black man eating watermelon is "ravenous."[31] The consumption is "intense" and eaten "as only Southern coons can."[32] In *The Watermelon Contest* (Edison, 1901) a black man is eating in such a rushed manner that he is regurgitating seeds and mush. In most of these films the consumption of melons is nothing short of frenzied. The connotation is that black men have uncontrollable desires. They are savage and gluttonous, so eager for the pink flesh of the watermelon that they revert to primitiveness and lose all sense of decorum. One of the earliest American Mutoscope releases was entitled *A Watermelon Feast* (1896). The catalog description simply states, "A family of darkies reveling in a feast of the favorite food of their race."[33] Charles Musser's research on *The Watermelon Patch* demonstrates that all these films emblazoned the threat of uncontrollable black male appetites to white civilization.[34]

Another common subgenre of film that prominently featured "real" African Americans were shorts involving dancing. Entertainment was one of the few public ways in which African Americans were able to enter white society in the pre–Civil War era. Entertainment was also one of the services slaves were expected to provide white southerners on the plantation. The way that black performers moved fascinated white entertainers and was one of the rationales behind the development of blackface. The unique musical ability of African Americans was one of the few positive qualities attributed to the race in the nineteenth century by mainstream white society.[35]

Both the Edison Company and Lubin released films titled *Buck Dance*. Although the "buck" in traditional racial iconography was a sexualized creature, in both of these films he is harmless and humorous. The 1898 Edison version is indecipherable because of the condition of the film, but Lubin's 1903 version is full of racial stereotypes. Sigmund Lubin was a founder of one of the most successful early film companies. He produced vaudevillian and blackface theatrical shows and was familiar with the racialized nature of popular entertainment. The Lubin catalog summary of the film read, "Here is seen a number of 'Smokes' dancing for their favorite 'watermelon' and they pound the floor with their cinderellas to beat the band. The luscious fruit is held by one of their number in plain view, and they finally stop dancing and engage in a tussle to see who can obtain the green fruit and devour it."[36] The animalistic nature of the African-American man is stressed. It is implied that he will do anything to get his "precious" watermelon, including dancing and fighting.

In *Love and Theft*, Eric Lott has argued that the objectification and vulgarization of black male stereotypes in forms of popular entertainment have been performed through the instrument of the "pale gaze."[37] This refers to

a Euro-American perspective that influenced the aesthetic and narrative functioning of American film. Film creators assumed that the typical moviegoing
spectator was a white man. The pale gaze maintained Euro-American male
hegemony, ridiculed black male power, and controlled black male sexuality
on the screen. Until the 1970s, the majority of American mainstream films
were made through the eyes of the "pale gaze" in that a Euro-American perspective influenced the aesthetic and narrative functioning of American film.
Manthia Diawara has argued that "the dominant cinema situates Black characters primarily for the pleasure of White spectators."[38]

"Dancing" films put African-American entertainers "on display" and
stressed the unnatural, foreign (read nonpale or nonwhite) aspects of their
physical movements. The supposed fundamental primitiveness of African
Americans implied their "difference." This becomes even more evident
when reading the film production company catalog descriptions of early
African-American dance films. The most common word used to describe the
dancing is "grotesque."[39] This deliberate word choice implies the freakish,
inhuman activity taking place on the screen. Even in films with respectable,
well-dressed African-American couples, the style is still referred to as
grotesque. What becomes important on the screen is not the physical act of
dancing, but who is doing the dance.

In early dancing shorts, African Americans usually performed the cakewalk. The cakewalk received national prominence in the 1890s. It was one
of the first African-American entertainment forms to gain widespread popularity. Originally, the cakewalk was a pre–Civil War parody of the way white
people danced, a form of reverse minstrelsy.[40] Slaves in the plantation South
mimicked the stiff formal dancing style of their white owners. A couple
would parade and strut their bodies in an expressive manner. The cakewalk
became prominent nationally in the 1890s when women began touring with
"colored" road show companies. Improvisation and experimentation were
part of the dance and countless early films demonstrated its popularity.[41]

Lubin's *Cake Walk* (1898) coincided with the first black stage musical to
perform in New York—*Clorindy*. This musical production dealt with the origins of the cakewalk. The stage show *A Trip to Coontown*, which also featured
the cakewalk, appeared in New York the same year.[42] The popular success of
the dance led to international touring groups. Black performers danced the
cakewalk all over Europe in the first few years of the twentieth century.[43]

Production company catalog descriptions give credit to African-American
dancers on the screen and at the same time denigrate and stereotype their
performance. In the Selig catalog description for *Cake Walk* (1903), the

writers acknowledge that the dancing is "well executed" but attribute the performance to instinct and not professionalism by arguing that it is accomplished "by people who have a reputation in this line."[44] Lubin's *Cake Walk* (1898) shows "colored professionals," but this is merely their "favorite pastime."[45] Edison's *Up to Date Cake Walk* (1900) is "novel and amusing" but the performers are "coon cakewalkers" who are "grotesque."[46] What is never mentioned in these catalog descriptions, yet is quite evident in the films, is the pride African Americans demonstrate in their dance and the fine clothes that are often worn for performing. Instead, the production companies stressed the novelty of "coon" dancers. A popular song of the period, *Under Southern Skies* seemed to be the inspiration of the filmmakers' activity:

> You'll hear the darkies singing.
> The songs they love the best,
> You'll hear the banjos ringing,
> While the old folks rest.
> The pickaninnies dancing,
> To see who'll win the prize,
> In the evening by the moonlight,
> Under southern skies.[47]

Cinematic portrayals were designed to meet the desires and wishes of the white audience. The filmmaker was not free to produce any moralistic or cultural fable he wanted to in the context of mainstream American moviemaking; he had to make a film that would pull in audiences and bring a profit to investors. The film had to conform to dominant standards of hegemonic acceptability. Such "coon" depictions were thought to be representative of Euro-American views of African Americans. Daniel Bernardi has argued that "there is no single or even dominant individual or film company responsible for integrating whiteness into United States cinema."[48] It simply became part of the American cultural mainstream.

By far, the largest subgenre of early films with black depictions were films that featured African-American men as chicken thieves. Chicken and watermelon were two foods to which African-American men apparently had an insatiable addiction. The food stereotype was consistently linked to thievery. Built within this broad-based stereotype was the assumption that African-American men had no other way of obtaining a pullet than to steal it.[49] The implication inherent within this racial slur was that African-American men could not honestly fulfill their own gastronomical desires, let alone feed their families. Charles Musser has argued that "the image of African-Americans as happy-go-lucky petty thieves, common to the minstrel show and the Sunday supplement of most newspapers, was unfortunately, if predictably, being broadened."[50]

One of the Edison Company's earliest films was entitled *Chicken Thieves* (1897). The catalog description of the film attempted to play the racial angle both ways. Arguing that the film "depict[ed] an occupation commonly attributed to" black men, it claimed it is "sometimes [even] proven against the colored race."[51] This technically primitive film shows a black man sneaking near a henhouse with a sack in his hand. As he approaches the window, an African-American accomplice hands him two chickens. He falls out of the henhouse window but is determined not to let one of the chickens go. Just as the thieves take off, two white farmers appear, one with a scythe and the other with a gun. The armed farmer fires two shots at the thieves but their fate is not determined. The irony of this is captured in the final line of the Edison catalog description: "The smoke effect from the gun at this close range is startling and beautiful, and the entire picture is one of the best composed and most ingenious we have made."[52] The cinematic depiction of a firing gun must have been thrilling for early film audiences, but even more so in knowing that an African-American man was the target for that bullet. *Chicken Thieves* had a simple binary racial structure: Black Thievery/White Protection.[53]

Lubin produced several films with the title *Chicken Thief*. One can assume that Lubin's constant remake of films with this theme must have been due to the immense popularity of these shorts. The 1903 version shows "the proverbial colored chicken thief."[54] Once again, a farmer's henhouse is struck, and once again, Lubin delivers racist depictions. The two black characters are Fatty and Skinny. They are often referred to as "boogy" and "smoke." Another Lubin production of 1903 was entitled *Dancing for a Chicken*. The film manages to combine two racial stereotypes into one extremely short film—the black love of chicken and dancing. The catalog's film description demonstrated the contempt that the Lubin Company had for African Americans: "A party of colored folks are engaged in a dancing contest for a chicken. Everyone knows that coons love chicken and each buck and wench is doing his or her utmost to win the prize. One imagines one can hear them smacking their lips while devouring the chicken that is yet to be won."[55]

The popularity of this subgenre of chicken thievery is well documented. Biograph's 1904 production *The Chicken Thief* was one of their largest grossing films of the year. It was also the first multireel film with actual black actors in the title roles produced in the United States.[56] *Chicken Thieves* was one of Biograph's first attempts at multireel story films. Unlike the 1897 Edison release, the film had a clear beginning, middle, and end. The opening shot of the film shows a black man happily devouring fried chicken. The film continues with a passage showing two African-American men capturing dozens of hens from a henhouse. The owner of the henhouse and his son hear noise and rush out of bed, but to no avail; the chickens are lost. The farmer then decides to get even. He places a large steel trap in the henhouse, bolts it down, and covers it with straw. The thieves are then shown sitting down at the head of their makeshift dinner table. Two children and other family members are enjoying the chicken. The next night the two chicken thieves attempt to replicate their previous success by returning to the same henhouse. One of the men gets his leg caught in the steel trap and his cries of pain wake up the farmer and his son. The two thieves run off into the woods, one with his leg still in the trap. He jumps a gate but the other thief is shot in the buttocks. He "tumbles in a heap and the pack of farmers is on him in a minute."[57] He is dragged away. The chicken thief with the trap on his leg then runs into his own home where a dancing party is taking place. He desperately looks for a place to hide and his wife suggests the attic. The black family members continue the party to make things look normal when the farmer and son appear. They burst in and begin looking for the thief. He finally appears when he falls through the attic with the trap caught in the rafters.

This appears to the modern viewer to be a morality play but was purposefully billed by Biograph as a slapstick comedy. An advertisement for the film proclaimed, "The film is one continuous bout of laughter."[58] Two intended morals are clearly demonstrated. Violent action toward African-American men was apparently amusing, if not hilarious, to early-twentieth-century viewers because the "coons" deserved it. This follows the Radical southern mentality of vengeance toward criminal African Americans. Second, the only apparent way that African-American men could feed their children was by thievery. Director Wallace McCutcheon purposefully shows the shoddiness of the black cabin and the poverty of the family but never sympathizes with their plight. Indeed, overt violence toward both of these men is the climax of the film. One can only imagine how African-American spectators felt when watching such a movie.

Between 1905 and 1909 the major motion picture companies seemed to give the black chicken thievery theme a rest. But between 1910 and 1914 no fewer than eight films emerged with this theme. The primary difference in this series of films is that African-American men did not portray themselves—almost all of the characterizations were done by white men in black-face.[59] As the industry expanded exponentially and became more professionalized, African Americans were deliberately left out of the equation, as in other industries that proved to be profitable.

Violence toward African-American men, particularly vigilante violence, is a common theme in many of these films. In *A College Chicken* (Essanay, 1910) the African-American theft of a chicken only begins the action. It is really the story of devil-may-care college boys who beat up an older black man who looks "suspicious." After pummeling him, they steal his stolen chicken and feast on it themselves.[60] *Hen House Hero* (Essanay, 1912) is the story of a romantic triangle between three rural whites. Farmer Schultz promises his daughter's hand to the man who can catch the chicken thief who has been raiding his ranch. Both of Schultz's hired hands, Henry and Dave, love his daughter Dinah. Henry eventually gets the girl, while disappointed Dave "is left to take it out on the coon."[61]

The fictional "Rastus" character, a variation on the Sambo stereotype, was prevalent in a number of films in this period. In *Rastus' Riotous Ride* (Pathe, 1914), Rastus must steal a chicken for his daughter's wedding present. In *The Tale of a Chicken* (Lubin, 1914), Rastus places a stolen chicken in a rival's house in order to obtain the hand of a woman. In *C-H-I-C-K-E-N Spells Chicken* (Essanay, 1910), Rastus pursues a young woman, not for her affections but for the chicken she is carrying with her. No matter what the situation, stealing a chicken seems to be the solution to the problem. In *Mandy's Chicken Dinner* (Lubin, 1914), a henpecked husband steals a chicken in order to impress the local preacher at Sunday dinner. But once again, an attempt by an African-American man to make a false impression leads to disaster.[62]

In only one film of the era is the issue of black chicken thievery seriously questioned. Kalem's short *Chased by Bloodhounds* (1912) is a quite subversive film. Mr. Bunny, a white man, is a breeder of quality chickens. One day he generously gives an impoverished fat black gentleman a suit of his clothes. The black man repays him by stealing one of his chickens. Bunny asks his next-door neighbor if he can use one of his bloodhounds to find the thief. He sends the dog after the black vagrant but he forgets that the thief is wearing his shoes. The dog responds by chasing Bunny all over the countryside. If the film had ended here, it would have been a comedy of mistaken identity. But after Bunny returns to his home, exhausted after being chased by the bloodhound, he has a series of nightmares reliving his horrible plight. Bunny tries to forget his trauma but he simply cannot. In *Chased by Blood-*

hounds, the black protagonist does not suffer. Instead, he makes off with the clothes and the chicken. It is the principal white subject who must question his choices and live with his actions.[63]

African-American thievery was not limited to chickens, according to early filmmakers. In *A Nigger in the Woodpile* (Biograph, 1904), two white men attempt to catch the thief who has been stealing the firewood. They drill a hole in a log, put in a stick of dynamite, and place it on the woodpile. A distinguished looking black man (in blackface) steals the planted wood. In the next scene, Mammy takes this piece of wood, places it in the stove, and an explosion occurs. The old black man falls on top of the stove and a large hole is blown through the cabin roof. Obviously, stealing does not pay. Film historian Charles Musser argues that there is a link between rural poverty and violence in the early Biograph narrative films.[64] If African Americans engage in criminal activity, violence tends to be either the result or the solution. Such cinematic depictions simply documented the Radical southern position that black men were naturally driven to criminality.[65]

The vast majority of early American cinematic portrayals of African-American men depicted them as harmless individuals, nonthreatening comic foils who appeared to be driven by appetite and emotion and not intellect. On the surface, this seems to contradict the popular southern sentiment that African-American men were criminals and rapists who were "retrogressing toward a natural state of savagery and bestiality."[66] In fact, there appeared to be two popular stereotypes of black manhood between 1896 and 1910—that of the cinema, which humanized the childlike black man, and that of a dominant social and political ideology of the South, which considered the black man the ultimate threat to white civilization.

The one element that tied these two stereotypes together was violence. In southern culture, lynching, imprisonment, and intimidation were all deemed necessary to keep the black man in his place. Within American motion pictures, violence toward African Americans was depicted as humorous and justifiable. Rather than demonstrating the horrible results of castration, beating, and hanging, these films downplayed the consequences of white racial aggression.

One can argue that since motion pictures were a form of mass entertainment, the white audience, which made up the vast majority of film patrons, would not wish to see authentic depictions of violence toward African-American men despite contemporary racial attitudes—this would force many individuals to ponder such results. But they would accept the humorous use of violence toward African-American men, which ultimately put them in their place. Early motion pictures, therefore, supported barbarism toward African-American men because the violence did not really appear to be harmful and because this use of force upheld the moral order.

A number of early silent films illustrate the supposed laziness and indolence of African-American men. White filmmakers argued that for black men, thievery was more natural than working for a living. This belief was dependent on the premise that African-American men were like children. Since children often avoided work, it was assumed that black men had an aversion to physical labor.[67] *Everybody Works but Father* (Biograph, 1905) was based on a popular song of the era. The company made two simultaneous productions of the film, one with white characters and one in blackface. The film's central figure is a lazy "pappy" character. Pappy yawns as he comes downstairs after a nap. Mammy washes clothes in a bucket while a daughter brings in more clothes. Instead of helping his family, Pappy sits down in a rocking chair and smokes a pipe. His son comes into the house after chopping wood. He complains about his father's laziness and threatens him with an ax. The daughter then begins yelling at her father, pointing a stick at him and eventually giving him a whack with it. Pappy responds by just sitting back down in his rocker. The son threatens his father once again, and Mammy responds by threatening Junior with a stick.[68] *Everybody Works but Father* supports the belief that the African-American family is matrifocal. Without the work and discipline of the black woman, it appears as if the black family is doomed. In an era when a basic premise of American masculinity was the ability to support one's family, the film illustrates that Pappy is less than a man.

Early silent films demonstrate that African-American men will do anything but work to make money. One alternative to thievery was shooting craps. This was a popular theme in a number of early films and continues to be an activity associated with African-American men in popular media.[69] In *The Tramp and the Crap Game* (Edison, 1902), African-American men play craps in back of a theater.[70] In *Interrupted Crap Game* (Selig, 1903), African-American men stop their crap game to chase a stray chicken.[71]

Eph's Dream (Powers, 1913) is a culmination of a number of racist generalizations regarding the African-American man in terms of work and industriousness. The company's promotional material for the film explained:

Eph is a black man of the crapshooting variety. He is industriously engaged in his favorite occupation of crapshooting and hoping for big winnings. He fares badly in the game and goes home. His mind still dwelling on his imaginary winnings, he goes to sleep and dreams. He finds money on the street—oodles of it—meets a "sweel" wench, visits the swellist cafes, throws money around promiscuously, and is the ideal of his class. But finally the crash comes. He awakens and comes back to the actual things. . . . He wanders out from his hovel, back past the old crap game and, hoping to realize something on his dream, he makes a "grab" at the stakes.[72]

This film could be seen as a brutal social commentary on the lack of economic opportunities available for African-American men in the beginning of the century but it was billed as a comedy. Rather than attempting to understand African-American male unemployment, the film demeans black men and expects them to take the easy way out.

In the early twentieth century, manhood and race were inextricably linked in American society. American motion pictures and popular culture at large "fixed" certain visions of masculinity. According to the early American cinematic canon, black manhood was clearly not on the same level as Euro-American manhood. Black men were considered immoral or lacking in initiative. The black man was also regarded as animalistic. The most blatant example of this is *Burlesque Lions and Their Tamer, Hagenbeck's Circus* (Lubin, 1903). A number of African-American men are crouched down in a cage and they "snarl and bite at each other like wild animals."[73] A white lion tamer appears and has enormous difficulty attempting to tame them. He stabs them with a pointed weapon and finally is aided by two white assistants. "The darkies [lions] are finally subdued," claimed the Lubin program.[74]

This "circus" allegory was a cinematic exercise in early-twentieth-century racial views. According to Radical southern ideology, African-American men were savages, if not animals. They were dangerous to each other but especially dangerous to white men. They had to be subdued; physical violence was to be used if necessary. This sentiment argued that white men should, must, control the African-American man. The "animalistic" nature of African-American men was illustrated in many realms of American popular culture.[75] Virginia journalist Phillip Alexander Bruce claimed that African-American men were "the most bestial and ferocious animals."[76] African-American ancestral ties to Africa were emphasized by scholars and journalists of the era. Harvard professor Nathaniel Shaler wrote, "There will naturally be a strong tendency for many generations to come, for them to revert to their ancestral conditions."[77] These conditions were, of course, bestial and savage. *Hagenbeck's Circus* stressed the danger that uncontrolled, untamed black men posed to white civilization.[78]

Euro-American filmmakers often defused this racially explosive situation by portraying African-American men as humorous rather than dangerous. By far, the comedy genre contained the majority of African-American male portrayals. One can argue that violent depictions of African Americans were simply part of the slapstick tradition of comedy that dominated early screen portrayals. Slapstick comedy can be defined as physical comedy with plenty of movement that involves cruel humor and violence. Virtually all of the great and minor silent comics of the pre-1920 era employed slapstick. The film studios of Mack Sennett (of Keystone Kops fame) are most closely associated with the genre. Steve Neale and Frank Krutnik point out in *Popular Film and Television Comedy* that "prior to 1906, slapstick was fundamental, not just to film comedy, but to the aesthetic nature, cultural function and institutional location of film as a whole."[79] The slapstick film depended heavily on a strong emotional arousal on the part of the viewer. Geared primarily toward a working-class immigrant audience, slapstick was considered lowbrow humor because it depended on pain and humiliation to gain an audience.

Violence directed toward African-American men was a staple theme in the first dozen years of American filmmaking. Violence has been an important element in American cinematic humor, but its relationship to historical context has largely been ignored by film historians until recently.[80] Racialized cinematic brutality was part of the larger slapstick comic tradition, but more important, it was an element of the Euro-American masochistic control of the black male body that dominated American race relations at the turn of the century.

Early silent films treated African-American men almost exclusively as humorous objects. This reflected the conservative southern sentiment that African-American men were not intelligent enough to be considered real men.[81] *Colored Sports* (Lubin, 1903) crystallized the dominant cinematic approach to African-American male representation. Two African-American men are telling funny stories to each other. The physical expressions of the men are considered "odd" by the filmmakers (and supposedly by the white audience). An element of difference defines the parameters of this film; not only are the men racially different, they are also physically dissimilar to white men. The second "humorous" type of such shorts usually involved the humiliation or physical abuse of black men. In this case the "stout" gentleman puts the lighted end of a cigar in his mouth. The degradation of African-American men was not exclusively intellectual; it involved the implementation of physical pain. Although this was the age of slapstick comedy, the physical maltreatment of African-American men closely mirrored real life, re-flecting a presumption that African-American men must be restrained.[82]

The sadistic tendency toward vicious physical abuse of African-American men is apparent in a significant number of early films. Black male pain meant white audience laughter in the minds of many filmmakers. This was not par-ticularly unusual in a period in which lynching had been ritualized into a form of mass entertainment in the South. Before a lynching, audiences gath-ered, promotional literature was distributed, and a "theater" was often es-tablished. Mass participation guaranteed audience satisfaction. Although lynching films were rare, motion pictures of the period often placed such racial hysteria on the screen.[83]

Once again, Lubin and Biograph led in the creation of such films. Lubin had a series of films produced in 1903 titled *Trick Donkey*. The premise of these films was that the donkey was more intelligent than a black man. An assorted number of African Americans are thrown, kicked, and pitched off a donkey's back, to the apparent delight of the audience. Even a young African-American boy is part of the violent action. The disdain for the par-ticipants is clear; in the catalog description of these films, they are described as "smokes," "dark clouds," "coons," and "darkies."[84]

The most dramatic example of this masochistic tendency toward African-American men is displayed in the short documentary *An Execution by Hang-ing* (Biograph, 1898). The film company proudly claimed that it was probably the only live hanging ever captured on film. The execution of an African-American man in the Jacksonville, Florida, jail is explicit and ghastly. The executioner adjusts a black cap over the prisoner's head. The noose is placed over his neck. After the man is hung, his body quivers and shakes from the tension. The nostalgic claim of the innocence of early silent cinema is clearly broken by this film. The death of an African-American man is clearly on the screen. His crime is never announced; his punishment is all the spectator understands.[85]

A number of comedy films with African-American characters (or men in blackface) revolved around mistaken identity. In *How Charlie Lost the Heiress* (Biograph, 1903), a young white man holds a carriage containing a black baby while the mother of the child chases after her hat, which has just blown off. His girlfriend just happens to stroll by at this time, and she is shocked, going off in a huff. The mere linkage of a white man with a black child, in any form, is obviously cause for scandal. In *The Subpoena Server* (Biograph, 1906), a white man tries to escape from receiving a subpoena. He cross-dresses and puts on blackface to escape the summons. The protagonist of the film is finally caught after dressing up as a black waiter. He attempts to stop a tramp from stealing food and is hit with a seltzer bottle. He wipes his wet face and the coal comes off.[86] This appears as a seemingly harmless farce, but one has to consider the fact that only the Euro-American man has the liberty to cross-dress or take on the characteristics of another race in early silent film. The ability to cross lines of gender or race is a demonstration of the Euro-American male control of the medium. The Other, be it Euro-American, African-American woman, or African-American man, is relegated to a position of regimented identity.

According to early motion pictures, the blackening of one's face immediately put an individual into an inferior position in American society. *A Burnt Cork* (Lubin, 1912) illustrates this better than most. In this film, Mr. and Mrs. Diggs are unaware that their disgruntled tenant, an unemployed actor who had recently been thrown out, has put blackface on them while they were asleep. The couple go throughout the community, ridiculed and harassed along the way because of their new skin color. Mrs. Diggs is proclaimed a "Negro Woman Maniac" by the local press because she attempts to attend her all-white church and is forced out by the women of the choir. Mr. Diggs suddenly becomes the "Negro Convict at Large." They are both eventually thrown in jail, where they plead with the police that they are truly white.[87] In *Drawing the Color Line* (Edison, 1909), Mr. Jack has his face blackened by his club members as a practical joke. He is unaware of his condition as he makes his way home. When he makes his regular stops along the way he is treated rudely. A police officer tells him to make himself scarce. His pals do not recognize him so they do not acknowledge his presence, and when he attempts to say hello to some female friends, their male companions beat him and throw him in the street. His own family members think he is a kidnapper and a thief and call for the police. Suddenly, Mr. Jack looks in a mirror and discovers his dilemma. Filmmakers never question the morality of the color line; it was just a natural part of the film's environment. Mr. Jack and the Diggs, as African Americans, do not know their place, and that is what gets them into trouble. The Edison Company billed *Drawing the Color Line* as a comedy, but any contemporary African-American spectator must have considered it a tragic reminder of real life.[88] A reviewer in the *Moving Picture News* wrote at the time, "An element of pathos can be found in it [the film]. . . . Merely putting a little black on a man's face changes his status."[89] *Drawing the Color Line* is, therefore, a powerful tale of the properties of whiteness.

Advertising for a Wife (Pathe-Freres, 1910) illustrates the lowly position that African-American men had within American culture. A young white man advertises for a wife. So many women appear at his doorstep that he has to find a way to get rid of all of them. He blackens up his face and all of the potential fiancées suddenly disappear. The mere thought of being romantically involved with a black man sends them fleeing from the house.

Occasionally a film dealt seriously with the color line in a liberal fashion. *A Close Call* (Biograph, 1912) is one such example. A white street vendor and a white banjo player realize they must change their act if they are going to survive. They decide that putting on blackface will do the trick. They become implicated in a scandal in which an African-American gardener, Jasper, is mistakenly accused of kidnapping a white baby. Just as Jasper is ready to be lynched (the noose is placed around his neck), the baby is found. This film is a powerful commentary on life in a southern town. African-American men were regularly blamed for crimes in which there was no evidence of guilt. Lynch mobs were a normal part of the racial pattern of the South and served as a form of vigilante justice. The only "untruth" of the film was mistaking the street vendors for real African-American men. Few Americans, black or white, would not be able to tell the difference between someone in blackface and real African-American men. This was one of the theatrical devices of the blackface routine: the audience's knowledge that the actor was really white. Yet in countless films made between 1896 and 1915, white men in blackface are thought to be real African-American men. This unfortunately contributed to the racist notion that "all blacks looked alike." By lumping all African-American men into one category of racialized gender norms, it was easier for white Americans to discriminate against and stereotype a diverse group of individuals. Negative qualities attributed to the black man excused the mechanisms of power and control that were in place.[90]

The superstitious and fearful nature of African-American men is a stereotype that lasted long into the sound era. This stereotype was a theatrical convention and was established in the early silent period in motion pictures. One of Biograph's earliest films, *Hallowe'en in Coontown* (1897), established the connection between African-American men and the ghostly holiday. In *Thirteen Club* (Biograph, 1905), the black(face) waiter is the epitome of fear, but he is also the character to which the audience clearly relates. This is the story of a secret men's club whose fraternal symbols are representative of popular superstitions. The white men meet at a coffin-shaped table with a skull and bones hanging overhead. The dungeonlike atmosphere frightens the African-American waiter. He quickly runs in and out of the room while serving the thirteen members of the club. They purposefully attempt to break superstition by shattering mirrors and opening an umbrella inside. The result is that one year later all thirteen members are dead. In the final scene the waiter returns to serve them and is horrified, realizing they are all skeletons.[91]

By 1910, films already had well established that black men were less "manly" because they were in constant fear. In *Dixie Duo Down South* (company unknown, 1910), two young girls decide to scare a black man by dressing in sheets and acting like ghosts. The man is so afraid he turns white (a common occurrence in films with black men). The girls then terrify an entire black community by running around the countryside in sheets (shades of the Ku Klux Klan?).[92] According to the film, these young girls are more intelligent than the frightened black men and, in a sense, superior, by being able to control their behavior. *In Zululand* (Lubin, 1915) involves two black princesses who dress as ghosts to persuade their mother the queen not to marry Zebo, a "good-for-nothing nigger."[93] They frighten Zebo so badly he will not go near the queen. The film ends happily for the princesses (with whom the audience is supposed to identify) because "the next day finds Zebo in the hands of the executioner, surrounded by the tribe, and the Queen on the throne ordering the execution."[94] The film was described by one reviewer as "cartoon humor."[95] These films demonstrated that black men could be manipulated by fear. Since they were of such a superstitious and fearful nature that even young girls could frighten them, this mechanism of control could be used in American society at large.

The supposedly superstitious nature of African-American men did not reflect the religiosity of the race. The cinema routinely mocked African-American spirituality, particularly in terms of church membership, participation, and leadership. In *Georgia Camp Meeting* (Lubin, 1903), the parson of a church is caught taking a swig from a bottle of alcohol by one of the members of the congregation while they are in prayer. Rather than admonish the minister, the congregation member simply demands a drink from the bottle.[96]

One of the most ridiculed aspects of African-American culture in early film is the portrayal of black romance. In early silent film the depiction of an African-American man and woman in love is considered an abnormality, an oddity. The freakish nature of black romantic love is evident in two Lubin shorts, *Whose Baby Is You* (1902) and *Darkies Kiss* (1903). In the first film, Erastus is kissing and holding his love, Dinah. Yet Lubin describes the film as "funny" since the couple are of the "old Virginny type."[97] *Darkies Kiss* is an even more obvious example of the "odd" nature of black romantic love. The film is an exotic excursion for the Euro-American spectator as he or she is exposed to visual representations of black sexual imagery. Lubin's promotional material claims, "It is probably that some of you have never seen a 'coon' and his best girl making love." This statement makes it abundantly clear that the spectator is assumed to be white. Thus, the "Other" is on display.[98]

Depictions of African-American romantic love are strikingly absent from silent films in the 1896–1915 era unless they are associated with violence, opportunism, and revenge or are portrayed in a humorous fashion. African-American married love is almost nonexistent. A number of films demonstrate the violent means that African-American men and women will use to maintain their relationship. This usually involves fighting a potential suitor. In *The Elite Ball* (Keystone, 1913), Rastus threatens a rival suitor with a huge razor. In *Darktown Razor* (Kalem, 1914), Sambo and Rastus engage in fisticuffs and thievery to "woo" Vebrena. In *The Black Prince* (Crystal, 1912), a jealous wife catches her husband, Ragtime Simmons, on the make with a young lady and chases him with a carving knife.[99]

The reasons why African-American couples get married are ridiculous, according to early cinematic texts. In *Darktown Duel* (Vitagraph, 1912), Eph Johnson and Rastus Simpson are rivals for the same woman. They decide to have a watermelon eating contest to decide who gets her hand. Maria Johnson, the young lady, rejects the winner of the contest because she fears he will eat too much once they are married.[100] The physical attributes of African-American romantic partners rarely match. The female is usually taller, larger, or more stout than her male companion. In Vitagraph's *A Georgia Wedding* (1909), the bride is so tall that she cannot make it through the cabin door where the wedding is to take place. The physical disparity between male and female partners implies the matriarchal domination of the African-American family.[101] According to early films, African Americans regularly pursue romance or marry for money or property. In *A Bucktown Romance* (Kalem, 1912), two African-American gentlemen vie for the hand of the widow Lane only because they believe she has money.[102]

The cinematic denigration of African-American romance and marriage is a direct attack upon African-American masculinity and femininity. Making African-American romance strictly humorous dehumanizes black men and women by arguing that they cannot have real human emotions or connections. Ridiculing African-American marriage implies that black men are unstable and irrational, either driven by money or controlled by dominant African-American women. Jacquie Jones argues that "the imaging of Black sexuality in mainstream film, particularly Black male heterosexuality, continues to be the most denormalizing factor in the definition of the Black screen character."[103]

Segregation between the races was stringently observed in the cinematic medium as it applied to romance or erotic physical contact. A series of films placed an African-American woman in the position of nonerotic comic relief.[104] In *Misdirected Kiss* (Biograph, 1904), a nearsighted boyfriend brings home flowers for his girl. She leaves the room while an African-American maid enters and arranges the flowers. The half-blind man begins kissing the maid's hand, startling both her and her mistress.[105] Another Biograph film, released in the same year, follows almost exactly the same premise. In *A Kiss in the Dark* (1904), a beautiful white woman comes to a window while her beau comes to woo her. She covers his eyes and a black mammy takes her place and kisses him. Everyone but the Romeo gets a good laugh; he is absolutely horrified. On the surface, this genre of film does not contain any direct portrayals of black masculinity.[106] But the genre contains an important subtext: The African-American woman is apparently undesirable. She provides nothing but sheer comic relief when confronted by a potential white male lover, who is "tricked" into propositioning her. This implies that only African-American men could possibly want such a woman. By placing the black woman on a much lower level of desirability than the white woman, the filmmaking establishment also lowers the social position of black men. This is a blatant disregard of the southern past. Thousands of black women were raped or forced into sexual relationships with white men in the antebellum and post–Civil War eras. By denying the sexual desirability of black women, one is denying the complicated and twisted pattern of racialized sexual relationships in American society. The racial roles are never reversed. An African-American man never accidentally kisses a white woman; this was the ultimate fear of white society and not a humorous subject. This genre of film demonstrates that the intended audience was a white audience. One of the appeals of this genre was that it elevated white womanhood and denied white male sexual desire for African-American women.[107]

The only African-American woman who was considered sexually desirable by the filmmaking establishment was the octoroon. An octoroon is an individual who is one-eighth black. This was obviously close enough to being fully white to distort the binary parameters of black/white relations. In the early silent film era she was always pursued by Euro-American men and never by African-American men.[108] The octoroon was always a woman and never a man. This structuralized absence of multiracial men is an interesting commentary on the ritualized patterns of gender and race in the early silent era. It allowed filmmakers to pigeonhole black male characters into stereotyped patterns without dealing with the racial, economic, and social diversity within the black community. Euro-American filmmakers could create simplistic portrayals of race and gender for intended white audiences that did not challenge the dominant racial system.[109]

Early American silent films also stereotyped African-American children. They were regarded as natural entertainers. One of American Mutoscope's first films, *Dancing Darkies* (1896), exploited the musical talents of African-American children. The catalog summary read: "A company of little darkies showing off their paces to the music of the banjo."[110] The Edison Company also exploited children. In *Dancing Darkey Boy* (1897), a crowd of jockeys and stable hands watches a "little darkey boy dance on a table."[111]

Early silent films considered African-American children as inferior to Euro-American children and dealt with them in animalistic terms. During the period 1896–1915, black children were not even considered children; they were "pickaninnies." Black children were always eating watermelon (*Watermelon Eating Contest*, Edison, 1900) or dancing (*Pickaninnies*, Edison, 1900) or playing tricks on others (*The Mailman in Coontown*, Biograph, 1906).[112] African-American children were also frequently "eliminated." In *The 'Gator and the Pickaninny* (Biograph, 1900) an alligator swallows a young African-American boy. Luckily, his father rushes to the rescue, chops the alligator open, and pulls his son out. The boy is described by Biograph as "none the worse for his experience."[113] Although the responsibility of the black father is firmly demonstrated, using a black child was a conscious choice. Black children were often considered "disposable." The physical and psychological trauma of being swallowed by an alligator in real life would obviously be dramatic. Even when the filmmakers are given artistic license through the suspension of belief, the fact that Euro-American children were not cast in such roles is a dramatic statement on the lack of worth of African-American children.

Edison's *Ten Pickaninnies* (1908) is the epitome of the cinematic dehumanization of African-American children. The story-poem reduces the number of African-American children from ten to zero in the text. Within the context of this "amusing subject" that is "funny all the way," African-American children are knocked out, kidnapped, beestung to death, shot, drowned, and eaten by an alligator.[114]

Why would the filmmakers be so intentionally cruel to innocent African-American children? Perhaps it was a form of wish fulfillment. In *White on Black,* Jan Nederveen Pieterse argues that children are often regarded as miniature adults. He points out that within Victorian anthropology, the psychology of the child and that of the savage were seen as twin themes.[115]

Thus, black children are symbols of their parents, who are also seen as child-like and savage (the children wear only loincloths). By eliminating the children, one potentially eliminates the adults. In the context of arguments of race relations at the turn of the century, when the deportation of all African Americans was seen seriously as a solution, the total removal of African Americans was not a particularly unusual theme. But the means employed by such films as *Ten Pickaninnies* illustrates the sadistic and violent tendencies that a segment of the Euro-American population had toward the African-American population. This was mainstream cinema. The act of murdering children in the context of a "humorous" film demonstrates the sociopathology of American race relations.

Like African-American women and men, black children were considered "inferior" when compared to Euro-American children. A number of films from the era dealt with the problem of "switched babies." In *Mixed Babies* (Biograph, 1908), a department store initiates a checking station for babies in carriages. The new head of the checking station is overwhelmed when the infant department has a big sale. He accidentally sends two children home to the wrong parents. Upon their arrival home, Mr. Jones thinks his baby is just sunburned, but his wife screams, "Good gracious, it's a coon!" The baby is immediately rushed back to the department store. In *Mixed Colors* (Pathe, 1913), a black baby is painted white and a white baby is painted black by mischievous boys. When the white mother finds the true race of her baby she makes a hurried exchange with the black mother. The theme of these and other similar films was not simply a matter of children being given to the wrong parents. At the center of these films was the understanding that white parents were given a child that was inferior to theirs. A black baby was an "Other"—a child they could not possibly raise or love. African-American men, women, and children were portrayed as inferior, primitive, and worthless by the early Euro-American film studios.

The majority of African-American screen portrayals of the early silent era were in slapstick films. Within the context of slapstick, the body is often treated as a type of inanimate object. One may be swallowed by an alligator or shot but no real danger appears to have taken place. The debasement and mutilation of the black body is a given in slapstick films involving African-American characters.

Popular comedy has often been closely associated with morbidity, but one cannot completely separate African-American cinematic depictions from the real lives of African Americans in the period of early filmmaking. Within slapstick comedies with African-American characters there was a dehumanizing aesthetic that contributed to the popular acceptance of the inferiority of blacks. Slapstick reflected real life; both the comedic genre and the racial codes of the era were based on derision of African Americans. Slapstick, therefore, was a psychologically compromised form of humor that did not preach disobedience but obedience to the racial norms of the era.

Slapstick has been described as "controlled nonconformity." Making the body into a plastic object that could be tortured in almost any way, the genre also ruthlessly argued for a return to racial and social order. Eileen Bowser points out that while slapstick gags often depend on subverting conventions, this rarely applies to racial conventions.[116] Slapstick comedy supported the status quo by giving comfort to Euro-American spectators. By punishing black thieves or eliminating black children, slapstick fulfilled the psychological needs of white society.

3

BLACK CINEMATIC RUPTURES
AND OLE UNCLE TOM

A litany of racial and gender stereotypes appeared on the early American silent screen. The cinema was, and has remained, an institution of popular culture that has held in place the Euro-American dominated symbolic order of "white" masculine supremacy. The development of racial masculinization in cinema has embodied tools of signification. The recurrence of certain resilient stereotypes, of both Euro-American and African-American portrayals, has created a narrative web with which the spectator is familiar and to which the viewer returns, with every new film he or she sees. This cinematic puppetry created black male stereotypes that pervaded American popular culture. Motion pictures, television programs, cartoons, postcards, popular literature, household accessories, and countless other material items of American popular culture reinforced the mythology of black male inferiority. What was original about the motion picture was not the message it delivered but the means by which the message was conveyed. The widespread distribution and popularity of the early motion picture ingrained such stereotypes in the minds of the American population. Early American silent film, therefore, needs to be considered not only as a form of entertainment but also as a disseminator of hegemonic mythology.

Watching a film does not necessarily mean accepting the ideology behind its construction. The relationship between the text and the spectator has been considered in two major ways. Structuralist analysis was organized in terms of binary oppositions of filmmaker/active and spectator/passive. Recent post-structuralist theorists have countered this simplistic scheme, arguing that narrative codes make no sense unless the spectator attempts to understand, evaluate, and comprehend what is on the screen. The spectator can accept, negotiate, or reject the system of power relations as displayed in the film. This gives the spectator the privileged position of power. Although the viewer is

41

limited to the cinematic text on the screen, he or she is in a position to accept or reject the film narrative and its issues of hegemony. In an influential article, "Black Spectatorship: Problems of Identification and Resistance," Manthia Diawara has argued that the terms "black spectator" and "resisting spectator" are interchangeable. This is owing, of course, to dominant derogatory stereotypes of African Americans in mainstream Hollywood films.[1]

Post-structuralist theorist Stuart Hall has emphasized the relationship between the encoding function of the filmmaker and the decoding function of the spectator. Quoted in Judith Mayne's book, he has argued that "the relationship between the ideology contained with texts and the various ways in which individuals 'decode' or interpret that ideology is based on their own social positioning."[2] One can accept the ideological positioning of the film's "message" or reject the theoretical underpinnings of the cinematic premise. Quite simply put, African-American and white audiences often saw the same film in different ways. In "The Oppositional Gaze," bell hooks has argued that "when most black people in the United States first had the opportunity to look at film . . . they did so fully aware that mass media as a symbol of knowledge and power was reproducing and maintaining white supremacy."[3] African-American spectators, therefore, developed an "oppositional gaze"; hooks claims, "Subordinates in relations of power learn experientially that there is a critical gaze . . . one learns to look a certain way in order to resist."[4]

The development of an oppositional gaze was one of the strategies African-American film viewers used to combat derogatory imagery on the screen. But there were also obvious ruptures from traditional racist stereotypes that existed in cinematic portrayals of African-American masculinity in the early silent era. This chapter will observe such ruptures or near-ruptures in film depictions of African-American men in the pre-1915 period. These will include African-American men in the military, the boxing exploits of Jack Johnson, films set in Africa, considerations of black male sexuality on the screen, and the Uncle Tom/faithful servant motif. Although the first two subjects made substantial breaks with the hegemonic cinematic canon, they were often controlled in their presentation onscreen. Although the final three subjects break away from the comedic genre where the vast majority of black male depictions lay, they fit into the oppressive marginalization of African-American men on film.

In the first five years of filmmaking, a realistic tradition dominated the medium. Filmmakers simply tried to record an occurrence, event, or personality; the filmic representation of the subject was in and of itself entertainment. Fictional narrative was of secondary importance to portrayals of everyday life, exotic locations, or the rich and famous. This documentary tradition often contradicted filmed representations of minstrel acts or blatant stereotypes of watermelons and chicken thievery. African-American men were filmed in a variety of settings, situations, and occupations, in opposition to the preordained, Euro-American images of such men. In simple terms, the reality of filmed life contradicted the woven, fictional filmic narrative.

African-American participation in the Spanish-American War was one such occurrence. The Spanish-American War was fought in 1898, just as films were starting to take hold in American culture. The war was of prime interest to American audiences, and film crews immediately rushed to the scene of the conflict or attempted to get footage of armed soldiers going off to war.[5] African Americans fought on both fronts in the war, in Cuba and in the Philippines, and their wide participation was bound to be captured by filmmakers. African-American soldiers were victims in the explosion of the *Maine,* one of the events directly leading to the outbreak of the war. Four regular regiments of Buffalo soldiers, serving in the American West, were transferred to the fronts during the war. *Colored Invincibles* (Lubin, 1898) showed the troops that aided Roosevelt's Rough Riders in taking San Juan Hill. The Lubin Company, well known for its abundance of racist films, gave black soldiers credit in their promotional material. The company proclaimed that black troops "fought with as much zeal as their white brothers."[6] In a rare progressive attitude, the Lubins claimed, "This is one of the scenes where the colored man is accepted as a brother in arms, for his work in the field was of equal, if not superior at times to his white companions."[7]

African-American participation in the acquisition and maintenance of control over the Philippines was also documented cinematically.[8] But following the Spanish-American War, African-American soldiers were rarely, if ever, portrayed on the screen in either documentary fashion or in a fictional narrative. Lubin's promotional material for *Ohio Colored Troops at Fort Algiers* (1903) acknowledged this fact. The company claimed that "colored troops are a novelty to the ordinary layman [implication, white] in that we rarely see them in battle array."[9] The soldiers are described as "proud." Yet this film is one of the few that portray African-American men as soldiers. Between 1903 and 1914, soldiering was exclusively a white male preserve on the screen. Kevin Gaines claims that "displays of military prowess and national loyalty . . . provid[ed] black men with a rare outlet for the assertion of strong, courageous masculinity."[10] The exclusion of cinematic portrayals of African-American soldiering was an attempt to restrict the parameters of black masculinity.

One of the most significant ruptures in Euro-American portrayals of black masculinity involved the boxing exploits of Jack Johnson. Johnson's repeated victories over white opponents, as captured on celluloid, challenged the hegemonic order of early silent film and consequently dealt a fatal blow to motion picture exhibition of filmed boxing matches. Daniel Bernardi argues that "Johnson's boxing victories produced a tension in the racial 'order of things.'"[11]

Johnson was an African-American heavyweight who quickly moved up the ranks in the boxing establishment in the first few years of the twentieth century. By 1904 he was considered a contender for the heavyweight championship. Jim Jeffries, the then-current heavyweight champion, argued that he would rather retire than fight a black man. Johnson became one of the first African-American boxers to break the racial barrier in the sport. In the nineteenth century, boxing had been strictly segregated, like most aspects of American life. Finis Farr, in his biography of Johnson, argued, "A prize fight between a white and a black man might well carry the symbolism of racial war. It was not a good thing; if the Negro lost, it could be taken by white people to mean that white superiority extended even to strength and speed of movement. . . . But when a Negro beat a white boxer, the loser's racial partisans could question the wisdom of trying to equal a black man in brute power when he stood closer to the savage, and even to the animal, than any white."[12]

Johnson's phenomenal ability in the ring and the promise of a large gate if he fought a white opponent led to the first significant interracial fight. In 1905, Johnson fought Marvin Hart, a well-known boxer. A controversial decision by the referee disqualified Johnson from the fight for not being aggressive enough. From 1904 to 1907 he toured the world, fighting boxers on both the east and west coasts of the United States and in Europe and Australia. Johnson's unbeaten record made it impossible for the sport's white professionals to ignore him. Tommy Burns, a white Canadian boxer, took the heavyweight crown in 1906. Burns avoided fighting Johnson. The black boxer responded by following the Canadian incessantly, mocking his cowardice for not meeting him in the ring. Finally, on 26 December 1908, Burns faced Johnson. The Canadian boxer was beaten to a bloody pulp. Jack Johnson, an African American, became the heavyweight champion of the world.[13]

Johnson's victory flew in the face of all contemporary racial ideology. It was now disproven that African-American men were physically and intellectually inferior to white men. Johnson's physical stamina and boxing expertise stunned Burns, who had based his strategy on the black man's supposed inferiority and lack of endurance. Johnson was able to defeat the prizefighter despite a jeering white mob at the match. The fact that a black man was now the heavyweight champion of the world was simply too much for many in power in the sports and political world. Jack London, the literary lion and a key journalist of the period, rallied for a "Great White Hope." He called on Jim Jeffries, the former heavyweight champion, to come out of retirement and face the black opponent. London pleaded, "Jeff, it is up to you. The White Man must be rescued."[14]

Jack Johnson also presented a public persona that was absent from the American cinema and almost nonexistent in mainstream American public life. He was the epitome of what one biographer, Al-Tony Gilmore, called "The Bad Nigger."[15] Johnson liked to wear colorful clothes and drive sports cars. He regularly flashed around money and frequently kept the company of white women. Johnson was boastful, proud, arrogant, and loud, qualities that defied how white society wanted the African American to behave. The public attention Johnson drew to himself caused the drive to find a Great White Hope to reach hysterical dimensions in a large segment of the white community.

Throughout Johnson's boxing career, the filmmaking establishment was present. Filmed prizefights were big box office in the days of the nickelodeon. In the early days of film, fights often were reenacted by other boxers, but by the time of Johnson's ascendancy, films of actual major prizefights could bring in crowds of spectators. Although prizefighting was illegal in many municipalities and states, exhibiting prizefighting films was not.[16] Segments of Johnson's fight with Burns were shown theatrically.[17] The *Richmond Planet,* an African-American newspaper, proclaimed, "No event in forty years has given more genuine satisfaction to the colored people of this country than . . . the victory of Jack Johnson."[18] Coming at a desperate time in African-American history, when lynching and racial violence were at a high point, Johnson's victory was a bright spot for African Americans.

The first groundbreaking film was the match between Johnson and the first "Great White Hope," Stanley Ketchel, a former middleweight champion. The Kalem Company had exclusive rights to the film and heavily advertised it in trade papers. In *The Making of a Champion* (1909) the company filmed a simple biography of the pugilist's life, showing him from infancy to champion of the world.[19] Johnson eventually beat Ketchel in a twelve-round match. *Variety* summed up the visual impact of seeing the boxers next to each other: "There can be no doubt in anyone's mind after

Jack Johnson and his wife. Jack Johnson's public persona contested the media-constructed image of proper African-American male behavior. (Library of Congress)

seeing the two men line up before the fight starts what a very slim chance
Ketchel had. The black fellow towers above him. The two when fighting
seem like a father fooling with his young son. Ketchel could not hit the black
man."[20] Dan Streible claims, "The *Johnson-Ketchel* pictures . . . presented
spectators with a sensational depiction of a fearsome, indomitable athlete."[21]
Johnson was now truly the man to beat.

The public exhibition of Johnson defeating his white opponents on film
was considered uniquely dangerous to the white establishment. Boxing
matches tended to be the preserve of adult white men. Nickelodeons and
motion picture theaters were populated by millions of young people, typi-
cally not present at boxing matches. Johnson's victory over his opponents
was a direct contradiction to the ideology of white male supremacy taught
in schools, propagandized by the mass media, and "scientifically established"
by experts. Streible argues that the image of "Johnson standing over an unconscious white hope, confronted viewers with an historically unprecedented image of black power."[22]

Johnson's success in the ring and his refusal to play the Uncle Tom character made him a hero to the African-American community but deeply an-
tagonized many white Americans. The *Chicago Defender* exclaimed,
"Johnson [is] a real champion. Nowhere in prize ring history is there
recorded an incident of pluck, patience and perseverance that compares fa-
vorably with Johnson's quest for the championship."[23] The Johnson-
Ketchel film played to packed audiences at the Pekin, Chicago's best-known
black theater. Although few examples of black audience reaction exist today,
it can be assumed that the response was overwhelming.[24] These early fight
films of Jack Johnson and his opponents clearly established that race mat-
tered when it came to spectatorial positioning.[25]

Jim Jeffries, former heavyweight champion and virulent racist, was finally
persuaded to redeem the white race and attempt to defeat Johnson. The
purse for the fight was the largest amount of money any sports figure had
ever been offered for a single event. The match took place on 4 July 1910
in the then-tiny backward town of Reno, Nevada. The media hype leading
up to the match was unprecedented in sports. The motion picture companies were there.[26] It was widely assumed that Jeffries would win and the
companies realized they would have a box-office hit on their hands. It was
estimated that thousands of white men would pay to see the defense of their
racial superiority. Prior to the match, the Chicago Film Picture Company released a film titled *Johnson Training for His Fight with Jeffries.* The match of
Jeffries versus Johnson was more than a prizefight. It was what the *Chicago*

Defender (the largest circulating black newspaper) characterized as "a fight against race hatred, and negro prejudice."[27] Literally thousands of spectators came to the desolate town to watch the battle. The largest press contingent in human history up to that time assembled, demonstrating the cultural significance of the match. Finis Farr argues, "The final week in Reno may have been the last stand of uninhibited American masculinity."[28] Both Johnson and Jeffries came into the boxing grounds in grand theatrical style. Johnson was the first boxer in the ring to strip. According to popular press reports of the period, a communal gasp came over the mostly white crowd as the spectators were able to examine the pure athletic perfection of Johnson's body. Rex E. Beach, a prominent author of the period, explained, "His image was a thing of surpassing beauty from the anatomist's point of view. [He had] a rounded symmetry more in line with the ideals of the ancient Greek artists."[29]

The match lasted fifteen rounds with an eventual victory for Johnson. The match was so culturally significant that the *Chicago Defender* advertised a theatrical presentation and blow-by-blow account of the events at the Coloseum. Every move and blow was acted out by illuminated electrical figures nine feet high on a colossal electrical board.[30] During much of the bout, Jeffries was staggering, bleeding profusely, with an eye that was permanently damaged due to Johnson's powerful hook. Some speculate that Johnson let the bout go on as long as it did for the benefit of the motion picture cameras.[31] That evening, African Americans celebrated as their hero triumphed against the Great White Hope, but massive race riots erupted in every major city in the United States. Many Euro-Americans retaliated by taking revenge against African-American fans. In Chicago, New Orleans, Atlanta, St. Louis, and countless other cities, innocent black men and women were beaten because Johnson had defeated Jeffries in the ring.[32] At least eighteen African Americans were killed.

Johnson's defeat of Jeffries also dealt a fatal blow to motion picture exhibition of filmed boxing matches. There was an immediate overwhelming reaction by the white community to ban any exhibition of the Johnson-Jeffries fight film. The *San Francisco Examiner* claimed that "within twenty-four hours" attempts to prohibit the screening of the Johnson-Jeffries match "assumed the proportions of a national crusade."[33] A national campaign to ban the film was led by the United Society for Christian Endeavor, a Protestant youth organization with over four million members. Letters were sent by the organization to governors across the nation to prohibit the showing of fight films.[34]

The viewing of such films by white Americans and African Americans was

considered dangerous by the organization and their supporters. One Johnson biographer claims that reformers argued that "the fight picture will be
worse than the fight."[35] A cartoon in the *Jackson Clarion-Ledger* depicts two
boys, one white and one African American, before a billboard promoting the
exhibition of the fight film. The byline asks, "Educational?"[36]

The one-word question summarized white fear of the exhibition of such
a film. The answer to the question must simply be "Yes." African-American
audiences were educated to the fact that white men were not naturally physically superior and dominant. Johnson's victory singlehandedly destroyed
the basis of white supremacy. Johnson's victory created remarkable racial
pride within the African-American community.

In both boxing matches and vaudeville shows, racialized stage performances are momentary. Film explodes the confines of time through the ability to visually document events (such as the victory of Jack Johnson).
Producers of films could isolate, distribute, replay, and save those frozen
moments. In Johnson's victory over Burns, the final knockout punch was
often eliminated from cinematic exhibition. But Johnson's victory over Jeffries was such a significant sporting and cultural event that African-American audiences demanded to see Johnson's victory.

The connection between the early black motion picture community and
Johnson was evident at this time. Robert T. Motts, owner of the Pekin Theater, one of the first black vaudeville theaters to exhibit motion pictures, was
head of the African-American community's reception committee when
Johnson returned to his hometown of Chicago after his victory over Jeffries.[37] Johnson obtained prints of the filmed match and they found their
way onto the black theatrical circuit.[38]

As Gilmore explains, "Within three days after the fight, nearly every major
city had seen fit to pass local ordinances prohibiting their [film productions
of the fight] exhibition."[39] Some African Americans also believed in censorship of the film out of fear of racial violence, but the majority of African-
American leaders supported the open exhibition of the film. The *St. Paul
Appeal,* a black newspaper, argued, "We are firmly of the opinion that the apparently country-wide objection to the film comes more from race prejudice
than from a moral standpoint."[40] The law had been quickly enacted after the
Jeffries-Johnson match to prevent any further filmed exhibitions of a black
man defeating a white man in the ring.[41] Supporters of the law justified it by
claiming it would prevent further race riots like those that followed the
match. Clearly connected with this campaign to prevent racial violence was
a determined effort by members of the white community to prohibit such an

undeniable image of black power and triumph. Letters to the editor in major newspapers reflected this sentiment. A writer to the *New York Times* called the fight and its result "a calamity to this country worse than the San Francisco earthquake."[42] A letter to the *New York Herald* was remorseful that "the best fight comes from the lowest and least developed race among us."[43] Despite attempts to stop the cinematic exhibition of the match, it was screened in a number of American cities, including New York, Philadelphia, St. Louis, and Kansas City, without any evidence of racial violence.

On 31 July 1912, Congress passed a law prohibiting the importation and interstate transportation of films or other pictorial representations of prizefights. The law, which remained on the books until 1940, was obviously aimed at Jack Johnson.[44] The federal courts, therefore, mandated that no African-American male boxer could successfully defend his title in front of motion picture cameras, eliminating a distinct, powerful portrayal of African-American masculinity.

Aggressive African-American men had not been allowed on the screen because they portrayed a real racial threat to white Americans. African-American physical retaliation or violence toward whites was strictly self-censored by Euro-American filmmakers. This was particularly true in the wake of early-twentieth-century race riots. If black violence was demonstrated on the screen, it was purely black-on-black violence. Selig produced two graphic demonstrations of this in 1903. In *A Night in Blackville*, a fight takes place at a dance. Razors are drawn, guns are pulled out, and a massive confrontation takes place. Selig claimed that this was "one continued round of laughter."[45] *Prize Fight in Coontown* had almost the same story line. The "exotic" nature of such a film (to a white audience) was clear in the promotional material. The company claimed, "Here it is, the real thing, a coon fight in a coon neighborhood by two bad coons."[46]

Such images of violence were directly related to Euro-American preconceptions of the "savage roots" of African Americans. African-American men were usually portrayed as primitive to justify the need for white male dominance.

The white male American hero has clearly been the standard figure in motion pictures. He has remained the protagonist for over a century of American film. As Joan Mellen explains in *Big Bad Wolves*, "Our films fostered the need for heroes, men larger than life." They have been "undomesticated . . . dominant . . . violent . . . strong . . . unthreatened . . . assertive."[47] This drive for heroic hegemony is a primitive desire for individual power over an alien environment.[48] To be in control, to dominate over the Other, it is necessary to contrast the cinematic image of the Other to that of a superior male image that implies he is a lesser man. Classic Hollywood film suggests that the Euro-American male hero must control and have power over his environment. Many classic genres, particularly the Western, revolve around the protagonist gaining mastery over his setting and its marginal Others. Whether the setting is a southern plantation, a tropical jungle, or an American city, the racialized Other has remained in a subservient and often countermasculine role. The marginalization of ethnic and racialized Otherness in masculinity formation is key in understanding how the Euro-American locus of cinematic control has functioned both as a gendering device and as a racializing device.

This was certainly the case in films that depicted Africa. British and American films made between 1896 and 1915 stressed the "African" roots of black people. Although on the surface this may appear as a rupture since it authenticates the African roots of black people, the actual ways and lifestyles of Africans were rarely portrayed; instead, the Africa shown in these films was an imaginary continent that existed only in the cinematic world.[49]

In American film, the black connection to the African motherland was never seen in a positive light. The Dark Continent was a foreboding, exotic, backward place, ruled by superstition and violence. The comedy *Rastus in Zululand* (Lubin, 1910) offers Rastus the choice between marrying the ugly princess of a Zulu chieftain or being boiled in a pot for the tribal dinner. Despite the humorous nature of the film, the association of cannibalism with Africans was deliberate. The lack of Christian morality and the primitive, savage heritage of the African American justified white imperial/racial domination. Euro-American cultural superiority was stressed through film by pitting the positive, strong, rational nature of white men against barbaric, ferocious black men.[50]

One of the most virulent fears of the white man was the supposed black male sexual desire for white women. For most of the period of silent cinema, American society seemed generally obsessed with black male sexuality. The irony of this situation is that the topic was rarely addressed by filmmakers even though newspapers and journals of the period covered it intensively.[51]

The Buck was the least filmed of the three dominant black male cinematic stereotypes. The Buck was a bestial, brutal, sex-crazed, violent criminal, forever willing to insult white womanhood and step out of his social place. With few notable exceptions, such as *The Birth of a Nation* (1915), the Buck was largely absent from the American screen. Black male sexuality was strictly avoided cinematically. Michel Foucault has argued that sexuality is an especially dense transfer point for relations of power. "[Sexuality] is [one of the elements in power relations] encoded with the greatest instrumentality; useful for the greatest number of maneuvers and capable of serving as a point of support, as a linchpin, for the most varied strategies."[52] Through the silent cinematic text, one would believe that the black man is almost asexual—the lack of close intimate relations with a woman or man makes him less than human. Jacquie Jones has gone so far as to say that "black male heterosexuality itself is a repressed discourse . . . characterized by powerlessness and reaction in the mainstream cinema."[53]

The first twenty years of American cinema also was the period of the most rampant lynching in the United States.[54] One can argue that the filmic prescription of asexuality to black men was an attempt to neuter them. The black male body was feminized (equated with the castrated body) to be put in a position of being mastered.[55] The Buck was an aberration in American film history but a pervasive threatening image to the white American public, particularly in the South. He was also a stereotype, but he was closer to the full complexity of the African-American man than the other two stereotypes because he was a man with a sexual drive. It is not accidental that the Uncle Tom and the Coon, the neutered African-American male stereotypes, were the longest lasting and most pervasive of these stereotypes. This ideology consisted of Euro-American sexual control and African-American male asexuality. One can argue that this was a wish fulfillment on the part of the moviemaking establishment and the American public or simply a gross simplification of the American racial hierarchy.

A racially based ideology of male sexual power was a key doctrine that Euro-American filmmakers attempted to fix on the screen. One rare example that contradicted this ideology was *Missionaries in Darkest Africa* (Kalem, 1912). In the film, two white missionaries, a father and his daughter, Faith, decide they are going to Christianize the Egyptians. They are able to win the trust of the local tribal chieftain, but he is interested in Faith only as a potential wife. After desperately falling in love with the girl, he bombards her father with presents. When the father refuses to give the chieftain Faith's hand in marriage, he kidnaps her. She commits suicide rather than "surrender her soul to the keeping of her master."[56] It is never revealed whether Faith is killing herself because she would be forced to marry a black man or a non-Christian. This is a clear association of heathenism with blackness.

The most frequently filmed story of the early silent era was *Uncle Tom's Cabin*. At least five versions of the story were filmed before 1915. Undoubtedly, the figure of Uncle Tom was the most recognizable and identifi-

An African-American man on slave auction block, from *Uncle Tom's Cabin* (1903). (Library of Congress)

able African-American male character in early film. *Uncle Tom's Cabin* is the story of a faithful, dedicated black slave and his relationship with Eliza, a young white girl. This widely influential abolitionist novel by Harriet Beecher Stowe was intended to be an indictment of the evils of slavery. It was highly influential in the abolitionist movement but it was also pivotal to American theatrical history. *Uncle Tom's Cabin* was the most popular stage play of the nineteenth century. As the twentieth century began, hundreds of *Uncle Tom* troupes were still traveling the country. One can argue that Uncle Tom was a rupture in the characterization of African-American masculinity in American popular culture because he was a sympathetic character with a sense of morality that equalled, or surpassed, that of the Euro-American characters. But the majority of these streamlined theatrical productions presented a satirized version of the original novel, far removed from its abolitionist discourse. Uncle Tom became the personification of a certain breed of African-American men—the loyal, subservient, "good" slave who remained dedicated to his white family. *Uncle Tom's Cabin* provided a Euro-American nostalgic turn to the past when African Americans were trusted and obedient.[57] Uncle Tom was the Conservative notion of a Negro who clearly knew his place. In an era of racial violence and rioting, he was a comforting image to the Euro-American spectator.

Uncle Tom's Cabin was the first novel to be turned into a screenplay and the first movie with subtitles.[58] Edwin S. Porter directed the first filmed version of the famous novel in 1903. This one-reel version was presented in tableaux style. Many moviegoers were familiar with the famous play, so large segments of the story were missing.[59] Instead, the more dramatic scenes from the novel were presented theatrically, each prefaced by a title that described the action and set the stage. A comparison between the original staged version of *Uncle Tom's Cabin* and the 1903 film of the play demonstrates how the motivations and message of the original novel had been gutted.[60] In the staged version, Eliza and George dramatically discuss the evils of slavery. The filmed version begins with Eliza pleading with Tom to run away. This 1903 version of *Uncle Tom's Cabin* was among the first storyfilms to use a white actor in the principal black role. Uncle Tom (in blackface) had skin color that was coal black in comparison with his snow-white hair. Yet "real" African-American male characters acted in secondary roles (such as the scene at the port of New Orleans). So much of the story is stripped down to its basic dramatic scenes that an individual unfamiliar with the novel would find it difficult to make sense of the film. Instead, the film displayed highly emotionally charged scenes from the book.

Porter's version of *Uncle Tom's Cabin* also lost Stowe's original sympathetic portrayal of African Americans. Instead, Porter utilized popular stereotypes of African Americans so that white Americans could "identify" with the story. A number of musical numbers in the film show African-American men and women dancing the cakewalk (one assumes these segments would have been accompanied by piano in the theater). Black couples even joyfully dance right before the auction sale of St. Clair's slaves. The auction scene is one of the most inverted scenes in the film. The cinematic version makes the institution of slavery look palatable rather than demonstrating its horrors. A number of black men are shown shooting craps before the auction. A black man actually arranges the auction block. The "slaves" are well dressed in late-nineteenth-century attire, an obvious travesty of history. The first slave sold is in a full woolen suit with a tie and hat. One of the slave owners admires the strength of the slave. After his auction, the black actor looks directly at the camera and smiles. Is this a subversive act on the part of the black actor? Is this wide grin of happiness an implication that he is being sold for such a high price? Immediately after this scene, the slave throws his master's hat on the ground, now seemingly unhappy.[61]

A clear dichotomy of African-American male characterization exists in Porter's version of *Uncle Tom's Cabin*. Uncle Tom is one of the rare "good niggers," whereas the majority of black men are shiftless, lazy, dancing fools, content to be sold into slavery. Thus, a contradictory message exists in the film. Although the film demonstrates some of the more horrific aspects of slavery in the personification of Simon Legree, it also excuses slavery by showing the need to control African-American men.

The final tableau of the death of Tom is quite revealing. Tom sees a beautiful *white* angel in the sky shortly before he dies. A painted scene of the Civil War follows. The final scene is that of Abraham Lincoln with a black male slave, on bended knee, praising the president. Lincoln is a heroic figure, rescuing the black man out of slavery. He is the epitome of white goodness and virtue. The film implies that white men are the instigators of slavery; they also save the nation from the institution's vices. African-American men simply play a passive role; they are enslaved and then rescued.[62]

Both the Thanhauser Film Corporation and Vitagraph released screen versions of *Uncle Tom's Cabin* in July 1910. Thanhauser stuck to the traditional one-reel format and Vitagraph experimented with a revolutionary three-reel multipart filmed play. The Vitagraph films were initially exhibited on successive days. Later in the year, all three reels were shown consecutively at one screening. This was a dramatic step in multireel feature film production.[63]

The critical and audience reaction to the Vitagraph release is interesting. The story still apparently packed an emotional punch. A contemporary reviewer in *Moving Picture World* claimed, "Probably few novels offer such a fertile field for exploitation in motion pictures as this. The incidents, as described, are dramatic, but they are more. They arouse the emotions more forcibly than almost any other book published, and in playing upon the emotions they excite interest."[64] The power of melodrama had been aptly established by 1910 and was used as a way to show the horrors of slavery. The filmmaking establishment would not adequately exploit this melodramatic exercise demonstrating the evils of racial prejudice and hatred until the post–World War II years in fear of losing a southern audience. Melodrama remained a staple of the silent film studio system but it was rarely used to demonstrate racial injustice.[65]

The feature film format began to sweep the American industry by 1914. Universal-Imp and World Pictures each produced two multireel films that attempted to tell Stowe's complete story.[66] The Universal-Imp production followed the pattern established by other film companies—a white man in black-face was hired to play the Uncle Tom role and real black men played second-ary characters.[67] World Pictures broke with this tradition by hiring an authentic African-American actor to play the Uncle Tom character. Sam Lucas, a seventy-two-year-old actor, was the first black actor to portray Tom on the stage. World Pictures hired him to replicate the role because he was widely recognized as one of the finest black actors of the age.[68] The World Film production was a five-reel adaptation. The director chose to follow the book rather than the stage version (the norm in film was to follow the stage version).[69]

Some prevalent themes in this version distinguish it from previous *Uncle Tom* films. First, the film stresses that Tom is a Christian. The opening title reads: "Tom—a religious nigger." In the first scene, Tom is shown on a chair citing Scripture with his hand raised in the air. He is castigated and punished in the film for his Christian beliefs. This is one of the primary ways in which the wickedness of Simon Legree is demonstrated (by appealing to the Chris-tian sensibilities of the white audience). In the film Legree yells, "I hate re-ligious niggers, damn you. Give that boy a hundred lashes, or I'll send you to that new Jerusalem you are always talking about." Tom, being a faithful Christian, cannot whip anyone.[70]

Second, Tom is less than a man. In several parts of the film he is a mere plaything for young white children. Eva dresses Tom, an elderly man, in rings of flowers. Later in the film, when Tom is sold to Haley, an evil slave dealer, a little white boy comes to Tom and in a comforting plea says, "When I'm grown up, I'll buy you back Uncle Tom." That Tom's fate can be determined by a young white child demonstrates the helplessness of black men in slavery.

Third, the characters of George and Eliza Shelby are more fully developed than in previous *Uncle Tom* films. George is an alternative version of African-American masculinity. Both George and Eliza are mulattoes portrayed by ac-tors in blackface. This was an obvious identification device the filmmakers used to make the white audience sympathetic to the characters. Filmmakers believed that mulatto characters were more palatable and identifiable than pure black characters. In the film, George and Eliza will do anything to save their child Harry from being sold to Haley. George is such a courageous man that he runs away from the Shelby plantation and attempts to free his wife and child. The black family is given respect in this filmed version; the cohesive unit of the nuclear family is shown in a positive light.

Fourth, white male characters are shown in a truly evil light. Both Haley and Simon Legree are depicted as horrible, immoral men. Emmaline has to fight off a drunken Legree who wants to rape her. Haley regards the mulatto boy Harry as a potential slave and not as a cute child. Legree is shot by a young black man, a daring cinematic act for a film in 1914.

The World Film version of *Uncle Tom's Cabin* demonstrated the complexity and conflicting messages inherent in Harriet Beecher Stowe's novel. Uncle Tom is an admirable, saintly character but also one who is less than a man. George is a strong man but he is clearly mulatto. The implication is that his white blood gives him strength and character.

Uncle Tom's Cabin played a pivotal role in one of the most important subgenres of African-American male characterization in silent film narrative (1903–1915)—that of the faithful slave/servant. The black male faithful slave/servant role conformed to the racially based ideology of sexuality; he was a eunuch. The faithful servant was a cinematic characterization, based on southern Conservative ideology, who lived only to please or save the white family that he served. The Euro-American community may have considered this a "positive" characterization of African-American manhood because the chief loyalty of this black servant was clearly to them. Loyalty to one's own family or racial group was secondary in the mind of the faithful servant. This demonstrated a straightforward hierarchy of priorities; the needs of Euro-Americans must always supersede those of African Americans.

Three parallel events contributed to the popularity of the faithful slave/servant subgenre—the increased use of the cinematic narrative, the coming of the fiftieth anniversary of the Civil War, and the entrance of David Wark Griffith into film directing.

American motion pictures began to undergo a series of dramatic changes in the period 1908–1909. The emergence of the story-film actually took place between 1904 and 1906, the height of the nickelodeon era. More documentary films were produced in this period than story-films, but story-films greatly outsold the nonfictional genre. Film production for story-films accelerated in the post-1907 era. The ability to develop a narrative that would be accessible and clear for the audience was a difficulty filmmakers had in producing story-films. A large non-English-speaking immigrant audience was attracted to nickelodeon features. Therefore, new filmmaking practices had to be developed to allow viewers to understand the narrative. Large numbers of theatrical and vaudevillian entertainers had also entered motion picture production by 1907. They brought experience in legitimate theater that tended to center on melodrama and not the re-creation of actual events. Filmmakers were also under pressure because of increased competition and the possible threat of governmental censorship.[71]

The Civil War provided a wealth of cinematic story lines for the filmmaking establishment. Beginning in 1908, a number of Civil War–related films began to be produced. This was an opportunity to take advantage of the growing interest in the war. A multitude of events were celebrated to commemorate the fiftieth anniversary of the most devastating war the country had ever fought. Many veterans of the war were still alive and many were in positions of power, so the commemoration of the Civil War became a masculine ritual, a demonstration of sectional compromise, and a display of racial solidarity. The generations born after the Civil War tended to mythologize it as a war of loyalty and romance, centered in the melodramatic form. From 1908 to 1917, the Civil War film was a genre as popular as the Western or the romantic melodrama. Kalem, Selig, Universal, Champion, Vitagraph, and Lubin produced this genre of films in the years before American involvement in World War I.[72] David Wark Griffith's widely popular and critically acclaimed Civil War films (produced for Biograph) were perhaps the most influential and will be dealt with first since the faithful slave/servant motif played such a large role in their plot development.

Griffith is recognized as one of America's leading silent film directors. He was a southerner and his father had served in the Confederate Army. His knowledge of history was limited but he was sympathetic to apologists for white supremacy.[73] Griffith's views on Reconstruction and the South were sentimental rather than violently racial like the ideology of white supremacists and southern Radicals.[74] He once commented on his heritage and the effect it had on film: "I used to get under the table and listen to my father [a Confederate colonel] and his friends talk about the battles and what they'd been through and their struggles. Those things impress you deeply."[75] Apparently, they made enough of an impact to mold some of Griffith's best-known films.

In keeping with the cinematic style of the period, none of the principal black male roles were actually played by African-American men. Occasionally, black men appeared as extras, particularly in crowd scenes, but they rarely were key to the plot. One of the most frequent themes in Griffith's Civil War films was intra-family conflict. The family was usually divided by association with the North or the South in regard to the Civil War. *In Old Kentucky* (1909) was an example of a film that used this plot device. Griffith's films completely break with any sense of historical accuracy in regard to slave reaction or to participation in the Civil War. In Griffith's films prior to *The Birth of a Nation,* black slaves support the southern cause and their masters, upholding the institution of slavery that binds their very existence. In Griffith's *The Honor of His Family* (1910), faithful servants gather around the old slaveowner as he bids good-bye to his son, who is going off to battle. They wave good-bye and wish him well, as if he was supporting their cause.[76]

Daniel Bernardi argues that the "voice of whiteness" was present in Griffith's filmmaking within three intermixed genres: stories of nonwhite servitude; stories of colonial love; and stories of the divinity of the white family and serenity of the white woman.[77] The faithful slave motif (which corresponds to Bernardi's stories of nonwhite servitude) was present in Griffith's earliest films. He began directing for the Biograph Company in the summer of 1908. Among his earliest releases was *The Guerilla*, in which a faithful slave with a kitchen knife protects his white mistress from a marauder. The moral of this story was quite simple—the purity and virginity of a white southern woman was certainly worth the sacrificial offering of a black male servant (corresponding to Bernardi's third genre).[78] *In Old Kentucky* has Uncle Jasper, the faithful slave, reuniting his white "family." Once again, the loyalty to one's white master or family came before one's own personal happiness or freedom.[79] Griffith's Biograph releases were widely popular because he was an excellent storyteller and he appealed to a racially conservative mentality.

The grand conclusion to Griffith's faithful slave/servant motif was the Biograph production of *His Trust* (1911) and its sequel, *His Trust Fulfilled* (1911). These films were about the "self-sacrificing love of the man [slave] for his master."[80] The promotional material for the films began, "In every southern home there was the old trusted body-servant, whose faithful devotion to his master and his master's family was extreme to the extent of even laying down his life if required."[81] The film begins with Colonel Frazier telling his trusty servant George to take good care of his wife and child as he goes off to war. George takes his responsibility seriously. He is completely subservient to the colonel's wife and daughter. Colonel Frazier is killed in battle. When Union soldiers finally come to the Frazier home, the slaves do not greet them but fight them off. George is beaten down by soldiers on the front steps as he tries to protect the home. Union soldiers loot the home and set fire to it with the child still inside. The title then reads: "George Risks His Life to Be Faithful to His Trust." He runs into the burning building and saves the girl. He collapses from exhaustion as he falls into the front yard but runs back into the house to rescue the master's almighty sword. This symbol of his dead master is apparently more important than his own life. His master's wife thanks him and then abandons the half-burned, physically exhausted slave. The next title reads: "Homeless—George Gives His All." He takes the white mother and child to his cabin, hangs up the

D. W. Griffith's *His Trust* (1911) and *His Trust Fulfilled* (1911) exemplified the "faithful darkie" genre. (Library of Congress)

sword, and tucks in the child. In the final scene of *His Trust,* George throws a blanket on the ground in front of the door of his cabin and sleeps outside while the white woman and child are inside. No sexual or racial taboos are broken here—obviously, everyone knows their place.[82]

His Trust Fulfilled begins four years later. The opening title reads: "The Emancipation—But George Remains True to His Trust." The white family still lives in George's cabin and he is still sleeping outside. A black congregation comes up to George outside the cabin. They are happy and enthusiastic about their newfound freedom. The white woman is so fearful of the multitude of blacks that she almost faints. George, trying to help her be strong, shows her her husband's sword. But instead she dies!

George is left with a white orphan girl. He provides support for the child with his savings, pretending it comes from her estate for appearance's sake. George pays $300 a year to send her to the Woodbury Seminary. He is still in the same old tattered clothes he was in before the war (while the white girl is dressed immaculately). After the girl graduates she wants to go to college. Thinking there is still money in her estate, she goes to a lawyer to inquire about the possibility. He informs her by letter that this is an impossibility. Just at this time a wealthy English cousin of the girl arrives in the United States. He goes to meet with the lawyer while George is there. George, not wanting to disappoint the young girl, steals the wallet of the English cousin, but not before he is detected. The lawyer lets him off, though, realizing his true intention. The English cousin ends up marrying the girl and George's trust is fulfilled. George is briefly thanked and then he goes home, penniless and alone. He returns to his cabin and looks at the sword, realizing he has done his duty.

The dramatic impact of this film can still be felt today. Yet Griffith's intentions are questionable. Did Griffith truly believe that this was the way it was in the South during the war? Apparently, many members of his audience believed so. A contemporary critic in *Moving Picture World* argued, "They [the Biograph Company] have reproduced accurately conditions which actually existed in thousands of instances all over the South while the war raged, and at its close."[83] Was Griffith attempting to portray an idealized, deferential, subservient Negro and compare him with the assertive, organized African American of the day? Was this an attempt to go back to a bygone era when race relations were arranged for the benefit of white men, women, and children? Was this a cry to stop the organized activities of this new breed of African Americans and an attempt to politically and economically restrain them? Griffith attempted to argue that African Americans and white Americans could live together, as long as blacks knew their place. Clearly, both of these films are set in the distant past, which questions Griffith's contemporary racialized political views.

Griffith and Biograph did not have a monopoly on the faithful slave/servant subgenre. In *The Confederate Spy* (Kalem, 1910), African Americans are depicted as quite satisfied under slavery. "Happy, contented, and well cared for, they are as joyous and happy as a bunch of school children just dismissed."[84] *For Massa's Sake* (Pathe, 1911) is one of the more incredible films of the genre. Colonel St. Clair leaves his entire estate to his son but manumits a family of eight who have been faithful to their former master. Harry has an addiction to gambling but he continues to employ the freed family until his inheritance runs out. Old Uncle Joe, patriarch of the African-American family, decides to sell himself and his entire family back into slavery in order to "meet his [Harry's] obligation."[85] The pure unbelievability of such films was a regular part of early silent film narrative. This was truly wish fulfillment on the part of white filmmakers. It is quite clear that "good" African-American male servants or slaves, the ones who were "faithful to their trusts" or "met their obligations" always seemed to live in the past. Such faithful African-American compatriots seemed not to exist in the modern era.

Between 1896 and 1915, the majority of American films depicting African-American masculinity confined black men to a narrow frame of reference. They were not part of an "unformed image" but reflected a tradition of literature, vaudeville, and popular culture that relegated them to a position of inferiority, degradation, or indolence.[86] In most instances, African-American men were not even worthy enough to play themselves on the screen; it was necessary for white men to depict them. Anyone watching a large body of early silent films would assume that all black men ate watermelon and stole chickens and in their spare time played craps and danced; black babies were worthless, black women were wenches, and the black family was nonexistent. According to early silent film, the white master's family was the only family that African Americans had. Black men were shot at, hung, eaten by alligators, bucked by donkeys, and beaten. Black men were always afraid (except when saving white families) and black romance was simply a joke. There were definite ruptures in early film (taken from real life) that threatened this unformed image but these ruptures were either legislated away, such as Jack Johnson's triumph over white boxers, or ignored, as with African Americans participating in the military.

The majority of silent films made between 1896 and 1915 were produced by northern-based urban companies. These motion picture studios not only aptly illustrated northern racism toward African Americans but much of the racial ideology of Conservative and Radical southerners.

David Wark Griffith's infamous *The Birth of a Nation* crystallized all of the worst stereotypes of African-American masculinity into a vicious diatribe of hatred illustrating the excesses of northern and southern racism. The African-American community had been aware of the powerfully negative cinematic imagery of themselves displayed on the screen and had protested against it sporadically. *The Birth of a Nation* would unite the African-American community against the film. The protest against the film included a call for censorship. Some African Americans would respond by creating their own films—the true renaissance of African-American filmmaking in this nation.

4

AFRICAN-AMERICAN CINEMA
AND *THE BIRTH OF A NATION*

Chicken-stealing, irresponsible, crap-shooting, lazy, watermelon-eating, tortured, dancing servants—this was the dominant imagery that African-American men saw of themselves on the screen when they were even allowed in movie theaters. This was the imagery that African-American men critically, economically, and artistically reacted to by beginning their own motion picture production in the 1910s. Black filmmaking was a reaction against this imagery but it was also an attempt by African-American men to reclaim their manhood. What black men saw on the screen did not reflect reality; it was an attack on African-American culture. Black men reacted to this imagery by reshaping images of themselves on the screen that reflected either reality or a more positive, even idealistic, view of black manhood. Kevin Gaines has argued, "Mass-media technologies and industries provided new, more powerful ways of telling the same old stories of black deviance and pathology. . . . It should be noted, however, that at the same time mass-culture industries provided opportunities for black cultural production, the construction, or reconstruction of black consciousness, and further struggle and contestation over representations of race."[1]

This desire and need to counter the negative cinematic imagery of African Americans became more critical following the release of *The Birth of a Nation*. The film was a tremendous catalyst to black filmmaking, demonstrating the political and societal need for more realistic cinematic representations of black people. *The Birth of a Nation* demonstrated to American society, African Americans in particular, the powerful influence of the new medium.

The Birth of a Nation was a milestone in the history of the cinema. The film became a cause célèbre, a topic on the tongues of politicians, moviegoers, and social workers. The film illustrated the pervasive power that motion pictures could have on the American social conscience. The film was based on two

63

of Thomas W. Dixon's novels—*The Leopard's Spots* (1901) and *The Clansman* (1903). Born in the midst of the Civil War, Dixon was eight years old when he accompanied his uncle to the state legislature in South Carolina, where he saw "ninety-four Negroes, seven native scalawags [white South Carolina Republicans] and twenty-three white men [presumably carpetbaggers from the North]."[2] This familial distortion of history was to have a profound impression on young Dixon. He was raised in an environment where African Americans were viewed as inherently inferior and not to be trusted. After working as an actor, clergyman, essayist, and lecturer, Dixon found his life work after hearing the Reverend John D. Fulton speak in Boston on "The Southern Problem" (by which Fulton meant the inability of the South to run its own government). Outraged at Fulton's derogatory remarks against the South, he interrupted the minister halfway through the lecture to denounce his remarks as "false and biased."[3] Dixon's main purpose in life became the desire to "set the record straight" regarding Reconstruction.[4] He became one of the best known and most vocal southern Radicals in the early twentieth century.

Dixon consequently turned to fiction to spread his message. His first novel, *The Leopard's Spots: A Romance of the White Man's Burden,* was an attempt to answer Harriet Beecher Stowe's abolitionist novel *Uncle Tom's Cabin.*[5] Whereas Stowe's novel attempted to show the nation the cruelties of slavery, Dixon attempted to demonstrate to the country the horrible anguish that southern white men suffered during the Reconstruction period. Stowe used her villain Simon Legree to illustrate the exploitation of blacks in a physical sense. Dixon took a character from Stowe's novel, a freed black slave, and transformed him into a graduate of Harvard who overreaches his societal boundaries when he asks to marry the daughter of a white defender of the Negro cause. Dixon's novel was an instantaneous success, selling over one hundred thousand copies in its first three months of publication.[6]

The Leopard's Spots established Dixon as an "expert" on southern life and Reconstruction. He believed there was an evolutionary gap between the black and white races and that racial peace could occur only with complete separation of the races. Dixon's nightmare was miscegenation, which he believed would lead to the mongrelization of the white race. Dixon believed that African colonization was the only hope; all freed slaves must be returned to their ancestral homeland. Dixon also despised the treatment that the North gave the South during Reconstruction.[7]

The success of *The Leopard's Spots* led to a constant demand for Dixon as a lecturer and writer. Tall and commanding, he preached his diatribe on race, Reconstruction, and the southern way of life across the nation. Outside the South, Dixon had to tone down his aversion toward northerners and immigrants, stressing instead his fear of freed, politicized black men. Dixon told audiences, "My object is to teach the north, the young north, what it has never known—the awful suffering of the white man during the dreadful reconstruction period. I believe that almighty God has anointed the white men of the South by their suffering . . . to demonstrate to the world that the white man must and shall be supreme."[8]

Within a few years Dixon completed his second and most famous novel, *The Clansman: An Historical Romance of the Ku Klux Klan. The Clansman* was a reworking and expansion of *The Leopard's Spots,* with a heavier stress on the heroics of the Ku Klux Klan and a vicious attack on Dixon's bête noir, Thaddeus Stevens, a leader of the Radical Republicans. In this book, Stevens is portrayed as a despicable character who lives with a mulatto mistress, contrary to most historical accounts. In the novel, he cast the Ku Klux Klan in a heroic role because they supposedly returned African-American men to their natural place of inferiority. *The Clansman* sold over one million copies, and its great success caused Dixon to consider its possibilities as a drama.[9] In 1905, Dixon converted *The Clansman* into a play that toured widely in the Midwest and the South.[10]

David Wark Griffith was also a product of the South. Like Dixon, he spent his childhood listening to tales of heroic sacrifices by Confederate soldiers and misdeeds and misconduct by scalawags, carpetbaggers, and, most of all, blacks. Griffith's view of the South was idealized, one based on "family mythology and a romantic literary and historical tradition."[11] Griffith's father actually served in a limited capacity in the war and grossly overdramatized his own contributions to the war effort (perhaps to counter his almost complete lack of financial support for his family). What was established in Griffith's mind was a white patriarchal ideal, a world in which white men protected white women and where African Americans stayed in their inferior place.

By 1914 Griffith was one of America's premier film directors. During his tenure at Biograph he directed hundreds of films, most of them traditional melodramas. The Civil War served as a backdrop for many of these films. In virtually all of the war films, a white male hero saves his family, girl, or nation in a time of crisis. Griffith and Dixon arranged to collaborate on filming *The Clansman* in 1914. Dixon recognized the potential of working in the new medium of motion pictures. He said: "The whole problem of swift universal education of public opinion is thus solved by this invention. Civilization will be saved if we can stir and teach the slumbering millions behind the politician. By this device we can reach them. We can make them see things happen before their eyes until they cry in anguish. We can teach them the true living history of the race. Its scenes will be vivid realities, not cold works on printed pages, but scenes wet with tears and winged with hope."[12]

The actual scenario of the film, based on Dixon's stage versions of *The Clansman* and *The Leopard's Spots*, was written by Griffith and Frank Woods. The traditional interpretation of the "origin" of the film is that Griffith was its "author," relying less on Dixon's novels than on his own childhood stories and research. Jeffrey Martin has argued that *The Birth of a Nation* borrows heavily from Dixon's plays and was changed only in the sense that Griffith took Dixon's theatrical treatment and filmed it in a more cinematic manner. Thus, *The Birth of a Nation* is actually a much closer adaptation of Dixon's novels than film historians had previously thought. This illustrates the cinematic transmission of Dixon's racist ideology directly into the film.[13]

The impact of *The Birth of a Nation* on American filmmaking cannot be overestimated. It became a critical stimulus in persuading dozens of African-American men of the absolute necessity of creating cinematic versions of themselves. *The Birth of a Nation*, in a sense, set the stage for a generation of cinematic portrayals of African-American men. African-American filmmakers fought strongly to counter its derogatory images.[14] White filmmakers were afraid of being called racist (which haunted Griffith to his grave) so they often eliminated or modified African-American male portrayals. Prior to *The Birth of a Nation*, white filmmakers seemed politically unconcerned with their portrayals of African-American men on the screen. The intense furor over the movie, which resulted in censorship, demonstrations, and race riots, awakened white directors to the "danger" of blatantly racist portrayals of African Americans. Following 1915, the number of black male portrayals in mainstream white productions dropped significantly. African-American men were much less frequently cast in major roles (even when they were portrayed by white actors in blackface). Through the 1920s, African-American men tended to serve as props or scenery in studio productions. As Manthia Diawara argues, "*The Birth of a Nation* constitutes the grammar book for Hollywood's representation of Black manhood. . . . White people must occupy the center, leaving Black people with only one choice—to exist in relation to Whiteness."[15]

A detailed analysis of the film is necessary in order to view the ways in which Griffith constructed racialized identity and to understand the specific images African Americans were acting against. Clyde Taylor claims that "mainstream cinema scholars and aestheticians . . . have kept the race issue at arm's length from their exploration of the film's technique."[16] I hope to alleviate part of this problem by analyzing the "production of meaning."

From the opening credits, Griffith makes it quite apparent that this story will be told in racialized terms. Of the leading characters, the three key African-American figures are described and defined in the credits by their race. Lydia is Stoneman's "Mulatto" housekeeper. Gus is a renegade "Negro." The pivotal white characters are described by their family relationship or by their profession. Therefore, African-American blood implies difference; white Americans are not defined racially since they are the "norm."

A number of film historians have illustrated the difference between Griffith's and Dixon's racial mentalities by using Williamson-like divisions to apologize for Griffith's "subtle" racism and to substantiate his genius. No doubt, Thomas Dixon is within the Radical camp; his rabid attacks on "uppity" African-American men and their lust for white women illustrated his support for African-American deportation to Africa. Griffith is usually placed in the "Conservative" camp; film scholars argue that his racist ideology was not as extreme as that of Dixon.[17] Apologist film scholars focus on Griffith's "genius" or discuss the "unconsciousness" of his racism.[18]

The opening scene illustrates Griffith's vision of the "place" of African Americans in society. The title reads: "The bringing of the African to America planted the first seeds of disunion." The establishing shot shows African slaves looking purposefully subservient to a man dressed in colonial garb. Through this opening title, Griffith is clearly arguing two of the major tenets of the Radical southerner's vision of race. First, he blames the disunion, in fact, the entire Civil War conflict, on the presence of African Americans. Thus, the victims become the conspirators, the individuals guilty for bringing on the bloodiest war the nation had ever witnessed. Second, Griffith argues that African Americans have no place in American society; their very presence can disrupt a nation and tear it apart. Thus, as Vincent Rocchio argues, *The Birth of a Nation* does not begin with the introduction of main characters but with an overt historical thesis.[19]

The second scene confuses the racial issue. The title reads: "The abolitionists of the nineteenth century demanding the freeing of the slaves." The scene shows a group of white abolitionists listening to a minister preach on the evils of slavery. The minister repeatedly points to an African-American man below him. The next shot shows a white man with his hands on the back of a twelve-year-old slave boy. An iris is placed around the two figures, cutting them off from the rest of the action. These scenes illustrate white paternalism over the black subject. In both shots, the African-American male characters are "below" the white male characters within the spatial framework of the shot but also within the evolution of society. Both the boy and the man are "children" who need to be protected by a white male authority figure. Thus, paternalism is the norm. But Griffith's racial ideology is complicated by the depiction of an older white abolitionist woman who is clearly moved by the minister's words. Griffith's momentary focus on this female character subverts the other parts of the scene. In a sense, Griffith demonstrates that the abolitionist's sympathy for the slave is a feminine emotion. The viewer questions whether these white men have been duped by women for the abolitionist cause.[20]

These two tableaux set the context of Griffith's historical argument for the rest of the film. Although the plight of the Cameron and Stoneman families in the Civil War and Reconstruction frames the main narrative, they are simply a device to espouse Griffith's views on race, sectionalism, and social order.

The film focuses on the relationship between a "good" family of the South, the Camerons, and their Pennsylvania cousins, the Stonemans. The Cameron family is a complete whole, that is, a two-parent family with loving brothers and sisters, but the Stonemans appear more fragmented, perhaps because they are motherless. The Camerons are given more screen time and there is more spectacle and dramatic intensity surrounding them. Austin Stoneman, the patriarch of the family, has risen to national prominence in the House of Representatives. He clearly loves his daughter Elsie, but Stoneman's deformities, which include a clubfoot and an ill-fitting toupee, make him look sinister. When the film moves to Piedmont, South Carolina, a title reads: "Life runs in a quaintly way that is no more." The Camerons are a happy, respectable, civilized family. Mr. Cameron, the kindly slavemaster, is surrounded by puppies and kittens that demonstrate his patience and goodwill. Two of the Stoneman sons come to visit their southern cousins. Griffith portrays the southern Cameron family as whole and complete whereas the northern Stoneman family appears "lacking." They lack not only a mother but a holistic environment, including slaves. Thus, the Stonemans and Camerons are allegorical figures, representing sectionalism and privilege. Griffith does not apologize for slavery but demonstrates it as a force that enhances the dynamics of the white family. In contrast, in the opening shots of the narrative, the African-American characters are treated in a fashion that implies they are less than human. In front of the Cameron home, two black children fall off a wagon. Their father, rather than comfort them, hits them with a switch (completing the slapstick motif).

Griffith divides his African-American characters into two categories. All of the pivotal African-American characters in the film, which include Lydia, Gus, Silas, and Mammy, are played by whites in blackface. All of the secondary characters, primarily actors that serve as extras, are played by real African Americans. This intermixture of racial portrayals is unsettling to modern viewers unused to blackface entertainment. It also demonstrates the instability of racial categorization. Defenders of Griffith argue that he used white actors in blackface because there were few black actors in southern California where the film was shot and that it was possible to save money by having a white actor play two roles—one in blackface and one in white. Whatever the case, Griffith's choice of having leading African-American characters played by white actors and by having real African Americans appear only in crowd scenes serves to reinforce his racist ideology. Griffith commented on his casting decision: "There have been questions as to why I did not pick real negroes or mulattoes for those three roles [Gus, Lydia, and Silas]. That matter was considered, and on careful weighing of every detail concerned, the decision was to have no black blood among the principals."[21] Thus, Griffith gives a nonexplanation.

Dr. Cameron and his sons are sturdy, benevolent fathers to their childlike servants, the slaves. The Camerons take the Stoneman siblings on a tour of their plantation. The slaves appear content on the Cameron plantation. In the slave quarters, they begin to cheerfully dance and sing for the white families, despite the fact that they have just worked twelve hours in the field. Griffith consciously underscores the black need to please and serve the white man and illustrates that this is an environment in which the natural order of race relations exists.

This scene is also crucial in the way that Griffith spatially organizes his characters. As the main white characters enter the frame, the African-American slaves are suddenly thrust into the background. Thus, they serve as a backdrop for the white figures.[22]

The proper racial order is clearly established when comparing Big Mammy of the Cameron plantation with Lydia, Stoneman's mulatto housekeeper. Big Mammy is robust and large, fiesty and strong; she contentedly does her chores. Lydia, on the other hand, is a conniving temptress, out to seduce her employer and disrupt the natural order of race relations. Stoneman eventually succumbs to Lydia's wiles, which are described as a "blight to the nation." The comparison of these women is necessary to understand the patriarchal framework of the film. In the clearly defined master/slave relationship of Griffith's idealized South, people know their place; lines of proper sexual/societal/racial behavior are never crossed (which completely denies the rape of thousands of black women in the South). In the North, where racial lines of demarcation were not clearly drawn, danger lurks everywhere. This is doubly true in the case of Lydia. Her mongrel ancestry makes her look wild-eyed and power hungry, an obvious example of the biological disaster that miscegenation can bring. In Griffith's patriarchal ideology, clearly defined racial roles have to exist for a society to survive.

The impending Civil War puts an end to the Stonemans' visit to the Cameron plantation. Griffith inserts the first of several historical facsimiles at this point in the film—Abraham Lincoln signs a proclamation calling for 75,000 volunteers for the war effort. The use of facsimiles and quotations from popularized histories of the day is an attempt to make the film appear authentic. Griffith personally felt that the Civil War and Reconstruction period had never been told through a truly southern (read "accurate") perspective. He claimed, "I felt driven to tell the story—the truth about the South, touched by its eternal romance I had learned to know so well."[23] In *The Birth of a Nation,* Griffith attempts to combine a personalized romantic account of the era with a sense of historical realism. He succinctly used historical facsimiles to reinforce his own vision of events.

The southern cause is portrayed as valiant and confident whereas northern mobilization appears dreary and dutiful. Both the Stonemans and the Camerons say farewell to the sons of the family as they volunteer to do their patriotic duty. Griffith vibrantly illustrates the glamour of southern gallantry. A grand ball is held in the Piedmont home of the Camerons after the First Battle of Bull Run. Men are handsomely dressed in their military uniforms and southern women parade in their finest. Bonfire celebrations are held in the streets. At daybreak, the southern troops depart for battle. Large crowds of southerners come out to greet them, including many African Americans (actual and blackface). At the Stoneman home, things are much more subdued. A blackfaced actor (with grotesque pancake makeup around his mouth) escorts Elsie to tell Stoneman that his sons are off to battle. The celebratory nature of southern pageantry is missing; so is the close personal relationship between parent and child.

Throughout the first third of the film, with slavery still in existence in the South and without the turbulence the Civil War would bring to the North, racial relations are seemingly static. All African-American male portrayals are passive and accommodating. When Piedmont is threatened by the war, this scheme of racial representation changes. A title reads: "An irregular [meaning racially mixed?] force of guerillas raid the town." Griffith points out that the first Negro regiments were raised in South Carolina (to give historical credence to the racial "threat"). There is chaos in the streets. The Cameron women are away from home and are desperate to return. The northern troops enter the town like monsters. They shoot down innocent citizens in the streets. In one of the most telling racialized scenes of the film, three African-American soldiers approach the Cameron front door. They move in an animalistic fashion as they carefully watch their backs. The African-American man who is in full frontal view of the spectator is half-dressed. He looks suspiciously around as he holds his rifle. The sexualized implication is not lost on the viewer: Griffith's racial depiction is clear; this half-dressed black animal is going to use force to enter the home where the white women have just entered. They break into the house and are confronted by old man Cameron. He orders them out, but the scalawag white captain demands that the three recruits obey his orders. The house is then overturned. Old man Cameron is shot and the soldiers scurry around the home like animals searching for food. They loot the Cameron's home and are purely malicious. The Cameron women hide in the cellar. Suddenly a "company" of Confederate troopers are informed of the raid. The Union irregulars set fire to the Cameron home but the Confederate troops arrive just in time to extinguish it. As Vincent Rocchio points out, this scene is short "but carries a high degree of narrative significance." It is a nightmare image of out-of-control blacks who threaten home, hearth, womanhood, and southern sanctity.[24]

The violence and horrors of the war are then illustrated by Griffith in a series of spectacular battle scenes. Both the Cameron and the Stoneman families lose sons in the war but the Camerons have it much worse. They have to sell their last possessions to make ends meet. The remaining women have nothing left to eat but parched corn. War is the breeder of hate, according to Griffith. However, just as the picture sinks into despair, a romance is kindled between Elsie Stoneman and the "Little Colonel" of the Cameron clan. She visits him in a hospital, not realizing that he has carried a picture of her that her brother gave him long ago. Mrs. Cameron comes to the military hospital where her son is a prisoner. She vows to enter even if she is shot and Elsie intercedes. She finds her son doing well but she also discovers he is going to be hung for treason. Elsie and Mrs. Cameron go to Abraham Lincoln's office and successfully beg a pardon from the great president.

Griffith's rewriting of history includes a saintly portrait of Abraham Lincoln. After a historical facsimile of the surrender at Appomattox, Lincoln proposes an easy readmittance of the South back into the Union. Stoneman and the Radical Republicans go to Lincoln to protest. Stoneman demands,

"Their leaders must be hung and the states treated as conquered provinces." Lincoln humbly responds, "I shall deal with them as if they had never been away." As a Radical Republican, Stoneman becomes one of the most powerful leaders in America. When the Camerons read of Lincoln's death, they ask themselves, "What is to become of us now?"

The second half of the film presents African-American male figures that are far more threatening to the social ideals of the period. In the second half of the film Griffith began to draw more heavily on material directly covered in Dixon's theatrical version of *The Clansman*. The opening title of the second half reads: "Reconstruction: the agony which the nation endured that a nation might be born. The blight of war does not end." Following rampant criticism of the film and threats of censorship, Griffith later added a second title at this point: "This is an historical representation of the Civil War and Reconstruction Period and is not meant to reflect on any race or people of today."

Griffith's prologue to the second half is quite lengthy. He takes an extensive excerpt from then current president and fellow southerner Woodrow Wilson's *History of the American People:* "Adventurers swarmed out of the north, as much the enemies of one race as of the other, to cozen, to beguile and use the negroes. . . . in the villages the negroes were the office holders, men who knew none of the uses of authority, except its insolences. . . . the policy of the congressional leaders wrought . . . a veritable overthrow of civilization in the South . . . in their determination to *put the white south under the heel of the black south.*" Griffith attempts to lend both historical and political credibility to his cinematic vision by quoting Wilson. But the message is decidedly mixed. African Americans are claimed to be ignorant, senseless human beings, simply manipulated and used by northerners. Yet Griffith demonstrates that African-American aggression is responsible for white southern suffering.

The corruption of Radical Republican politicians and their manipulation of race is displayed. Stoneman is the uncrowned king of Washington. His mulatto mistress is now the courtesan of his parlor. Stoneman's protégé, Silas Lynch, is the mulatto leader of the blacks. Lynch enters Stoneman's office and in deference to the mentor bends to kiss his ring. Stoneman reprimands him, "Don't scrape to me. You are the equal of any man here." The next title reads: "The great radical delivers the edict that the blacks shall be raised to full equality." Senator Charles Sumner comes to call on Stoneman. He refuses to accept Sumner's mulatto mistress. He also urges a "less dangerous" policy in the extension of power to the freed race. Stoneman, of course, rejects this proposal. Instead he proclaims, "I shall make this man, Silas Lynch as a symbol of his race, the peer of any white man living." With this statement, Griffith takes the agency of power and clearly places it in the control of white men. White men make or create power for black men. They are in the position to give or completely take away this power. Thus, as Dr. Frankenstein makes his monster not fully realizing what he is doing, Stoneman makes Lynch.

Griffith illustrates the danger of giving African-American men power. Stoneman becomes ill and sends Lynch south to aid the carpetbaggers and to organize the black voters. Lynch takes the very bastion of white southern civilization—Piedmont—and makes it his home.

Radical Republican control of the South breaks down race relations and the "natural" order of things. A title reads: "The ferment begins." Carpet-baggers induce African Americans to quit work. Instead, black men are now dancing in the streets. A "Forty Acres and a Mule" sign is shown in the background, illustrating Republican promises. Griffith implies that the Freedmen's Bureau caused a complete breakdown in the labor system. Black men are not responsible; they must be induced to work. African Americans also begin to receive handouts from the North. A title reads: "The charity of a generous north misused to delude the ignorant." The ravages of war are nowhere to be found. Problems with homelessness, hunger, and physical de-struction of the immediate postwar South are strikingly absent in this de-piction of government handouts.

Griffith deliberately attempts to sentimentalize and aestheticize the princi-pal characters as *white people*. In one early scene in the second half of the film, the Little Colonel is standing on a sidewalk with his sister. Black soldiers come by and push them—or at least make them physically get off the side-walk. Lynch observes the action and in a peaceful manner informs the Colonel, "This sidewalk belongs to us as much as it does to you, Colonel Cameron." Griffith anticipates outrage from the spectator—the very thought that a white male may have to demonstrate common courtesy or re-spect for a black man in uniform is unheard of. White spectators are expected to sympathize with the Colonel, whereas contemporary African-American spectators may have absolutely agreed with Lynch's remark.[25]

Griffith divides African-American male characters into three categories—northern blacks, southern blacks who are disloyal to the white man, and southern black men who know their place (the faithful souls). All northern black men are portrayed in a negative light in the film, with Silas Lynch as the prime example. One illustration of this takes place after Stoneman is advised by his physician to find a milder climate for his health. He goes to Piedmont. His northern black valet meets Big Mammy. The valet tries to hand her his bag and she exclaims, "Yo northern lowdown black trash, don't try no airs on me." She looks as if she will attack him but instead she kicks him and sends him upstairs with his own case. She has put him in his place. Later, when he raises his eyebrows at her in the hallway, she says to herself, "Dem free niggers f'um de No'f am sho' crazy." The valet's very freedom makes him suspect, even dangerous, according to the cultural code of the South.

Griffith depicts southern black men in a negative light by demonstrating their supposed animalistic passions, ignorance, and ability to be easily duped. When Silas Lynch heads south, he organizes the black vote. Set in a meeting hall, there is much anarchy and chaos taking place in this scene. Lynch informs the mob that the franchise is for all black men and the crowd goes wild. Now that the primitiveness of African-American men has been established in regard to voting, Griffith demonstrates overall African-American political ignorance. An elderly black man explains at a Freedmen's Bureau supply giveaway, "Et I doan' get nuf franchise to fill mah bucket, I do'an want it nohow." This is an important political statement. Spoken in 1915, in a period of time in which African-American men were almost completely denied the right of suffrage in the South, Griffith argued for the continued denial of basic constitutional rights for African Americans.

Griffith consistently defended *The Birth of a Nation* by arguing that he included both positive and negative portrayals of African Americans. But as Vincent Rocchio argues, "*The Birth of a Nation* is organized around constructing a very basic meaning that it presents as truth: that blacks are uncivilized."[26] For Griffith, the only positive portrayal of black masculinity was that of an elderly faithful black slave, modeled after Uncle Tom, who along with Mammy, conspires to save the Cameron family. With this exception, every other black male character in the film is either a northern or southern African American who cannot be trusted.

The sidewalk scene with Lynch and the Colonel is one of many scenes in which a contemporary African-American viewer could have used a negotiated or oppositional strategy. A second such scene takes place when Lynch comes to Piedmont and formally meets the Little Colonel. Lynch puts out his hand in a gentlemanly fashion of equal respect and Cameron refuses to take it; he simply looks away and pouts. Stoneman, who is present for this rude gesture, is insulted. A contemporary African-American spectator may have also been insulted by this action. But to guarantee that the spectator would identify with the Little Colonel's moral high ground of black nonac-

The Birth of a Nation (1915). (Library of Congress)

ceptance, Griffith immediately follows the scene with a title that reads: "Lynch, a traitor to his white patron and a greater traitor to his own people whom he plans to lead to an evil way to build himself a throne of vaulting power." This is a turning point in the film regarding racial representation. Prior to this scene, Lynch has been in complete deference to Stoneman. He has gone south to help African Americans by mobilizing the vote and helping out in the Reconstruction process. But Griffith argues that when Lynch attempts to give himself this agency of power he steps over the line of proper racial behavior. No acceptable African-American man should ever empower himself, according to Griffith's doctrine on race.

Once African-American men are given political power, the South digresses into a state of anarchy. The fact that African-American men are given the vote while former white Confederates are denied it (following the Congressional Reconstruction Act of 1867) is demonstrated. But Griffith does not stop with this fact, he carries it one step further toward racial antagonism.

African Americans not only vote, they cheat at the ballot box by casting several votes each. Respectable white men are denied not only the right to vote, they are forcibly pushed away by black soldiers still in Union uniforms. The result of their actions is that African Americans and carpetbaggers sweep the state of South Carolina and Lynch is elected as lieutenant governor. The news is reported to Stoneman, who is pleased with his protégé. African Americans celebrate their victory at the polls.

Meanwhile, the South is morally overturned. Hints are made that Lynch is secretly in love with Elsie, Stoneman's daughter. Thus, political power is a means to the inevitable black male desire—the right to possess a white woman. Lynch is proclaimed a hero to the people. Black crowds occupy the streets outside his home; many of them are black men in uniform. The celebratory nature of the scene takes on a sinister twist when the Little Colonel relates a series of "outrages" that have recently occurred. An all-black jury and judge find a white man guilty of a crime in court (white control of the judicial process before this period is never addressed). While the Little Colonel relates these transgressions, his own faithful family servant is punished for not voting with the Union League and the carpetbaggers. He is tied to a tree where he is whipped by black soldiers. A white man tries to stop them but is shot. The Camerons' "Faithful Old Soul" watches the action and relates the injustices to the Little Colonel.

The most telling, historically inaccurate, and blatantly racist scene of the film follows. A title reads: "The Riot in the Master Hall—the Negro Party in Control of the State House of Representatives. 101 Blacks against 23 whites. Session of 1871—historic incidents from the House of Representatives." This infamous scene begins with a dissolve in which countless numbers of African-American men appear suddenly in the House. An African-American legislator is eating chicken in the chamber. Yet another member takes off his shoes and is reprimanded by the Speaker. Another legislator takes a swig of whiskey from a bottle. A congressman then proposes a bill requiring all whites to salute black officers on the street. The overwhelmingly black legislature heartily approves the proposal as a title reads: "The helpless white minority." Griffith describes this legislative meeting as a "riot." A riot can be defined as an "assemblage of three or more persons in a public place for the purpose of accomplishing a concerted action in a turbulent and disorderly manner for a common purpose irrespective of the lawlessness of the purpose."[27] Lawlessness is purely an objective stance in this scene. All of the activity is being held in a representative body through the lawmaking process. Griffith would consider this a riot because the legislation

The quintessential fear of the white man: African-American male desire for white women. (*The Birth of a Nation*, 1915). (Museum of Modern Art)

passed is offensive to him. African-American men are to be placed under the thumb of the law, not behind the law.

The South Carolina legislature then passes a bill providing for the intermarriage of blacks and whites. White respectable citizens (many of them women) observe the proceedings despairingly in the gallery. When several black legislators start to leer at the white women in the gallery, a white man removes the women he had accompanied to the building. Griffith used actual African-American men in this entire scene, making the black male drive for white female flesh that much more intense for white audiences. Griffith's choice of real African-American men in this scene is not accidental; it is an aesthetic punch that underlines his theme that black male political power leads to sexual aggression.[28] All the legislature begins cheering; Lynch is treated like a hero. The gallery and state house are totally out of control; the ultimate plum prize of political power and equality has been won—the right of miscegenation.

Griffith clearly defines the real battleground of Reconstruction—black versus white. Boundaries between white Republicans and Democrats, northerners and southerners, carpetbaggers and secessionist conservatives, are meaningless. Racial cohesiveness is what is mandatory. Griffith does a brilliant job throwing off the artificial boundaries in the white race from this section of the film onward.

Griffith immediately solidifies racial loyalty by demonstrating the dangers the Radical Republican–dominated government brought to the South. The next title informs the viewer: "Later the grim reaping." The film introduces "Gus, the renegade, a product of the vicious doctrine spread by the carpetbaggers." Gus is shown in a close-up shot leering at Elsie and the younger Cameron sister. In the next scene, Griffith has Elsie and Little Sister meet Lynch on the street. Elsie, raised in an abolitionist household, believes in racial equality and shakes Lynch's hand. Little Sister is shocked and so is the Little Colonel, who is in the background. Lynch appears pleased that the Colonel sees this. Little Sister, in disbelief, asks Elsie why she would possibly extend this formality. At this very moment, Gus walks by and looks at Little Sister as she goes inside. The Little Colonel threatens him to stay away from his sister. Lynch sees this verbal confrontation and comes to the rescue. He threatens the Little Colonel. Two important morals are developed here: all black men will stick together so white men must too, and all black men want white women.

At this point the South appears lost, but white southern manhood comes to the rescue. The Little Colonel retreats to a bluff where he agonizes over "the degradation and ruin of his people." While he ruminates, the Colonel witnesses two white children dressing up in a sheet and scaring four black children who think they are a ghost, giving the Little Colonel his inspiration for the Ku Klux Klan. The Klan begins to frighten and terrorize the black population. Lynch's supporters score "first blood" as they shoot at Klansmen. Lynch describes the vigilante organization to Stoneman and Stoneman proclaims, "We shall crush the white South under the heel of the Black South." At this point, Stoneman informs his daughter that her fiancé, the Little Colonel, is a terrorist and she promptly breaks off the engagement.

The most dramatic scene of the film follows. Against her brother's warning, Little Sister goes to a spring with a bucket. She is walking through the woods when Gus spies her. He backs off for a while. The innocence of Little Sister is accentuated by her captivation with a squirrel; she is more of a little girl than a woman. When Mrs. Cameron informs the Little Colonel that his sister is alone, he immediately begins to look for her. Gus comes up to Little Sister and says, "You see I'm a capt. now and I want to marry." Gus delivers this line in a nonthreatening way and gently touches her arm. If he had been a white male character this would have been considered a moment of innocent naïveté. Little Sister then proceeds to knock him down. She begins to shriek for help and runs away. He yells after her, "Wait, Missy, I won't hurt yeh!" and follows her.[29]

Considering the racial climate of the period, Gus would certainly have been lynched for even approaching Little Sister. He had more to fear than Little Sister did. The Little Colonel is right behind them; he finds her bucket and shawl. Little Sister heads for the top of a cliff. Gus approaches the ledge while Little Sister screams for him to stay away or she will jump. This particular scene has been considered as a potential rape scene. The interpretation is that Gus follows Little Sister in an attempt to sexually have his way with her. The foregone conclusion was that all black men want white women and what all black men are interested in, in terms of white women, is sexual conquest. An oppositional reading implies nothing of the sort. Gus never implies anything provocative, he never makes any sexual advances. He indirectly proposes marriage so his intentions appear honorable. For Little Sister, who has presumably been fed a steady diet of the mythology of black licentiousness, death is better than any physical or emotional contact with Gus, so she jumps.[30] Griffith attempts to whip the audience into a furor of revenge and racial hatred. The Little Colonel finds her body, but she is able to reveal her "killer" before she dies. The protection of white women becomes one of the central themes in *The Birth of a Nation*. Little Sister is a symbol of white womanhood and white civilization.

Gus, meanwhile, hides in a gin mill full of black men. The Little Colonel goes to a blacksmith shop to enlist white townsmen to search for the accused Gus. They are going to "give him a fair trial in the dim halls of the Invisible Empire." The comparison between these two groups of men is important. The African-American men are sitting drinking while the white men are all hard at work. A white blacksmith enters the gin mill looking for Gus and proceeds to fight everyone there. At least eight African-American men fight him. He is victorious against all of them, illustrating the physical supremacy of white masculinity. But Gus, who does not play by the rules, shoots the blacksmith in the back and rides off on a horse. The Klansmen eventually find Gus and dump his dead body on Silas Lynch's doorstep.

The racial lines are now clearly drawn. Lynch considers Gus's murder a racial challenge. He orders black militia reinforcements to fill the streets. Stoneman, quite aware of the consequences, decides to slip out of town. Piedmont is now embroiled in a racial war. The Little Colonel preaches to his fellow Klan members, "Brethren, this flag bears the red stain of the life of a southern woman, a priceless sacrifice on the altar of outraged civilization." Thus, the Klan is at war to protect white womanhood. But there is more—he appeals to his fellow Klan members' sense of religious and masculine pride. Holding up a cross, he exclaims, "Here I raise the ancient symbol of the unconquered race of men." These former members of the Confederacy may have been defeated in the Civil War but they will not be defeated racially.

Lynch responds by promising death to anyone in possession of a Klan costume. He is happy to wreak vengeance on Cameron House. Old Man Cameron is arrested by a scalawag officer and two black soldiers. His former slaves laugh at the old man as he is physically and verbally abused. Mammy and the Faithful Soul decide they are going to help their former master. They pretend to be black mockers in order to rescue him. They are successful in leading their former (present?) master to escape. Griffith demonstrates that African Americans can be controlled and tamed, as long as they remain loyal to white authority. They hurriedly leave in a cart that is followed closely by black Union soldiers. The cart breaks down in front of a cabin owned by two Union veterans. It becomes their refuge, the former enemies become their allies. Perhaps the most telling title of the film reads: "The former enemies of North and South are united again in common defense of the Aryan birthright." The symbolic unification of racial solidarity is complete; the artificial and meaningless alliance between black and white is broken.

Griffith then begins an ingenious crosscutting scenario, interspersing shots of black soldiers attacking the cabin with Lynch's proposal of marriage and eventual violence toward Elsie. Griffith's furious editing heightens the suspense. The racial threat becomes more menacing and disturbing as the scene progresses; both aesthetic and textual attributes contribute to this emotion. Elsie goes to see Lynch. He is surrounded by the "new Black power base," well dressed in postbellum "white" fashion. When Lynch looks at Elsie he does so in a romantic, nonthreatening manner (much like Gus). He proposes marriage and appears sincere, truthful, honest, and calm. Elsie's response is that of horror. Lynch locks the door to the room and his mood suddenly changes. He is taken aback by her rejection; she vows she will never marry him. Lynch threatens her with a horsewhipping for her insolence. Pointing to African-American rioters outside, he exclaims, "With them I will build a black Empire and you as my queen shall be by my side." In this scene, Griffith crystallizes his worst racial fantasies—black corruption and the misuse of the political process, black male dominance and sexual conquest over white women, and black arrogance. The scene shifts to outside Lynch's residence where the streets are full of African Americans shooting guns in the air. The mood is that of lawlessness and chaos. Griffith illustrates that the transmission of any power to African-American men will lead to anarchy. The shot then shifts again to inside the house. Lynch smells Elsie's dress and she goes berserk. She pleads with him to leave her alone and screams. The sexual tension (and outrage) heightens as he leers at her in a provocative fashion. Griffith then tells the viewer not all is lost in the South, the great heroic force of white masculinity is to ride to the rescue. In one brief title: "The Klan is summoned," Griffith illustrates the magnificence and overawing power of southern white manhood.

The action then shifts back to Elsie and Lynch. Lynch is described as "drunk with wine and power." He prepares for a forced wedding, and this makes Elsie take action. She tries to escape but he chases her around the room. Interspersing shots of the Klan and the Elsie/Lynch saga are depicted. Elsie finally swoons and Lynch holds her in his arms. At this point, Stoneman, her father, arrives. Black soldiers guard the door to the room where Elsie and Lynch are. Lynch then locks her in a room with black confidants. He enters an anteroom and tells Stoneman, "I want to marry a white woman." Stoneman approves of this action, not knowing that it is his daughter he wants to marry. Lynch announces, "The lady I want to marry is your daughter." Stoneman then becomes angry; the racial solidarity is now complete.[31]

Silas Lynch is portrayed by a white man in blackface. One assumes that Griffith never would have allowed close physical contact between Lillian

Gish/Elsie and a real African-American man. This creates an interesting phenomenon in the spectator's mind. On a narratological level, one is terrified by the premise that the black man may have his way with Elsie; on the other hand, this is relieved when the viewer realizes that she is not really threatened because this is simply a white actor. It is a cinematic casting coup for Griffith; he both antagonizes and pacifies the white spectator at the same time.

Griffith's editing then proceeds in a flurry of activity. Four interspersing scenarios appear in rapid order. First, Elsie tries to break a window and escape from Lynch. She is forcibly restrained by Lydia, who tries to control her, and Stoneman is physically overtaken by Lynch. Second, black soldiers attack the cabin and threaten the inhabitants. Cameron wants to surrender but the Union veterans refuse to allow him. The message is clear—all white men must stick together. The third scene shows the town of Piedmont. A title reads: "The town given over to crazed Negroes brought in by Lynch and Stoneman to overcome the whites." Thousands of black men are armed; the scenes are extremely crowded. Griffith paints a picture similar to that of cockroaches or bees swarming over a victim. In a brief provocative shot, two African-American men fight over a black woman. She is helpless as they begin tearing at her clothes in an attempt to rape her. The fourth locus of action centers on the Klan. In five minutes of action they proceed to clean up the racial disaster. The Klan first overwhelms the black mob and then they rescue Elsie from Lynch. At the cabin, the action is still extreme. African-American men furiously attempt to break into the cabin, and it appears that they will be successful. Cameron holds a gunstock to his daughter's head; he would rather kill her than have her molested by a black man. But the Klan arrives to rescue the party.

The restoration of order is now complete. The Klan forces the African-American population to give up their arms, and the Klan parades through the streets as "Dixie" plays and the white inhabitants of Piedmont cheer on. African Americans run off into hiding, back into submission. At the next election, Klan members carry guns with them to the ballot box to prevent African-American men from voting. The coda of the film is an allegorical representation of Mars dissolving into the Prince of Peace. As Thomas Cripps brilliantly states, "The coda at once embraces pacificism, Christianity, Klan terrorism and the virtues of the white race."[32]

The Birth of a Nation was an epic of white supremacist mythology. Griffith's ability to link the visual imagery of cinema to human emotion was a landmark; the director was able to tap into a familiar assemblage of racial, sexual, and cultural symbolism that entranced the white filmgoing public. Griffith, the southern Conservative, became Griffith, the Radical racist, with the production of *The Birth of a Nation*. Richard Dyer argues that the film "shows the forging of a national identity, in which geographical division [North versus South] is transcended through a realization of a common white racial identity."[33] The director composes his film around the obsessive fear of the Radical mentality—that black men would use political, military, or physical power to rape white women.

The Birth of a Nation opened in mid-February 1915 in Los Angeles, moved to New York in early spring, and to Boston in April, where African Americans "mounted a stand against it."[34] Jesse Rhines argues that "protest against this film brought blacks and whites together in the first major contest over racial discrimination in the motion picture industry."[35]

The viciousness of *The Birth of a Nation* mobilized the African-American population. The NAACP launched a vigorous campaign to halt the exhibition of the film.[36] The controversy over *The Birth of a Nation* swelled the ranks of the civil rights organization, giving it a rallying point to attract more members. The organizational and mobilizing impulse already present within the African-American community was heightened by the sensationalistic film. *The Chicago Defender* proclaimed, "It is meant to create a greater race prejudice than obviously exists."[37] An editorial in the *Crisis*, the official journal of the NAACP, claimed, "It is gratifying to know that in this work [against the film] we have the cooperation of all elements of colored people. The *New York Age* [a black newspaper] and the *Crisis* worked hand in hand with Harlem, Brooklyn, and Jersey City. We know of no factions in the righting of this great wrong."[38] The fight against the film was carried out on both a national and a local level. The national leadership of the NAACP worked diligently to encourage the National Board of Review not to approve the film.[39] Branch chapters in Oakland, Tacoma, Boston, Portland, Pittsburgh, Chicago, Atlantic City, Dayton, and other cities worked enthusiastically to force the prohibition of the exhibition of the film in their regions.[40] The Boston branch published a pamphlet titled, "Fighting a Vicious Film," which it distributed throughout the nation. The tract contained letters, speeches, and "evidence" against the film.[41] The *Crisis* covered these local campaigns with the hope of spreading reaction against the film. As Jane Gaines has noted, the NAACP leadership hoped that the fight against the film would translate into a larger struggle against segregation and racism in the public sphere.[42]

African-American criticism of the film focused on the negative depiction of African-American men. An editorial in the *Crisis* claimed that "the negro [is] represented either as an ignorant fool, a vicious rapist, a venal and unscrupulous politician or a faithful but doddering old idiot."[43] A strongly gendered tone was present in the arguments against the film. The *New York Evening Globe* argued that "white men in this country have never been just to black men."[44] For others, the status of women was at issue. W. Allison Sweeney believed that the fight against *The Birth of a Nation* was a fight to protect African-American womanhood. She argued, "Why ask that we moisten our tears over the graves of the Ku Klux Klan, the midnight murderers . . . despoilers of helpless womanhood—rapers of the queens of a race—queens, mark you, just as surely as those with eyes of blue and flaxen hair."[45] What connected all of these attacks on the film was the contention that it did not reflect the reality of African-American life.[46]

The Birth of a Nation illustrated to the African-American community that the visual imagery of the cinema was a powerful tool to oppress African Americans. In their sixth annual report, the NAACP argued, "People grew to hate their neighbors for not carefully stated reasons or carefully investigated facts, but for the very lack of reasons and facts. That makes the power of suggestion and slander all the more dangerous. . . . A peculiarly aggravating case of this during the last year has been the motion picture play *Birth of a Nation*."[47] From state to state and city to city, *The Birth of a Nation*'s overwhelming popularity persuaded many motion picture censorship boards to release the film, sometimes with cuts, to meet the clamor of movie fans.[48] Many African Americans opposed to the film believed that the film could have real behavioral effects, reinforcing attitudes or causing racial strife. *The Birth of a Nation* was an attempt, therefore, not only to provoke but to disrupt public peace. The *Crisis* argued, "The Play is leaving the cities and going into the smaller towns where its influence may be greater than in the larger cities."[49] This statement illustrates that NAACP leaders realized the power of motion pictures to disseminate ideology and influence the public. Clyde Taylor refers to the African-American reaction and organized resistance against the film as an "unprecedented new force of resistance that demonstrated an altered historical terrain in which racial Radicalism was removed further from the center and placed on the defensive."[50] The leaders and rank and file of the NAACP knew all too well that lynchings usually took place in rural areas and not big cities. The African-American community soon realized that boycotts and calls for censorship would have only a marginal effect.[51] What was really needed were alternative cinematic portrayals of African-

American life that were both realistic and uplifting. Attempting to prevent such racist films was a limited reaction to the dissemination of prejudicial viewpoints. But the sixth annual NAACP report claimed, "If Negroes and all their friends were free to answer in the same channels, by the same methods in which the attack is made, the path would be easy."[52] *The Birth of a Nation,* thus, indirectly led to a proliferation of African-American filmmaking.[53]

The Birth of a Nation initiated a serious discussion in the African-American community over white control of African-American imagery in film. One month after the release of the film, Edward Sheldon's old stage play *The Nigger* was translated into film. African Americans greeted the film with a hostile reception because of the word "nigger" in the title. A number of NAACP branches called for the banning of the film. But *The Nigger* was important for another reason—it caused African-American journalists, activists, and club members to debate whether the portrayal of African Americans in the film was objectionable. *The Birth of a Nation* had made African Americans seriously consider how they were portrayed on the screen; no longer would white filmmakers be able to portray African-American men in any way they chose without organized action against such films. *The Nigger* was actually an exposé of racial prejudice. Phillip Morrow, the protagonist of the film, grows up with the understanding that he possesses the finest lineage of white southern manhood. He decides to run for governor with the help of a local whiskey distiller, Cliff Noyes, who makes his fortune by supplying African Americans with demon rum. Morrow signs a Prohibition bill after his election, believing that alcohol consumption is un-Christian and immoral. This destroys Noyes's business. He decides to ruin his protégé by exposing the fact that Morrow has black blood in him. Morrow resigns the governorship but decides he is going to help his newfound "people" rather than be destroyed.[54] Once the true message of the film was revealed, a number of prominent African Americans ended their attack on the film. May Childs Nerney of the NAACP said, "A friend of mine went to see it and says that it shows the other side, that is, the white man's responsibility for existing conditions."[55]

The African-American community immediately attempted a number of cinematic responses to *The Birth of a Nation.* Jane Gaines argues that "early black filmmaking is inextricably tied to the release of this film."[56] Booker T. Washington strongly suggested that his successful autobiography *Up from Slavery* be translated into film. *Up from Slavery,* a highly fictionalized story of Washington's life, helped establish the Tuskegee leader as the spokesman of his race in the eyes of white America. Primarily a rags-to-riches story, *Up from Slavery* was a hopeful, purposeful book that preached African-American economic nationalism at the same time it acquiesced to whites. A friend of Washington's argued that it "might quite properly be used as a counter-irritant to *Birth of a Nation*."[57] But the story went unfilmed.

In the summer of 1915, both Booker T. Washington and W. E. B. DuBois expressed interest in a cinematic alternative to *The Birth of a Nation*.[58] Their intention was strictly political and not monetary.[59] The New York branch of the NAACP openly courted Elaine Sterne of Universal Pictures to develop a script that would be "thoroughly sympathetic to the Negro."[60] The NAACP first considered a twelve-reel film titled *Lincoln's Dream*, but the film shrank to five reels when the organization failed to secure financial banking for the potential project from their white members. Like *Up from Slavery*, it was never produced.[61]

Booker T. Washington and his private secretary Emmett J. Scott made an attempt to create an alternate film. Washington's control of the National Negro Business League guaranteed a forum for distribution and his presidency of the world-famous Tuskegee Institute would give the project a sense of esteem. After *The Birth of a Nation* experienced censorship attacks, D. W. Griffith contacted Washington about the possibility of shooting a conciliatory prologue to the film to be shot at Tuskegee. Washington, already under attack from DuBois and his camp, refused to deal with the director. Scott and Washington opened negotiations with Carl Laemmle of Universal. Elaine Sterne began pitching *Lincoln's Dream* to the Tuskegee camp after the NAACP failed to secure financing. Unfortunately, Washington died before the project became a reality, and without his clout, the proposed film simply faded away.[62]

Griffith's production company also contacted Hampton Institute, another leading African-American institution of higher education, about producing an epilogue to *The Birth of a Nation*. The college administration agreed to Griffith's proposal and the film was produced in the spring of 1916. No existing copy of this epilogue exists, but by all contemporary accounts it demonstrated black progress since Reconstruction. The tagged-on footage had little connection to the original film; apparently it was a five- to six-minute series of shots of the training taking place at Hampton.[63] This addition to *The Birth of a Nation* was a deliberate attempt by Griffith and his production company to squelch African-American protest against the film. It was also a naïve attempt by the leaders of Hampton to dilute the poisonous message of the original film. Contemporary sources claim that the short epilogue was a disjointed piece of filmmaking, simply added to pacify state and local censorship boards.[64]

Many African Americans, most notably leaders in the NAACP, strongly protested the addition of the footage. In the *Crisis,* W. E. B. DuBois publicly criticized Hampton for its decision. Oswald Garrison Villard, chairperson of the NAACP board of directors, argued: "That Hampton should ally itself in any way with so vile a play as *The Birth of a Nation* is a compromise which I must condemn without reservation."[65] Many African-American leaders would not agree to the modification of racist tracts like *The Birth of a Nation* as cinematic alternatives of African-American imagery.

Previous attempts at pitching an independent project to Hollywood may have been unsuccessful, but Emmett J. Scott, Washington's protégé, was determined to become involved in the filmmaking industry. Scott corresponded with Edwin L. Barker of the Advance Motion Picture Company of Chicago. One month after Washington's death, Scott signed a contract with the Advance Company promising access to National Negro Business League chapters, African-American newspapers, the Tuskegee Institute, and his own "colored man's viewpoint." In return, Scott would become a writer-consultant on an unspecified project and would receive a percentage of the royalties from the project. The film never got off the ground.

In 1916 and 1917 the newly organized *The Birth of a Race* Photoplay Organization attempted to raise funds from both black and white investors to film a grand epic of racial progress. The prospectus for the company promised:

Never in the history of motion pictures has a proposed photoplay created so much interest. *The Birth of a Race* will be 12 reels in length— a full evenings entertainment—and the plans are to make this the greatest feature photoplay ever presented to the public. It will be exhibited in practically every civilized country in the world. Because of its truthfulness, and of its proclamation of social betterment and understanding, *The Birth of a Race* will not be prohibited by any state or city, and children as well as grownups will see it.[66]

The press material argued: "In prophetic vision it *[Birth of a Race]* will bring close the future, in which the races—all races—will see each other as they are."[67]

Supporters of the project included Julius Rosenwald of Sears and Roebuck, Frank O. Lowdon, governor of Illinois, and a pantheon of African-

American journalists, academics, physicians, and professionals. The project was supported by African Americans and Euro-Americans.

Filming began in 1917 but dragged on for over a year. Due to a lack of financial support, *The Birth of a Race* was abandoned by a host of film companies. These companies included Selig, the Frohman Amusement Company, and Rothacker Film Manufacturing Company. The film stock was simply passed on from company to company and the original intention of the film was drastically changed. Successive film companies found themselves caught up in an expensive project. Therefore, appealing to a mass audience to recoup investment costs became more critical than strictly appealing to African-American political consciousness. Thomas Cripps claims, "As whites were divided by differing economics and politics, so blacks were divided by the wish to make either great art or great profits."[68] By the time the film was completed in 1918, the United States had become heavily involved in World War I and war propaganda played an influential role in the finished product.[69]

The Birth of a Race has traditionally been denigrated by film critics and historians. It was a disappointment to many African-American investors who had expected a direct assault on Griffith's *The Birth of a Nation*. Contemporary critics described the film as "grotesque," "uninteresting," "disconnected," "without form," and "a terrible waste."[70] This criticism was often based on what the film originally promised rather than on the final product. The partial film that remains today is a little disjointed at times but it remains a remarkable work, considering that *The Birth of a Nation,* Griffith's fierce racial diatribe, had been produced only three years earlier.[71]

The film is epic in structure. It bears a strong resemblance to Griffith's masterpiece, *Intolerance* (1916). *The Birth of a Race* begins with the creation of "man." A title reads: "Man is created, but it is a white man." The film begins with a strongly racist premise, but by the time it reaches the age of Noah, the film argues that "the sons of man multiplied and spread all over the earth and divided into groups and tribes. . . . they had forgotten God's thought in Creation—Equality—and gave themselves over to the folly of envy and prejudice." The directors show the beginnings of warfare. In this section there is the first appearance of an African-American man, in a caveman costume. A title reads: "And they fought like beasts—these men to whom God had given dominion over all things." A black tribe is shown fighting a white tribe.

The next major scene depicts the Egyptians holding the Israelites in bondage. The film bears a strong resemblance to Cecil B. DeMille's *Ten*

Commandments (which would not be produced for another nine years). In Egypt, all of the servants are black. But the wrongs of slavery are clearly shown. In fact, the allegorical similarities between slavery in Egypt and America are induced. The evils of slavery are further shown in a segment on ancient Rome. The directors argue that Jesus Christ comes to earth to save the millions in slavery persecuted by the Romans. Jesus Christ is shown preaching to a wide variety of people. Many African, Chinese, and Asian peoples are purposefully depicted in close-up. A title reads: "Christ made no distinctions between them—His teachings were for all." As Christ is crucified, a black Simon of Cyrene is shown carrying Jesus' cross.

These basic themes of equality, freedom, and peace are carried throughout the rest of the historical evolution of "mankind" (American mankind). The voyages of Christopher Columbus, the Revolutionary War, the Declaration of Independence, Lincoln and the Emancipation Proclamation, and World War I are all painted with a proequality brush. One of the last scenes of the film depicts a black man and a white man tilling the soil of a farm. The film dissolves and they are suddenly in military uniform. Although this scene is an argument in favor of African-American participation and support of the war effort, *The Birth of a Race* puts African-American men on an even plane with white men as both farmers and soldiers, which is remarkable for 1918.

Despite the "good intentions" of the numerous filmmakers who worked on *The Birth of a Race,* many African Americans were disappointed with the final product. Tuskegee administrator Emmett J. Scott, who had bought stock in the company, claimed:

> The venture was conceived . . . by a group of promoters who were lured by the pinnacle attained by David W. Griffith. Griffith was content with chronicling the birth of a nation. This group . . . proposed to take in a race. For stock selling purposes, that race was the Negro race. The picture was started on the premise of a nationwide defence of the Negro race. . . . A large quantity of film picturing the advancement of the Negro race was dropped.[72]

From 1915 to 1918, the controversy over *The Birth of a Nation* marked a radical change in the relationship between African Americans and the cinematic medium. For the first time, the African-American population mobilized a massive propaganda campaign against a motion picture. This campaign was carried out in newly established black newspapers and organizational journals like the *Crisis*. The fight was led by African Americans, with a segment of the white Progressive community providing assistance. The NAACP became a national voice for the black population because of the furor over *The Birth of a Nation* and would remain a leading civil rights organization. Moreover, the cinematic attempts at dispelling the falsehoods over *The Birth of a Nation* illustrated to African Americans that neither the major motion picture studios, white financiers, nor white creative talent could be trusted with providing a more realistic depiction of African-American manhood. Therefore, African Americans would have to develop a cinematic apparatus of their own.

5
THE DEFENSE OF BLACK MANHOOD
ON THE SCREEN

The Birth of a Nation's vicious message of racial intolerance persuaded many African-American men that an independent black cinema was necessary for the social and cultural betterment of the black population. But African-American filmmaking actually had begun before Griffith's classic film with the formation of the Foster Photoplay Company in 1910.

This chapter will address the African-American cinematic response to Euro-American filmic stereotypes. African-American men portrayed themselves in both documentaries and fictional narratives. Documentary films proved conclusively that Euro-American stereotypes of black men had little in common with their real lives. Fictional films gave African-American film audiences black male role models to epitomize and idolize. This chapter will support my central thesis—that a redefinition of black manhood was the major theme in black independent silent cinema. Through the cinematic medium, African-American male filmmakers reflected on the attributes of positive black manhood. These sentiments were perfected by the Lincoln Motion Picture Company, one of the most successful and prolific of the early black motion picture companies, whose oeuvre focused on a cinematic reworking of black masculinity.

William Foster was the first African American to form a motion picture production company. Sources vary concerning the origins of the Foster Photoplay Company, but it is known that it was organized in Chicago between 1910 and 1912. Foster was a multitalented man, active in the African-American community in Chicago in a number of cultural capacities. He was an actor (under the stage name Juli Jones), a sportswriter for the *Chicago Defender*, and a theatrical promoter.[1] Foster produced a number of one- and two-reel films between 1912 and 1916. These included the comedies *The Railroad Porter* (1912) and *The Fall Guy* (1913), the detective film *The Butler* (1913), and the melodrama *The Grafter and the Maid* (1913). Foster also produced the first African-American newsreel.[2]

The 20 December 1913 edition of the *Indianapolis Freeman* explains Foster's rationale for entering the industry. This article is enlightening because it details his reasons for breaking into an industry that had been exclusively controlled by Euro-Americans for seventeen years. This article also contains important information about black spectatorship in the early silent era.

Foster declared two major reasons for entering the motion picture industry. One was his reaction to "the traditional caricatures . . . projected on the screen [that] was not true to life." Foster argued that American motion pictures had a significant impact on the African-American community, which "resented" the "traditional portrayal presented everywhere of the Negro." Foster claimed that in predominantly black sections of major cities, theater owners had to remove certain derogatory depictions of African Americans because African-American patrons protested these caricatures. Therefore, the passive black spectator has to be removed from the lexicon of American moviegoing, even in this racially precarious period of American history. Foster argued for positive, realistic portrayals of African-American culture and life. He explained, "Our brother is born blind and unwilling to see the finer aspects and qualities of American Negro Life." Foster argued that motion pictures should portray "interesting phases" of African-American life— "those of a realistic nature."[3]

Foster's second rationale for entering motion picture production was purely economic. He saw filmmaking as a potentially lucrative enterprise for African-American investment. He predicted "phenomenal success for those among us who have the bravery and foresight to wrestle with the problems of production and presentation."[4] He estimated that in 1909 there were about 112 "colored" theaters in the United States.[5] Foster realized that the majority of these theaters were owned and operated by white men and recognized that motion picture production and distribution was completely controlled by Euro-Americans or Europeans. He believed this "rich commercial plum" should not be grabbed exclusively by white men and that it was the right and responsibility of African Americans to produce films for their own racial group. Foster knew it would be a difficult endeavor, but with "bravery and foresight" African Americans could "reap [their] portion of reward."[6]

Foster's first film, *The Railroad Porter* (1912), had much in common thematically with the black violence-ridden clichés that white producers were churning out. The film featured an all-black cast, a rarity in that period. A wife invites a "fashionably dressed chap" (a waiter at one of the colored cafés) to lunch when she believes her husband is out of town. The wife is accidentally caught with this man by her husband and in a moment of fury he pulls out his revolver. The waiter runs home and also gets his gun but apparently no one is hurt in the end.[7] On the surface, the film appears to fit many of the racial and gender stereotypes of the era's white-produced films.[8] But Mark A. Reid accurately points out some fundamental differences. In the black film, men are employed, marriages do take place, businesses are owned and operated by blacks, and violence does not conclude the film.[9]

Little is known about Foster's other films.[10] White trade publications did not review such films and many black newspapers did not yet concern themselves with movie reviews. Foster's willingness to experiment in a number of genres—comedies, detective films, and melodramas—demonstrated a broadening range of African-American male cinematic roles. In a 9 September 1915 article in the *Chicago Defender*, Foster (writing under the pen name Juli Jones) claimed, "In a moving picture the Negro would off-set so many insults to the race—could tell their side of the birth of this great race."[11]

Following Foster, a number of African-American men, among them George and Noble Johnson and Oscar Micheaux, were willing to invest and experiment in motion picture production for both economic and political reasons. The potentially lucrative African-American film audience, the overwhelmingly negative portrayals of African-American masculinity on the screen, and the developing multifaceted movement of black self-help and racial organization were all key factors leading to the distribution of films starring African Americans by African Americans. Though many African-American production companies were short-lived, they demonstrated the persistence on the part of many African-American men to develop a more well-rounded conception of African-American society and manhood.

Any discussion of "black filmmaking" or "black cinematic imagery" is fraught with pitfalls and definitional controversies. Until recently, when film historians considered "black" portrayals, they were almost exclusively dealing with motion pictures made by white filmmakers. From Peter Noble's *The Negro in Film* (1947) through Thomas Cripps's *Slow Fade to Black* (1975), black imagery in American film was largely discussed only in relation to films directed, written, and produced by white filmmakers. "Black" filmmaking is also laden with aesthetic or politicized difficulties. To some theorists, "true" black filmmaking would include only the production of films by African Americans, totally uninhibited by white loci of power and control over the filmmaking process (either financially or artistically). The intended audience would be assumed to be African American. Thus, *true* black film would be made exclusively by black writers, producers, and directors for an intended black audience. This is the definition of a racially nationalistic ideal rather than a description of what occurred. The problem with this definition of black filmmaking is that it excludes the majority of films in which African Americans had a major role in the creative process.[12]

I distinguish between three predominant artistic forms of black cinematic imagery. The first category includes films produced by companies owned and controlled by African Americans. The second category includes all-black films produced by independent companies owned by Euro-Americans but with African-American creative participation. These companies were outside the Hollywood studio system. The third category includes films produced by major (white) motion picture studios.

These categories will help to explain the characteristics that developed black cultural projection through filmmaking in the decades of the 1910s and 1920s. Richard Merelman has defined cultural projection as "the conscious or unconscious effort by a social group and its allies to place new images of itself before other social groups and before the general public."[13] Between 1913 and 1929, African-American screenwriters, producers, directors, actors, and cinematographers used the medium of film as a way to display a more realistic black culture to an African-American moviegoing audience. African-American production teams simultaneously produced idealized norms of African-American cultural attributes, particularly in regard to imagery of black manhood. These new images of black masculinity sharply contrasted with the negative imagery of white studio productions. New cinematic projections of black manhood placed African-American men in a role almost exclusively relegated to white men in studio productions—that of the heroic warrior, the moral family man, the passionate lover, and the patriotic citizen. Much of this new imagery was placed in an all-black cinematic world, free of the interference of racism of white America.

Black cultural projection is a form of mental production. It forces African-American cinematic artists to create a world that is more "realistic" than that portrayed by mainstream Hollywood productions. It also forces African-American filmmakers to seriously examine values, morals, and judgments they believe the audience should consider. In this sense, black cultural projection directly challenges mainstream white filmmaking. Film scholar Gladstone Yearwood argues that "the aesthetic criteria of a black cinematic tradition must be based on a demythification and demystification of institutionalized cinema."[14] I would add two corollaries to this argument. First, black cultural projection can exist without white cultural projection. All black cultural production is not simply a "reaction" to white values or artistic sensibilities. Black cultural projection can be independently conceived, free from Euro-American cultural norms. By establishing a model in which African-American cultural projection is simply a reaction to white artistic production denies the creativity, artistry, and genius of African-American filmmakers.[15] Second, African Americans often collaborated with Euro-Americans to produce black cinema. White Americans have served as sources of capital and have been artistic copartners in the formation of some black cultural projections. Thus, whether something is an "authentic" black cultural projection is a moot argument.

Silent black cinema was far from independent. Even when African-American producers and directors were able to acquire black financing and control over the productive process, filmmakers were often limited by the dominant cinematic artistic styles of the period.[16] Most black theaters tended to screen more Hollywood films than they did black independent films. Black films could reflect a black sensibility, but on some level they still had to "look like" white films in terms of production values to bring in an audience.[17] Since the beginning of filmmaking, the production, distribution, and exhibition arms of the industry have been almost exclusively controlled by Euro-American sources. The founding of black film companies in the 1910s and 1920s was an attempt to develop production. But these same film companies also had to develop a distribution network. Mainstream movie distributors would rarely handle all-black films; therefore, few copies of black films were ever duplicated. This means that individuals like Hunter Haynes, William Foster, George P. Johnson, and Oscar Micheaux (all black filmmakers) often had to sell their own product by touring the country with several copies of their films. Pearl Bowser and Louise Spence have demonstrated how this process was part of a larger economic pattern within African-American culture in which black businessmen "developed many separate, though seldom fully autonomous, commercial institutions."[18]

The exhibition of all-black films was limited. In 1914, filmmaker Hunter Haynes estimated that there were only 283 motion picture houses that exclusively catered to African-American movie patrons.[19] A number of mainstream movie houses had midnight showings of all-black features (thus the name of one early black film company—Midnight Productions). The number of theaters that would exhibit all-black features was only a small segment of the entire exhibition network. In the silent era, most African-

American directors believed they were making pictures exclusively for black audiences.[20]

A fundamental premise of black filmmaking in this period was the financial and creative constraints that society placed on African-American filmmakers. As Charlene Regester has noted, "African-American motion producers had to contend with limited theaters catering to black audiences, minimal capital for producing pictures, inadequate resources, lack of filmmaking training and skill, poorly trained scriptwriters, producers, directors and actors, and distribution practices that were severely limited in comparison to those employed by major motion picture studios."[21] Independent black films were never as commercially successful as mainstream studio releases. Artistic expression was limited because of lack of money and the absolute necessity of finding an audience. The failure of a countless number of black film companies demonstrates this economic vulnerability.[22]

During the silent era, black filmmakers used much of the symbolic imagery and production modes used by the white filmmaking establishment. What is unique and important to this discussion is that African Americans produced and directed films that created strikingly different worldviews. In the formative period, African-American filmmaking may not have been earthshaking aesthetically, but it was ideologically. Early African-American cinema challenged the dominant culture's portrayal of black life. If Euro-American society used cinema as a means to control social messages and imagery, African-American filmmakers proved that cinema also could be revolutionary. By attempting to disrupt hegemonic film practices, African-American artists used the same codes to create counternarratives. In her landmark *Fire and Desire*, Jane Gaines has described "the deep significance of the all-black cast film[s] for the members of the black audience in terms of the image validation and reciprocity, [and] the return of their own image to them."[23] This model of a mirror cinema was groundbreaking in the way it addressed and transformed the contours of mainstream Hollywood cinematic language.

African-American men constantly move between majority and minority cultures. This was absolutely true of black filmmakers. African-American directors and writers had to negotiate the racism and discrimination they faced on a daily basis. Some films produced a utopian landscape where such problems did not exist. Other directors decided to deal with such issues head-on. African-American men had to define their own masculinity in a society that largely denied them access to dominant white middle-class notions of manhood. This tendency to self-define manhood became the dominant theme in the era of black silent film.

Silent black film served a dual purpose: to make money for the production company and to challenge racist notions of black manhood. Some black filmmakers seemed to be concerned only with the capitalistic notions of filmmaking, but often the early black films that "stand out" are those that challenged dominant imagery. *Close-Up* columnist Geraldyn Dismond argued that "these 'race movies' have the same motive . . . to present Negro films about and for Negroes . . . showing them not as fools and servants, but as human beings with the same emotions, desires and weaknesses as other peoples; and to share in the profits of this great industry."[24]

Black filmmakers reflected their perceptions of the world through the medium of film. It is important to realize that in the silent era, men made almost all films produced and directed by African Americans. Black silent film was both racialized and gendered; only on rare occasions were black female perceptions transmitted through the medium.[25] Issues of gender, race, class, political ideology, and white interference in the creative process (or lack of it) had an impact on African-American film. Any discussion of silent black cinema must address the male control of the artistic medium. Both race and gender served as designations of reality in this filmmaking.

African-American men used the medium of film to create a world in which they set the boundaries and conduct for black manhood. The sociocultural background of these filmmakers played a major role in their cinematic productions. Oscar Micheaux's rural roots and the Johnson brothers' fascination with the "complete" family served as formative tendencies in their films.

Black culture has always been a multifaceted, polyphonic social group that must be discussed in its entirety. Thus, there is not one black culture but black cultures. There is also not one black silent cinema, but forms or modes of black silent cinema. Black filmmakers reflected the many layers of African-American culture—rural and urban; upper class, middle class, and lower class; educated and uneducated. Northern migration during the World War I years and the 1920s had a dramatic impact upon African-American moviegoing habits. Discretionary income and more leisure time in urban metropolises contributed a ready-made audience for early race films.[26]

Class played a major role in many films of the silent era. Filmmakers stressed the urban bourgeois values of DuBois's Talented Tenth over a rural sharecropper lifestyle. David Lewis has documented the growing strength of the black professional class in the era.[27] African Americans were also increasingly going to college. These opportunities for economic advancement were not available to all African Americans, though. Class differences and frustrations would play themselves out through the medium, revealing the changing nature of African-American life in the early period of the Great Migration.

Gladstone Yearwood argues that black film can be defined as "any film whose signifying practice or whose making of symbolic images emanate from an essential cultural matrix drawing from a collective black socio-cultural and historical experience and [that] uses black expressive tradition as a means through which artistic language is mediated."[28] Yearwood's position throws the defining process of black film into the context of the African-American community as a whole; spectators legitimize films based on their own sociocultural or historical background. This empowers the black majority and marginalizes members of the black minority (radical, feminist, gay, and lesbian). Black silent film was a commercial enterprise; therefore, filmmakers attempted to produce a movie that would appeal to a mass black audience. This productive process included iconic imagery and political and social sentiments with which the mass racialized audience could identify. As Jane Gaines claims, "African-American audiences 'wanted something back' from the imagery on the screen."[29] Black silent film had to have meaning. Audience members had to be able to understand and interpret the plot, characterizations, and moral framework of the film. The most successful filmmakers, particularly Oscar Micheaux, were able to implement "issues of social reality within the black community" in the narrative structure of their films, giving spectators an identifiable moral sense of the film.[30]

Silent black cinema did not attempt to interpret only reality; mythology also played a major role in the filmmaking process. African film critic Madubuko Diakite explains that myth making served three major purposes in black film: to provide viewers a form of entertainment, to provide viewers a degree of emotional relief through vicarious experience, and to offer support for key features of behavior within the sociocultural community.[31] I argue that within black silent cinema, myth making served a dual purpose—to challenge many aspects of the dominant community but at the same time to try to create some system of social order and meaning (and relief) within the African-American culture. Black silent film was escapist, yet reflected political and social values of the black community. Black cinematic myths and mythical characters attempted to produce a consciousness of meaning within an American society that was segregated, racist, confrontational—and irrational.[32]

Black silent cinema also produced a number of artistic "styles." There was not one unique style in black filmmaking in the silent period. Some directors corresponded to a cinematic style that closely mimicked white studio standards, whereas other filmmakers (such as Micheaux at times) were more experimental. Style differed in white-produced and black-produced films in regard to body language, dress, language (or titles), and individual performance style. Black cinematic style was a reflection of the African-American culture. It was a way to orient the viewer to a lifestyle or a community with which they were familiar or could identify.

African-American male filmmakers challenged dominant stereotypical depictions of themselves through both documentary and fictional means. One of the ways in which African-American filmmakers reformulated the cultural imagery of black men was by filming the exploits of African-American soldiers in war. During the Spanish-American War, a few short films captured black soldiers on celluloid. During World War I, a number of newsreels and documentaries displayed black heroics and military identity. At least six all-black companies—the Toussaint, Peter P. Jones, Downing, Turpin, Filhey, and Frederick Douglass Companies cinematically captured black men in uniform during the late 1910s. In fact, the Peter P. Jones Company continued to exploit the military activities of black soldiers during the Spanish-American War as late as the 1910s. A three-reel documentary, *For the Honor of the 8th Illinois Regiment* (1916), showed the infamous African-American regiment at battle in Cuba and being warmly received by the governor of Illinois. The preparedness movement and the renewed interest in militarization prior to the U.S. entry into World War I convinced the Peter P. Jones Company that such footage could profitably be brought out of mothballs.[33] The same company bought footage from the conflict in Mexico with Pancho Villa. The two-reel documentary *Colored Soldiers Fighting in Mexico* (1916) showed the same 8th Illinois regiment under the command of a white colonel.[34]

More than one hundred thousand black soldiers were sent to France during World War I. Out of a total African-American population of twelve million, this meant that practically every black American family knew someone or felt the direct impact of black participation in the war. Although more than 80 percent of all African-American men who served were stevedores or in other manual labor positions, a number of black military divisions distinguished themselves during the war.[35] The Peter P. Jones Company did not even wait for the soldiers to get to Europe. In *Negro Soldiers Fighting for Uncle Sam* (1916) the company showed black soldiers training for active duty.[36] The Downing Company produced *Our Colored Fighters,* proudly illustrating the military exploits of black soldiers. The promotional literature for the company claimed: "By communicating with this corporation, colored patriotic organizations can secure this film and give the people of every

section of the country an opportunity to see it and to assist in raising funds
for the various war relief agencies that are conducting 'drives' for the benefit of our boys at the front."[37] The black press recognized that motion pictures were important in the war effort, particularly in regard to racial
change. Journalist Lester A. Walton argued that "race hatred, color prejudice, greed for gold for territory, for unbridled power are some of the con-
tributory causes which bring about war. . . . what the movies must do . . . is
to teach the people that it is wrong for them to hate one another because of
color race."[38] Another critic argued that cinematic representations of black
soldiers in World War I would "affect the damage and mischief that has and
is being done to the colored race by unscrupulous productions such as *The
Birth of a Nation*."[39] It was recognized that participation in World War I
and the filming of this participation would demonstrate African-American
loyalty, patriotism, and worthiness of full citizenship. As Pearl Bowser and
Louise Spence have documented, African-American newsreels of soldiers
often countered derogatory mainstream newsreels that depicted African-
American men as bumbling fools.[40]

Because of the logistical problem of acquiring footage of black soldiers
from overseas and the necessity of cooperation with the U.S. War Department, many of the films with depictions of black soldiers did not actually appear until the war was over. *The Heroic Negro Soldiers of the War* (Frederick
Douglass Company) documented the black male experience in the war by
showing men leaving their homes and joining the army, training for duty,
going overseas, fighting in France, and eventually returning triumphantly to
the United States.[41] The film was not released until 1919. The traditional
historical interpretation has been that military pictures were box-office poison for the majority of the American moviegoing public following the war.
Millions of feet of documentary and fictional footage of military-themed
material had been filmed during the war, but almost as soon as 1919 began,
military pictures were considered dead material.[42] However, this was not
true in the African-American community. Military-themed pictures continued to be important in the black community through 1921 as a reminder of
the sacrifices and contributions that black men had made to the war effort.[43]
Doing Their Bit (Toussaint Film Company, 1918) demonstrated the wide
range of roles black soldiers played during the war. The documentary
showed black soldiers training both at home and in Europe. It illustrated the
life of the common field soldier and showed Emmett J. Scott in his role as
Special Assistant to the Secretary of War. The film did tremendously well at
the box office in the black community.[44]

Many African-American men had a difficult transition returning to domestic life after a racially freer existence in Europe. In the summer of 1919, the country exploded in a series of racial disturbances, most notably in Chicago. Hundreds of thousands of African Americans had moved north during the war seeking good-paying jobs in the defense industry. Many northern whites feared the ever-growing influx of African Americans.[45]

Despite the racial disturbances, the documentary tradition was alive and well in the late 1910s and early 1920s among black film companies. Not simply relegating their footage to military activities, these documentaries strongly contrasted the fictionalized studio portrayals of black manhood with "real life." These newsreels and documentaries were almost exclusively viewed by African-American audiences.

Progress in black education was a common theme in these documentaries. School officials at both Tuskegee and Hampton Institutes, the two most well-known black educational institutions of the era, used the medium of motion pictures to promote their schools. In 1913, the Anderson Watkins Company produced *A Day at Tuskegee,* a three-reel film showing the diversity of industry within the school. In 1923, Crusader Films produced *Tuskegee Finds the Way Out.* The "out" can only be assumed to be an escape from the wrenching poverty of sharecropping, which the majority of African Americans still participated in as the decade began. In 1921, the T. H. B. Walkins Company produced a newsreel illustrating scenes from seventeen black colleges.[46]

Economic progress and self-sufficiency were two common themes in black newsreels. *Walker Newsreel No. 1* (1921) illustrated black-owned banks and factories. The Colored Business League and the National Negro Business League also were filmed frequently.[47] Black filmmakers captured the activities of black social and fraternal orders that bound thousands of men together in brotherhood. In 1916, the Haynes Photoplay Company filmed the BMC and Odd Fellows (two black fraternal orders) on parade in Boston, Massachusetts, in one of their newsreels. In 1915, the Peter P. Jones Company filmed a Grand Elks parade and a Baptist convention. In 1921, the Renaissance Newsreel Company showed an Imperial Elks Lodge meeting. The same newsreel illustrated other forms of black self-sufficiency by documenting a black YMCA and the Booker T. Washington Sanitarium.[48]

Documentary makers also filmed black politicians and civic leaders. *Monumental Newsreel No. 2* (1921) showed President Warren Harding receiving black political leaders at the White House. In 1914, Haynes Photoplay Company illustrated pictorials of famous black politicians. In *Turpin's Real*

Reels (1916), Charles H. Turpin filmed himself as "the first black man ever elected to the office of constable in the state of Missouri."[49]

This plethora of documentaries depicted African-American men in a wide variety of political, economic, and social activities. They directly countered the narrow range of cinematic roles African-American men occupied in mainstream studio productions. They were crucial in demonstrating the reality of black life.

Black men were also depicted participating in a number of spectator sports. In the 1910s and 1920s, the mainstream media still portrayed African-American men as physically weak, inferior, and lazy, so heroic exploits of black athletic prowess were remarkable challenges to the dominant ideology. Boxing, the least segregated of all of the spectator sports, produced black stars like Joe Wolcott and Sam Langford, who were admirably cast in newsreels. In 1921, Peacock Films showed footage of Ned Gourden, a famous Howard University athlete, who broke the world's record for the one-hundred-yard dash. In the same year, Monumental Pictures showed the New York Giants baseball team play an exhibition game against an unnamed black professional team in Atlanta.[50] These films lionized African-American athletes and refuted the myth of the feebleness of African-American men.

As discussed in Chapter 3, Jack Johnson, the first black heavyweight champion, was a popular subject for black filmmakers. Johnson was one of the best-known African-American men during the silent film era. In 1912, he was convicted of violating the Mann Act by transporting his white wife across state lines before their marriage. He was sentenced to a year in prison and was released on bond pending appeal. This happened shortly after his victory over former champion Jim Jeffries while he was at the height of his career. Johnson disguised himself as a member of a black baseball team and fled the country to keep from going to prison; he was afraid of being killed by white inmates or prison officials. From 1913 to 1920 he was a fugitive from the law. Between 1913 and 1915 he defended his title in Europe. On 5 April 1915, Johnson fought Jess Willard, a white man, in Havana, Cuba. He deliberately threw the fight, believing a loss would mean U.S. federal authorities would drop charges against him. He was mistaken, and in 1920 he finally surrendered to U.S. marshals and was sentenced to the federal penitentiary in Leavenworth, Kansas, for one year. Johnson continued to fight professionally until 1928 but redirected much of his energy toward the world of show business.[51]

In 1921 Johnson appeared in *As the World Rolls On,* a six-reel feature film produced by Andlauer Company of Kansas City, Missouri. Johnson was the

main attraction, but the film also showed members of the Kansas City Monarchs, one of Negro baseball's premiere teams. *As the World Rolls On* was an
important black silent feature for its wide-ranging depictions of the diversity
of African-American life and for its idealistic story line.

As the World Rolls On showed a number of prominent scenes of African-
American life in the early 1920s—the cultural life of Kansas City, a major
African-American hub; Negro League baseball and its stars; black fraternal or-
ganizations like the Odd Fellows and the Knights of Pythias (who gave the
Monarchs their prize); and the former heavyweight champion, Jack Johnson.

As the World Rolls On stressed the physicality of black manhood—the ability to beat one's opponent in the ring, on the field, and for the hand of a
woman. For the production team, a strong body made for a strong mind.
Johnson is a role model in the film who seems to have all of the answers.
Nothing is mentioned of his larger-than-life escapades, his marital and financial difficulties, his flight from the law, or his time in prison. Instead, the
film applauds his caring nature and sheer physical prowess. The film synopsis promised "close-ups of his great muscles and masculine body of steel."[52]
The current obsession with the athletic skills of African-American men is not
unique to the early twenty-first century.[53]

Films of Johnson's victory over Jeffries continued to be exhibited some ten
years after its completion despite the technical illegality. A 1922 ad in the
Chicago Defender advertised the great contest as "15 gripping rounds." The
"catch" for this decade-old fight was an enlargement process in which moviegoers could watch Johnson's brutal defeat of Jeffries in close-up. The racial
victory still held special significance for the African-American community.[54]

In 1922, as film spectators were rewatching the historic fight, they were
also seeing Johnson in another feature film, *For His Mother's Sake*. This
Blackburn-Velde production "of filial devotion, replete with pathos and stir-
ring scenes" was a prodigal son story.[55] In the film, Johnson's younger
brother steals a valuable package. Knowing the truth would kill his mother,
Johnson's character takes the blame and flees to Mexico. While there, he
wins thousands of dollars prizefighting, pays for his brother's mistake, and
everyone ends up happy. The producers of the film wanted to capitalize on
Johnson's pugilist skills. *For His Mother's Sake* reiterated the idea that the
only way to right a wrong, to have a happy balance, was through physical
strength. Jack Johnson demonstrated to a generation of African-American
male youth that athletics was one of the few ways out of the ghetto or off
the sharecropper's farm through these two fictional feature films and his
prizefighting films.[56]

The Frederick Douglass Corporation was one of the best organized of the early black independent companies. The company was organized as a reaction to the harmful effects of *The Birth of a Nation*. Drawing their name from one of the best-known African-American historical figures of the nineteenth century, the company associated their films with a man who was well educated and self-emancipated. Operating out of Jersey City, New Jersey, the company's first film was *The Colored American Winning His Suit* (1916). The Frederick Douglass Film Corporation listed some basic principles they wanted their films to evoke: "Affect the evil effects of certain photo plays that have labeled the Negro and criticized his friends. To bring about a better and more friendly understanding between the white and colored races. To show the better side of negro life [and] to inspire the negro a desire to climb higher in good citizenship, business, education and religion."⁵⁷ However, by no means were the organizers of the company revolutionary in their racial politics. They tempered their cinematic principles with accommodationist language. Claiming their films were "void of bitterness," they argued that they depicted "the true American white man with a spirit of charity and justice of whom there are many such to whom the [black] race owes a debt of gratitude. The play *[The Colored American]* at no point seeks to enhance the value of one race at the expense of the other."⁵⁸

The Colored American Winning His Suit is a classic example of the promotion of bourgeois self-help. A multigenerational story, the film explains that through hard work and education, a black family can succeed. The central figure is Bob Winall. The story begins shortly after the Civil War with Bob's "free but poverty-stricken" parents. Bob's father is a "determined man," "not to be daunted."⁵⁹ He is the masculine role model in the film, the one who sacrifices himself for his children. There are two children in the family, Bob and Bessie. During their childhood, their father accumulates enough money to buy his former master's homestead and becomes a property owner. Bob's father ensures that both his children get a proper education. Bessie graduates from Spelman and Bob gets a law degree from Howard University. The film stressed parental sacrifice, the value of education, and thrift. In the end of the film Bob Winall *wins all* due to his intelligence, respected friends, and nurturing parents.

The Colored American Winning His Suit illustrated an interesting variation on class differences. The film attempted to instruct African Americans on how to succeed; yet the filmmakers also argued that money was not valuable when it came to romantic love. Publicity in the *New York Age* assured the readers that the actors were inexperienced although the cast was "made up of young men and women of the race from the homes of the best families at Jersey."[60] Some of the filming was also completed at Howard University, giving the film racial authenticity and a further association with bourgeois values. The *New York Age* argued that "the picture is developed with the idea of overcoming the effects of certain vicious photo plays which have created antagonistic propaganda against the race in the past few months. The showing of this first picture indicates that object will undoubtedly be attained by the company."[61]

The second film the company released was *The Scapegoat*, which premiered on 15 May 1917. *The Scapegoat* was adapted from a story by Paul Laurence Dunbar, a prominent African-American author and poet of the era. The film was one of the first taken from a "known" black literary source. The film starred well-known black theatrical people (Abbie Mitchell, Walker Thompson, and Maude Jones) but the film's adaptation was apparently not successful. A *New York Age* reporter argued that the film lacked a certain cohesiveness (the protagonist was single in one scene and married with a child in the next). The reporter also criticized the film because black middle-class characters used a lower-class dialect in the titles. He argued that a colored firm producing primarily for colored theaters should know better.[62] This proved that African-American spectators were a discriminating audience, not accepting negative imagery of black people or poor production values. Although widespread criticism of all-black productions in the black press was rare, it did occur.[63]

The World War I and postwar era was full of all-black productions that attempted to explain to African-American audiences what characteristics were needed to create a "good man." *Shadowed by the Devil* (Unique Film Company, 1916) was not subtle in making its point. The film contrasted the characteristics of three individuals—a spoiled "princess," a man possessed by the devil [literally], and Everett, "a good industrious son of poor parents, a quiet and sober young man, a loving husband and . . . father [who] shows the traits of his early learning."[64]

Intraracial problems in the African-American community were often depicted at the same time definitions of masculinity were being cinematically constructed. In 1920, the Royal Gardens Film Company of Chicago released a six-reel film titled *In the Depths of Our Hearts*. The principal theme is the condemnation of intraracial discrimination based on skin color. A mother raises her son and daughter "to believe that any one of a darker hue is unfit as an associate."[65] The film portrays this as a serious problem within the African-American community. The son falls in love with a darker-skinned girl and rebels against his mother's racial prejudices. He is sent to the farm of an abusive uncle to forget the romance. He eventually escapes, goes to the big city, and finds his former sweetheart working as a waitress in a restaurant. The lovers are reunited. According to the principles of the producers, a true man shows no color-conscious discrimination against members of his own race.

A number of black independent features illustrated idealistic virtues of manhood against the classic generic archetype of American cinema—the Western. Joan Mellen has argued that Westerns have been integral in defining masculinity on the screen. She claims the genre "provided male heroes with that precivilized environment in which they could exercise potency free of emasculating restrictions, those imposed by class, law and education."[66] For black independent filmmakers, Westerns also offered freedom from the "emasculating restriction" of race distinction. Westerns had a compelling capacity to dwell on male pride and self-esteem, offering black moviegoers an opportunity to actually cheer on black manhood.

The $10,000 Trail (Bookertee Film Company, 1921) was one of the first black Westerns ever produced. The film packed in black audiences, anxious to see black cowboys ride the range.[67] The film's protagonist was Smiling Bob Woodson, a "big-hearted two fisted" rancher. He was crude but possessed "rugged chivalry." His lack of manners eventually frustrates his fiancée, Kate Atkinson, Bob's snobbish eastern belle. Another woman, Rosemary Vale, sees the virtues in Bob's character and falls for him. A band of villains takes Rosemary and Bob captive. Bob is eventually released but he must save his new sweetheart. He tears up $10,000 in cash, leaving a trail of mutilated currency while being led out of the hidden encampment. Bob is described as "generous," "resourceful," and "self-sacrificing." He gives up all the money he has to rescue Rosemary. When Kate finds out he is penniless she breaks off the engagement, "leaving him free to declare his love for the girl whose life he has saved."[68]

Monarch Productions' *The Flaming Crisis* (1924) throws an eastern newspaperman into the rural West to prove his moral fortitude. There "he becomes involved in a number of adventures which try his courage and bring him victory."[69] These adventures include rescuing a child from a cattle stampede and winning the heart of a lovely, wealthy woman. The atmosphere of the West tested the rugged attributes of black manhood.

Absent (Rosebud Film Corporation, 1928) places another stranger in the wilderness to prove his manhood, but under slightly different circumstances.

Clarence Brooks, one of the best-known black leading men of the silent era, plays a shell-shocked veteran from World War I who loses his memory during the war. Brooks was a veteran in real life. While in the West, the Brooks character is taken care of by an old miner and his daughter. He eventually regains his memory and strength and wins the heart of the daughter. The principal commercial appeal was the star power of Brooks. The *Los Angeles New Age Dispatch* described him as a "nationally known star."[70] The *Los Angeles Age* said he was "the world's foremost Negro star."[71]

Black manhood was tested in the urban jungle as well as in the rural wilderness. The Maurice Company produced three features during the 1920s that were set in an underworld milieu, in many ways foreshadowing the popularity of the gangster genre of the 1930s. The company was founded by Richard Maurice, who also starred in each of the feature films. Maurice films were unique in their hard-edged, often grim depictions of urban life. Maurice's first film released was *Our Christianity and Nobody's Children* (1920). The film told the story of two illegitimate children, a brother and sister. The brother promised his mother on her deathbed that he would watch over his sibling. The children have a stepfather who is "destitute," "unnatural," and a "no-account type."[72] He kidnaps the sister and her brother is determined to find her. The boy is eventually accused, tried, convicted, and sentenced to hang for a murder that he has not committed. The actual killer is a drug addict who decides he will help the boy escape from prison and find his sister. They find her in a brothel, and through a series of courageous fights, rescue her. The film was described as a formidable thriller and did well in the African-American community.[73]

According to his cinematic legacy, Richard Maurice had a pessimistic view of life but he was also a spiritual man. *Our Christianity and Nobody's Children* reflected this sentiment. It was even more prevalent in *Eleven P.M.*, one of the few all-black silent features that is still available for viewing. A detailed analysis of the film is available in the appendix.[74]

Eleven P.M. creates three strongly contrasting characterizations of black masculinity in the personae of Perry, Sundaisy, and Clyde. Perry is a multi-talented superman. A handsome athlete and superb boxer, an educated and talented writer, and a devoted boyfriend, Perry illustrates through his dream imagery his moral strength and respect for women. He defends his girlfriend against a masher and stays away from places of "evil repute."

The character of Clyde and his father Roy were played by the same actor (as adults). This was not coincidental; this device was used to demonstrate the transmission of undesirable character traits from generation to generation.

Although Clyde may have been nurtured into a life of crime by the Reverend Hackett (another notoriously corrupt man and part of the literary/cinematic legacy of the despicable preacher), the film stresses the negative genetic attributes that Roy transmits to his son. Clyde is a man without a moral bone in his body. He is willing to use both a mother and daughter for sexual pleasure and financial gain. He is willing to break up a home and double-cross the only man that truly cared about him in life—Sundaisy. Drawn to flashy cars and expensive suits, Clyde is willing to turn to a life of crime to acquire his material pleasures. Clyde proves that he is not above the spiritual world, though; his own demons and ghastly apparitions eventually destroy him.

Sundaisy is the most interesting of the male characters and the most complicated in the matrix. Given an apparently feminine name, Sundaisy's adrogynous look and flowery name make him "less than a man" on a superficial level. Forced to become a street entertainer to make a living, Sundaisy's mulatto status also means that he does not fully "fit" into the African-American community. But Sundaisy is a morally respectable character. He cares for the son of a criminal and a girl-waif whom he marries to save her from a life of poverty and degradation. Sundaisy is faithful to his no-good stepson, his runaway wife, and his corruptible daughter Hope—and this makes him a tragic figure. He sacrifices himself for others who do not return the favor. Eventually his "worries, sorrows and disappointments" make him die of a broken heart. This leads the spectator to an interesting moral dilemma. Is Sundaisy a fool? Is caring for nonblood relatives in the African-American community a waste of time? *Eleven P.M.* demonstrates that African-American melodrama in the silent era did not always offer easy answers to life's dilemmas.

The majority of films produced by independent film companies between 1913 and 1929 were dramatic in nature. Almost all of the characterizations of African Americans in white-controlled film productions were comedic. Serious drama communicated a sense of legitimacy to the black community. African-American film corporations did produce some comedies in the silent era but they often used humor to deal with serious social problems.

One comedic subgenre addressed the growing divide between the urban and rural black experience. *Uncle Remus' First Visit to New York* (Hunter Haynes Photoplay Company, 1914) was comedic in style, but it also contrasted the lifestyles and traits of the "old" Negro with those of the "new" Negro, who was urban and urbane. Rastus, the "new" Negro in the film, is a successful New York businessman who is "high-tone" and has "stylish friends" (but he cannot escape the derogatory slave plantation/minstrel name).[75] He and his wife invite Uncle Remus (an unsophisticated farmer from Awfulville, Mississippi) to visit them in the big city. Uncle Remus and his wife suffer a series of misadventures in New York City owing to their inexperience in dealing with the modern trappings of life. A reporter from the *Indianapolis Freeman* reported that *Uncle Remus* "is a faithful portrait that contrasts the New Negro with the Old and forges a chain of circumstances that vividly point out the progress the race has made in his 50 years of freedom . . . the modern and the antebellum Negro as shown in sharp differentiation, imparting a lesson that cannot fail to inspire."[76] Although white studio productions emphasized the desirable characteristics of the "old" Negro, films directed by African Americans often ridiculed such figures. In *Why Worry* (Lone Star Motion Picture Producers, 1923), the leading characters are rural hicks who come to the big city. They are described as "both so dumb that they think Rex Beach is a summer resort," and many supposedly amusing incidents come out of their stupidity.[77] *Uncle Remus* and *Why Worry* were two cultural products of the era that denigrated the rural southern Negro and showed the more sophisticated life of the urban African American. In his masterly *Straight Lick: The Cinema of Oscar Micheaux,* J. Ronald Green places rube movies in the context of the Great Migration. He argues that these films "articulated the sense of awkwardness and the lack of sophistication of many Americans, including the kind of social ambivalence that country people might feel upon going to the city."[78]

The Lincoln Motion Picture Company is significant for several fundamental reasons. It was not the first film company owned and managed by African Americans, but it was the first to offer a startlingly different portrayal of African-American masculinity that strongly contradicted the chicken-stealing, watermelon-eating Sambos of the early silent era or the sex-crazed bucks of *The Birth of a Nation.*[79] The Lincoln Motion Picture Company made redefining black masculinity one of their central themes; Lincoln's emphasis on black manhood structured the discourse of the early African-American film industry. The company is also significant because it was one of the few black motion picture companies to produce a coherent body of work. In addition, it also produced two African-American male stars—Noble Johnson and Clarence Brooks. Johnson became the preeminent African-American silent film star, cast in a number of all-black features and costarring in countless secondary roles in major Hollywood releases. Clarence Brooks also acted in a number of mainstream Hollywood productions as well as significant African-American productions.

The Lincoln Motion Picture Company was organized on 24 May 1916 in

Los Angeles, California.[80] Noble Johnson was the leading figure in the formation of the company. He was born on 18 April 1891 to an African-American father and a white mother. He grew up in Colorado Springs, Colorado, where he helped raise and train horses with his father, who was an expert in the field. Johnson's mother died giving birth to his younger brother, so Johnson's father became the major parental force in his life. He was raised as a child of the West, spending his time working on cattle ranches, trapping animals, and saddling horses.[81] He went to school with Lon Chaney, with whom he would later cross paths in the filmmaking industry. Johnson regularly traveled for his father's business once he reached adolescence and early adulthood. Upon arriving home to Colorado Springs in June 1914, Johnson found a great deal of activity because the Lubin Film Manufacturing Company was producing a film in the area. The film was an eight-reel Western, *Eagles Nest*. One of the leading actors was injured completing a horse stunt on the set and a casting call was made to replace him. Johnson applied, and his years of experience in handling and training horses enabled him to secure the position. He starred as a Native American in the film, a trend which, once established, continued throughout his life. In the early part of his career, Johnson played nonblack characters more frequently than he did black ones.[82] His horsemanship and performance in *Eagles Nest* brought him to the attention of the Lubin Company, who asked him to come to the company headquarters in Philadelphia.[83]

Besides Johnson, other prominent members of the Lincoln Motion Picture Company staff included Dr. J. Thomas Smith, vice president and treasurer; Clarence Brooks, secretary; Dudley A. Brooks, assistant secretary; William O. Tyler, attorney, and George Johnson, Noble's brother, who took care of distribution and screenwriting. Mark Reid argues that the division of labor within the Lincoln Company resembles a film collective in which members performed more than one task.[84] The only white member of the organization was Harry Gant, a cameraman whom Noble had met while working at Universal Pictures. Therefore, the content of the films was controlled by African Americans but the cinematography was controlled by Gant, who filmed all of the Lincoln features.[85]

The company's first two-reel feature was *The Realization of a Negroes Ambition*, released in 1916. The title alone indicated that this would be a film that would be significantly different. In a letter to owners of theaters with black patrons, Clarence Brooks explained: "The purpose of this company is to produce pictures like all other companies, that will satisfy and be accepted by any other person in this country, regardless of nationality. And mainly to display the Negro as *he is in his every day life,* a human being, with human inclinations."[86] In their attempt at realism, Brooks argued: "It is seldom that the Negro has been displayed as anything else but a bootblack, waiter, porter or servant of some kind, yet in reality they have men of all walks of life."[87] Thus, the purpose of the company was to cinematically readjust conceptions of black manhood. It was, as Brooks argued, "to satisfy this desire . . . for the Negro 'movie going public.'"[88]

The Realization of a Negroes Ambition starred three members of the Lincoln Motion Picture staff—Noble M. Johnson, Clarence Brooks, and Brooks's brother Dudley. This was done for several reasons. First, the Lincoln Company was extremely short on cash. The company did not incorporate until 20 January 1917, so the filmmakers were literally subsidizing the film with their own funds. Second, both Johnson and Clarence Brooks had acting experience that qualified them to fill the roles.

Ideologically, *The Realization of a Negroes Ambition* is part Horatio Alger and part Booker T. Washington. The film's protagonist is a Tuskegee-educated young man, James Burton (played by Noble Johnson). This was the first time in screen history that a college-educated African American had ever been depicted. James has been trained as a civil engineer but there is no work for him on his father's farm after graduation. He decides to head west and make his fortune. James's ingenuity and ambition are stressed.

When he arrives in California, he is turned down for a position at an oil field, for which he is well qualified, because he is an African American. Employment discrimination based on race had never been addressed in a film before. Despondent, James walks away from the oil office but spots a young white woman in a runaway cart. He makes a daring rescue, jumping from the back of a horse onto the rig to save her (Johnson's remarkable horsemanship skills came in handy). The young woman turns out to be the daughter of the oil field owner (the Algeristic twist). He is so grateful to James that he gives him a job. Once the owner discovers he is a trained civil engineer (and not just a shiftless Negro), he is placed in charge of an oil expedition. James learns about the industry and discovers that the soil on his father's farm is remarkably close to the type of soil on which the oil company has been drilling. James gets his boss to stake him the money to drill on his father's land, well aware of the possible economic opportunities this might provide for his family.

James returns home to stake his claim. He eventually strikes oil, which "make[s] him independent." (This is screenwriter George Johnson's word choice and is critical to understand the dynamics of the film.) He no longer

needs to rely on his boss. Johnson makes enough money to buy a house and
marry his sweetheart. The final scene shows "James in later years, with ambition realized, home and family, a nice country to live in and nice people to
live and enjoy it with."[89] George Johnson's summary sentence contained a
litany of masculine ideals critical to the Lincoln ideology. Lincoln men were
ambitious and strong, dedicated to their families, patriotic, supported by
their friends because of their outstanding character, and African American.[90]
Using Kevin Gaines's analysis of social uplift, the Lincoln team would distinguish themselves as "bourgeois agents of civilization," attempting to inspire the undeveloped black majority.[91] In my analysis, this should not be a
criticism of the Lincoln team, who were operating under enormous pres-
sures both economically and artistically and who were using the medium of
film as a tool of empowerment.

The black community's reaction to the film was overwhelming. Countless
letters praising the film poured into the office of Tony Langston, entertainment editor of the *Chicago Defender*, the largest circulating African-American newspaper of the period. J. Dooley, owner of the Grand Theater,
claimed that "the Lincoln Motion Picture Company has done something in
getting away from the cheap and low stuff called 'comedy' of other producers. It is great stuff."[92] A reporter for the *Chicago Defender* declared that
"this educational and interesting picture marks the beginning of a new era
in the production of Race pictures."[93] He argued that African Americans
were sick and tired of "insulting, humiliating and undignified portrayals of
the cheap burlesque slap-stick comedies so universally shown as characteristics of Afro-American ideals." The reporter believed that *The Realization of
a Negroes Ambition* was a milestone in African-American cinema.[94] From
Tuskegee to Chicago, the film received overwhelmingly favorable praise.

The quality of Lincoln motion pictures and Noble Johnson's growing
fame and popularity were two of the critical factors leading to the company's
success. Much of the success was also due to the distribution network established by George Johnson. He had Tony Langston, editor of the *Chicago
Defender*, and Romeo Daugherty, editor of the *New York Amsterdam News*,
working as agents for the company.[95]

The genre was unique because it was an African-American production
that was not a comedy. African-American men had appeared in dramas before but the cast was usually predominantly white and the African-American
man was usually portrayed as a faithful slave. In this production, the African-
American man was the hero and the protagonist. *The Realization of a Negroes Ambition* appealed to the African-American community because it was

both realistic and idealistic. Many African-American spectators saw *Realization* as a deliberate counternarrative. The film expressed idealized notions of African-American manhood. It was "interesting, inspiring, commendable and educational."[96]

The Lincoln Motion Picture Company was in business longer than most African-American film companies because of the quality of their products and their knack for distribution. *Realization* was the opening attraction at the annual meeting of the National Negro Business League on 14 August 1916. Thousands of African-American businessmen were in attendance, an excellent forum for potential distribution of the film.[97] A journalist who attended claimed:

> This educational and interesting picture marks the beginning of a new era in the production of Race pictures. Feeling that the trend of public sentiment among the Race lover of the silent drama is growing so antagonistic to the insulting, humiliating and undignified portrayal of the cheap burlesque, slap-stick comedies so universally shown as characteristic of the Afro-American ideals, the Lincoln Motion Picture Company of Los Angeles, California, a Race firm, has in their first release successfully eliminated these undesirable features and produced a really interesting, inspiring and commendable educational love drama featuring the business and social life of the Negro—as it really is and not as our jealous contemporaries would have it appear.[98]

The film proved to be a huge moneymaker in many black film houses. Teenan Jones, operator of the Star Theater in Chicago, claimed that it was breaking house records. He enthusiastically stated, "To say our patrons were surprised and delighted is putting it mildly."[99] The demand for the picture was so great that the Lincoln Company had to print four additional copies. Countless letters poured into their office from theater managers asking them to keep them informed of when a new Lincoln film was being released.

The Realization of a Negroes Ambition, like Lincoln's other films, would fit into the genre of uplift narrative. A strongly male-dominated genre, these films, according to Jane Gaines, "were moral tales of self-reliance, resourcefulness, and exceptionality in which the hero's ambitions are achieved in the same way that race prejudice is thought to be overcome—by demonstration of the way in which he is just as accomplished as or just like a white hero."[100] Gaines's definition is slightly overdeterministic, but the genre did emphasize the valiant heroics and moral strength of an

African-American man who was able to overcome the racial and social barriers society placed before him.

The second production of the Lincoln Company was *The Trooper of Troop K*. The film was released in late 1916 at the height of the conflict with Mexico. The Lincoln Company decided to capitalize on the current interest in the crisis, giving the film a particular racialized appeal. This three-reel film featured the Battle of Carrizal, which involved two all-black cavalry troops— Troops K and C. *The Trooper of Troop K* was a far more ambitious project than the previous release. An advertisement for the film promised "350 People, Ex-Ninth and Tenth Cavalrymen, Mexicans, Cowboys, Horses."[101]

The film was important for several reasons. First, Lincoln attempted to give an epic feel to the adventure. The company hired a number of extras and genuine military equipment—guns, uniforms, and cannons—to give the film a sense of authenticity (though it was actually filmed in San Gabriel, California). The Lincoln Company purposefully attempted to cash in on the adventure angle of the film. One promotion read: "It is a very realistic reproduction of the historical incident [of Carrizal] featuring in detail, the mowing down of the charging troopers' ranks by the deadly machine gun fire."[102]

Second, the film was critically important for depicting reenactments of the heroics of real-life African-American men rather than the dramatic adventures of fictional characters like James Barton in *Realization*. The film involves three main characters—"Shiftless" Joe (Noble Johnson), Clara Holens (Beaulah Hall), and James Warner (Jimmy Smith). Shiftless Joe is of a lower class than Clara and Jimmy. He does not know how to take care of his appearance. Clara, of a "good family," takes an interest in Joe because of his unselfishness and humaneness. She always advises him on how he can better himself. Jimmy, a popular well-dressed young man, is romantically interested in Clara and cannot understand why she would bother with Joe. Joe gets a job but is late to work one day because of his deep sympathy for animals. He eventually shows up for work, messes up on the job, and is fired. He tells Clara, who is disappointed in him. She believes he should enter the army, where "regularity, discipline and training" will make him into a man. Jimmy likes this plan because he will now have Clara to himself.[103]

Upon arriving in Casas Grandes, Mexico, Joe becomes a good soldier. "Although [he] is still a little crude and shiftless, he has won the heart of his captain by his constant good nature and love and care of his horse."[104] Joe is heroic in the war, even saving his captain. Jimmy, on the other hand, finds that Clara is not attracted to him. Joe is greeted with open arms by Clara upon his arrival home.

In the beginning of the film, Shiftless Joe is certainly not a desirable man. He is a "good-for-nothing fellow." Jimmy, on the other hand, has all of the attributes of bourgeois male status—fine clothes, respectable friends, a good family, and spending money. As the film progresses, audience identification with the protagonist, Joe, becomes complete. He may be a little lazy and un-couth but he is kind to animals and brave when faced with danger. As one newspaper journalist put it, "he finds himself all man with a big heart and good enough for a little girl who is waiting home for him."[105] It is Joe's compassion and willingness to sacrifice himself for others that makes him a "real" African-American man. Mark Reid argues that Joe "is a redeemed black hero" who presents an alternative image to both the coon and Tom stereotypes of mainstream white filmmaking.[106] I argue that he also prob-lematizes the concept of a bourgeois black hero because of his class origins and the figure of Jimmy, a member of the African-American middle class.

The film also received countless telegrams and letters of ringing endorse-ment. C. H. Turpan of the Booker Washington Theater of St. Louis claimed, "*Trooper of Troop K* has convinced me the colored people will not only accept Dramas by all colored casts but will eat them up."[107] The manager of the Bryar Amusement Company of Nashville, Tennessee, explained, "We played the picture during the worst possible weather but nevertheless we played to capacity business."[108]

The third Lincoln film, *The Law of Nature,* was released in 1917. It was released at a turning point in the company's existence—it was the first film made after the production company had incorporated but was the last film starring Noble Johnson.

The Law of Nature further developed Lincoln's themes of the proper role for men and women in society and defining qualities that embodied a true man. Jane Gaines in *Fire and Desire* discusses the utopian characteristics of Lincoln's racial uplift melodramas. She claims that these films of racial em-powerment were often "narratives of sentimentality."[109] These narratives, cen-tered on romantic love and the moral cohesiveness of the family, prized African-American heterosexual love, which culminated in marriage and family.

The film focused on a character played by Albertine Brooks (Clarence Brooks's wife). She is a former eastern society lady, who, working as a gov-erness out West, marries her employer, a wealthy cattleman. She misses the excitement of the East and eventually persuades her husband to take the family back to the big city. Her husband, a rural cowman, cannot fit into the gentility of eastern society. A former suitor pursues her persistently back East, well aware that she is married. These factors persuade her husband to take their son and return to the West. The heroine ends up alone as "she realizes her folly and the inevitable consequences of 'Nature's Law,'" and returns West to her husband and children. According to the promotional material, she "succumbs to the will of God."[110]

The patriarchal ideal and the inevitable conclusion of a happy, unified family are hallmarks of the Lincoln oeuvre. Although the focus of *The Law of Nature* is on Albertine Brooks's character, the basic theme remains the same—the unification and preservation of the nuclear family. *The Realization of a Negroes Ambition*, *The Trooper of Troop K*, and *The Law of Nature* all conclude with a romance and marriage between the protagonist and his or her paramour. A coupling between man and woman was standard to the melodramatic form in white-controlled studio films. However, the African-American romantic couple and marriage were almost nonexistent in studio films. The Lincoln Motion Picture Company deliberately presented the wholeness of African-American family life, complete with romantic love and tenderness toward children.

The Lincoln Company built its economic foundation on three things—the quality of their productions, the positive messages they portrayed, and the stardom of Noble Johnson.[111] *The Law of Nature*'s advertising used all three. Lincoln offered a "Satisfaction Guaranteed" policy to their patrons and exhibitors, arguing that everyone would be pleased with the "class, photography, dignity and morals" of a Lincoln production.[112] The company claimed that the all-black Lincoln Theatre in Memphis, Tennessee, brought in $322 in gross receipts in two days (4–5 August 1917), a tremendous amount of money for a black theater in this period. *The Law of Nature*, like previous Lincoln pictures, was a financial success.[113]

The release of *The Law of Nature* in the summer of 1917 coincided with a major campaign by the Lincoln Company to get African Americans to buy stock in the company. They based their sales campaign on two premises. First, it was advertised as an ideal financial opportunity for African-American investors (the title of one promotional ad read "The Secret of Getting Rich"). The Lincoln Company attempted to demonstrate how lucrative stock investment could be by comparing previous stock growth rates in other key industries. The company demonstrated the potential financial growth of the motion picture industry by rattling off a list of figures relating to the industry (including a claim of "8,000,000 Negroes of Movie Age").

The second premise was an appeal to racial pride and solidarity. The company argued, "To obtain this we could borrow from the white banking houses by mortgaging our plant etc. but we would rather ask a few members of our Race who want to make a SAFE and GOOD INVESTMENT to join us."[114] The company strongly applied this racialized angle. They claimed, "[We are] the ONLY producing company at present that is accurately producing high grade motion pictures featuring the Race in photoplays of merit minus all humiliating burlesque."[115] Lincoln positioned itself as providing an alternative to mainstream cinematic depictions of African Americans. In attempting to explain why the company had broken house records across the country, they claimed, "Why? Because we have what the people want. They are disgusted in seeing themselves burlesqued and made the 'goat.' Listen! Reader. We are not telling you what we prepare to do. We are telling you what we are doing."[116] The company collected a series of ringing endorsements from prominent African Americans (Madame C. J. Walker and leaders of Tuskegee and Hampton Institutes) and black periodicals. The Honorable R. R. Church, Jr., from Memphis claimed, "Your two pictures shown at my Theatre week of March 26 are the best Negro pictures I have ever seen. I have been disgusted with most Negro pictures until I saw yours."[117]

A great deal of the success of Lincoln productions was due to their star (and president) Noble Johnson. By 1917, Johnson was the first true African-American film star. He was a known commodity in the black community and could pull in audiences. Johnson's movie-star good looks and skill in action/adventure stunt work brought him widespread recognition. The Lincoln Motion Picture Company recognized Johnson's widespread appeal. "Make a 'Noble M. Johnson Day' at your theater," they appealed. "Let this popular coming star demonstrate his remarkable ability to increase your profits."[118]

Johnson quit as president (and star) of the Lincoln Company on 3 August 1918 at a Lincoln board meeting. His explanation was that there was not financial capital to produce the next picture and that he did not have the "time" and "capacity" to attend to the financial needs of the company.[119]

There has been a great deal of speculation as to whether there were other reasons why Johnson resigned from the company. Henry T. Sampson in *Blacks in Black and White* argues that Johnson's immense popularity in the African-American community caused distress at Universal Pictures. Johnson was often featured in lithographs and large pictures of Lincoln films. During his years at Lincoln he was also playing secondary roles in several of Universal's highly popular serials. In an advertisement for *The Bull's Eye,* an eighteen-episode Universal serial starring one of the company's leading players, Eddie Polo, it is Johnson who is prominently featured in African-American publications. Many black theaters that exhibited Universal productions featured Noble Johnson as the cowboy-hero over other players even when he was not the leading man. In fact, one such advertisement in the *Chicago Defender* exclaimed, "Wednesdays! Come and See the Race's Daredevil Movie Star, Noble M. Johnson, 'supported' by Eddie Polo."[120] There have been claims that Universal pressured Johnson to resign because Lincoln motion pictures were outdrawing Universal releases in many African-American communities. The "racial angle" of Johnson's billing was aptly demonstrated in a letter from W. H. Tamppert to George Johnson. Tamppert, manager of the Savoy Theater in Birmingham, Alabama, claimed, "I have just finished *[The Bull's Eye]* featuring Polo and Johnson and will state it was the biggest box office attraction I have ever had due mostly to Johnson whom I have advertised extensively as THE movie star (colored)."[121]

Universal did not capitalize on Johnson's "success" because it strictly went against racialized cinematic norms of the time. The "necessity" of having and promoting a white star over a black costar seemed mandatory to the company. Johnson was probably forced to resign from Lincoln in order to refigure proper racial positioning. (Was it assumed that the African-American community would still see Johnson's Universal productions?) George Johnson claimed that Noble was "our most valuable asset. [He] was compelled to resign from the Lincoln organization due to his increased demand in the large white organization [Universal]."[122] It can be assumed that Noble Johnson would have also been guaranteed a steadier, higher paying income at Universal.

Noble Johnson's departure left a void at Lincoln. The executive and financial aspects of his job were assumed by George P. Johnson, Noble's brother. Johnson became the general booking manager for the Lincoln Company. He established the first national film booking organization operated by African Americans.[123] Noble was largely in front of the camera, and George remained behind the scenes. George made a number of important contacts in the black theatrical circuit while continuing to work at a full-time position in the Omaha, Nebraska, post office. The Lincoln Company continued to promote and circulate the three previously filmed Lincoln productions throughout 1918 and 1919, capitalizing on Noble's continued popularity. George's business relationship with Tony Langston, theatrical editor of the *Chicago Defender,* the largest circulating black newspaper of the country, was crucial to the company's success. Langston arranged to have Lincoln's films screened for black theater owners in exchange for a percentage of the gross.

In 1919, the Lincoln Company released its fourth full-length fictional feature film, *A Man's Duty.* Clarence Brooks starred in the film and assumed the leading man position in Lincoln's stock company.[124] *A Man's Duty* had the themes of class, morality, and male responsibility, so common in the Lincoln genre. The protagonist is Richard Beverly, "a vigorous athletic inclined chap," who is from a high social class in his hometown."[125] He is the rival for the affection of a young girl with Herbert Gordon, a man of devious means. Herbert gets Richard drunk and leaves him in a bordello. Richard is publicly humiliated and defends his honor. He fights Herbert, who hits his head on a rock and supposedly dies. Richard immediately leaves town, afraid of being charged with murder. Richard mentally and physically falls apart "after months of exposure, dissipation, and drinking." He then falls in love with Merriam Given, a lower-class woman who has borne a child out of wedlock. Richard realizes he can never marry Merriam with the threat of murder over his head so he writes home to find out Herbert's status. Herbert is alive but Richard is faced with another predicament—he had impregnated a prostitute, Helen, in the bordello. Merriam informs Richard that her child is also illegitimate and that it is "a man's duty" to go home and marry Helen. He then discovers that Herbert is the real father of Helen's child. He immediately contacts Merriam and the two are married. As the film synopsis explains, "From the hardships of the past they now emerge into a great joy and happiness which is derived by months of privation and suffering." The nuclear family is assembled and the hero has completed "A Man's Duty."[126]

The film was a success. George Paul, owner of the States Theater in Chicago, claimed: "We have run all of your other pictures to big business and this feature is one of the best pictures ever shown in our theater and has done more business in our four days run at the State Theater than any feature we have ever had for the same number of days."[127] The Lincoln Motion Picture appealed to a much neglected need in the African-American community—the need for a black hero. Paul explained: "We smashed all attendance records. The crowds were tremendous and created such a jam that several windows in our doors caved in and our railings bent over; but we don't mind such repair bills when a picture gets the business and completely satisfied the audience like yours did."[128]

The promotional material for the film asked the question, "What Is a Man's Duty? To his unfaithful fiancée? To his relatives? To his fickle friends? To his self-respect?"[129] Like the Sundaisy characterization in *Eleven P.M.*, the Lincoln Motion Picture Company wanted to present the confusing and conflicting loyalties with which the modern African-American man had to contend. The Lincoln Motion Picture Company also stressed the necessity of having African-American men be held responsible for the children they bring into the world. During a period of increased internal migration, the traditional African-American ways of life were being transformed. Illegitimacy and abandoned children were real problems in the African-American community and the Lincoln Company stressed the duties of black men toward their offspring.

The final Lincoln production, *By Right of Birth*, was released in 1921. A convoluted tale of mistaken identities, greed, and rediscovered ancestral roots, the film is significant for three major reasons. Clarence Brooks, the hero in the film, portrays Philip Jones, "a brilliant law student and popular athlete."[130] Once again, the Lincoln Company expanded the professional careers that were available to black men on the screen (thus, replicating "real" professions African-American men held).[131] Second, the film dealt with an authentic problem in African-American life—attempts by white businessmen or governmental officials to steal land that belonged to freedmen. Finally, *By Right of Birth* completes the series of Lincoln films by once again concluding with a "happy family reunion" and a unified structure.[132]

In 1923 the Lincoln Company announced that their next production would be *The Heart of a Negro*. Shortly after the announcement, the Lincoln Company discontinued operations. Like other all-black production companies, Lincoln was short on capital and found the distribution network almost impossible to manage. Lincoln films brought financial gains to African-American movie houses that displayed them, but limited financial returns to the company itself. The limited number of duplicated copies and the logistical problem of getting these films to theaters that would exhibit them were insurmountable obstacles for the company. Jane Gaines argues that the flu epidemic and increased competition from white producers also added to the film company's problems.[133] The company did not have the financial capital to open all-black theaters to show their films or to develop an adequate distribution network.

The overall impact of the Lincoln Motion Picture Company cannot be overestimated. Lincoln motion pictures played in all forty-eight U.S. states, the Hawaiian Islands, the Bahamas, and Cuba. The Lincoln Company showed a radically different portrayal of African-American men from white studio productions of the era. The company's films concluded with a "whole" nuclear family, illustrating the love between African-American parents and children and between man and woman.[134]

African-American men used filmmaking as a means to assert and define their own sense of manhood. Film served as an important gendering device.

As major motion picture studios were elevating white manhood by contrasting it with an inferior, animalistic, slothful black man, African-American men were delivering the cinematic equivalent of an ebony hero, an African-American man who worked, was educated, took care of his wife and children, and worked for the betterment of society. Although the political discourse in black silent filmmaking varied, the motivation to portray a "different" African-American male characterization was almost universal. Oscar Micheaux would prove to be the most prolific and controversial of all African-American filmmakers in the silent era. His black male characterizations would challenge both the dominant white studio system and the African-American community at large.

6

OSCAR MICHEAUX:
FROM HOMESTEAD TO LYNCH MOB

Oscar Micheaux is the preeminent figure in African-American silent cinema. He was the most prolific black filmmaker of the silent era, directing at least twenty-eight silent features or reedited versions of films between 1919 and 1929. He remained in the industry longer than any other African-American filmmaker, producing and directing films until 1948. Micheaux is seminal to African-American silent cinema because of the dramatically complex ways in which he tackled subjects sensitive to both Euro-Americans and African Americans. Most African-American directors of the silent era were afraid to deal with controversial issues, particularly those involving racism or discrimination, but Micheaux addressed lynching, job discrimination, interracial romance, mob violence, intraracial prejudice, rape, and religious hypocrisy. As Pearl Bowser and Louise Spence argue, "He persistently chose themes that were explosive at the time."[1]

Three recent works have fundamentally changed the landscape of Micheaux scholarship: Pearl Bowser and Louise Spence's *Writing Himself into History: Oscar Micheaux, His Silent Films, and His Audiences,* J. Ronald Green's *Straight Lick: The Cinema of Oscar Micheaux,* and Jane M. Gaines's *Fire and Desire: Mixed-Race Movies in the Silent Era.* These books represent the second wave of Micheaux scholarship, rightfully giving him the central place he deserves in African-American film history.[2]

These four scholars contradicted and displayed the problematics of much of the criticism that the first generation of scholars lobbed at Micheaux. This first generation charged that Micheaux's films were aesthetically inferior, recapitulated white racial stereotypes, or were bourgeois in their value systems. However, what many film scholars failed to do (and continue to fail to do) is to separate Micheaux's early body of work, his silent films, from his sound films of the 1930s and 1940s, which were much more commercial and exploitive in their appeal. Micheaux's silent features, however, were revolutionary when compared to white-produced or black-produced films of the era for the hard-hitting themes he considered and for the variety of black male roles he displayed in his productions.[3] In his silent films, Micheaux's political, social, and racial edge made him a dramatically different type of African-American director. As J. Ronald Green has argued, Micheaux achieved greatness.[4]

A number of theoretical problems present themselves when dealing with Oscar Micheaux and his body of work. These have been aptly demonstrated by film critics and historians over the years. One of the least discussed issues is the lack of material available for screening. Of Micheaux's twenty-eight silent feature films, only three are still in good condition—*Within Our Gates* (1920), *Symbol of the Unconquered* (1921), and *Body and Soul* (1924). The first generation of scholars had access only to *Body and Soul*. As a result of this "lack" of an available historical product, theorists focused their attention on Micheaux's sound films that were available for viewing, skewing the politicized nature of his cinematic rhetoric. Donald Bogle, Thomas Cripps, Gary Null, Daniel Leab, and others based their harsh critiques of Micheaux on his sound films.[5]

Another issue concerns Micheaux's aesthetically "poor" filmmaking techniques. Micheaux operated on a tight production budget. Lacking outside financing, he was often dependent on advances from black urban theater owners to pay for his next production. This meant that film continuity, editing, and characterization often suffered because of Micheaux's need to save film stock. Micheaux's productions included off-camera directorial remarks, poor lighting, and missed cues. This was because Micheaux often refused to shoot a film more than once. Silent film star Lorenzo Tucker claimed, "Micheaux would laugh when he saw some of the money that white producers were putting into black-cast films. He knew that the market wouldn't support the investment. He would put just so much and nothing more into a film because he knew he would only make so much money. That's why his films were technically poor."[6] Critics have pointed out that his sound films particularly reflected "the limitation of his technique, capital and concept."[7]

In addition, Micheaux's productions were often criticized for replicating racial stereotypes that were remarkably similar to white independent or studio productions. This included a color-coded dynamic that established the hero and heroine as light-skinned and the buffoon or villain as dark-skinned. The light-skinned ideal has been problematic in dealing with Micheaux's films.[8] Richard Gehr argued that "Micheaux's was a world of dichotomies—

black/white, light/dark, rural/urban, rich/poor . . . productive/shiftless."9
This led to the production of films that included negative portrayals of African-
American men, some as severe as those that were observed in mainstream
white productions. J. Ronald Green has recently demonstrated that in
Micheaux's films a simplistic color-coded dichotomy does not hold true. Although the majority of Micheaux's heroes and heroines are light-skinned,
there are also favorable characters that are dark-skinned.10 Gaines and Green
have both pointed out that Micheaux was working in a system in which the
convention in race movies was to have dark-skinned antagonists and light-
skinned heroes.11 Yet one cannot deny that there was contemporary criticism
of Micheaux's incorporation of this dynamic. In the *Chicago Defender* in 1922,
columnist D. Ireland Thomas commented on Micheaux's film *The Dungeon:*
"The advertising matter for this production has nothing to indicate that the
feature is colored, as the characters are very bright, in fact, almost white. . . .
Possibly Mr. Micheaux is relying on his name alone to tell the public that this
is a Race production or maybe he is after backing it in white theaters."12

Micheaux's presentation of African Americans in the leading roles of his
films substantially changed African-American moviegoers' reception. An
African-American spectator watching a black actor or actress in danger, in
love, or successful in a profession probably watched such a production with
a different emotional framework or response as opposed to films that were
white-cast. Thomas Cripps argues that the central problem for Micheaux and
other black producers was the "temptation to make mirror images of white
movies."13 Although genre and characterization may have been borrowed
from white movies, they were often set in a milieu with a black sensibility that
changed the dynamics of the film's receptive structure. Charlene Regester
maintains that some of Micheaux's depictions of African-American men were
those of a "bad" character but that such portrayals were important because
they went against the one-dimensionality of white-produced imagery of
African-American men.14 In Micheaux's films, black men may have been evil
or corrupt or vindictive, but there was often (but not always) a motivation
to such emotional qualities. J. Ronald Green claims, "Micheaux mounted a
persistent, career-long critique directed at perceived character traits in people of his own race."15 But unlike in white productions, such negative characteristics were not portrayed as "natural" to the black man.

Micheaux's films also have been critiqued for promoting "bourgeois" values. His films incorporated such concepts as self-help, education, and economic advancement but they were often placed against the realities of
African-American life, in contrast to films by other black filmmakers.

Micheaux was often criticized for using only members of the black middle class in his productions. This argument must be placed against the fact of black directors' counterhegemonic stance when it came to characterization. Most white-produced films portrayed only lower-class African Americans. Micheaux and other black directors showed the African-American bourgeoisie, who were playing such a pivotal role in the Harlem Renaissance of the 1920s. Eileen Landay claimed that "while some of [Micheaux's] films dealt with the problem of being black, this was never from the point of view of the ghetto dweller or sharecropper; his subjects were the black bourgeoisie."[16] A closer examination of Micheaux's films proves that this was not true. His films also praised the working man and woman.

Landay claims that Micheaux's focus on the black bourgeoisie was an attempt to create racial pride but she never explains how. His class characterizations were deliberate. By showing the "problems" the black bourgeoisie faced, lower-class African Americans could identify and unite with their racial brothers and sisters rather than be antagonistic toward them because of their socioeconomic status. One of the characteristics of middle-class culture and sensibility was the notion of uplift, of providing an example. This was especially true of the African-American middle class. Micheaux's and other race films of the period were often about assimilation into American society, which was consistent with the racial politics in one strand of the African-American community of the period. Micheaux attempted to give the black audience morals and issues that would lead to their success. In his first novel, *The Conquest*, Micheaux argued, "One of the greatest tasks of my life has been to convince a certain class of my racial acquaintances that a colored man can be anything."[17] He was, of course, a commercial producer, but he did instill his own ideology into his filmmaking. Micheaux claimed, "I have always tried to make my photoplays present the truth, to lay before the race a cross section of its own life, to view the colored heart from close range. . . . It is only by presenting those portions of the race portrayed in my picture in the light and background of their true state, that we can raise our people to greater heights."[18]

Micheaux's films did not have the same aesthetic workmanship as mainstream studio productions. He may have expanded racial characterization in "white" oriented genres. He may have reflected a morally suspect spectrum of African-American men. Moreover, Micheaux did focus on the black bourgeoisie, whom he believed, like DuBois, would lead the African-American population to economic and social success. But he also challenged conventional norms of filmmaking by incorporating a black sensibility that showed the complex problems and issues facing African-American men in the post-war years. As Jesse Rhines claims, Micheaux was a race man—an individual who wanted to uplift African Americans as a race.[19] Micheaux was a businessman out to make a profit but he was also an important social commentator, using the commercial medium of motion pictures to express his viewpoint.

In *Fire and Desire,* Jane Gaines rightfully considers the problems associated with using auteur theory to discuss the works of Oscar Micheaux. Certainly, the African-American audience "made" meaning when viewing his films. But Gaines insightfully argues, "The case of Oscar Micheaux represents an opportunity to challenge not only the elitism of authorship theory by shifting attention to the race movie audience but a chance to redefine the motion picture producer as an instigator and an actualizer, someone who not only designs the work but orchestrates its reception."[20] Oscar Micheaux presented material on the screen that was all too familiar to African-American audiences, but since this material had never been explored cinematically, as Gaines argues, Micheaux orchestrated meaning.

This chapter demonstrates how Oscar Micheaux's screen portrayals of African-American men challenged the dominant imagery of white-produced cinema. It will investigate the major themes and issues that Micheaux explored. Micheaux's films fall into five major thematic categories—Westerns, Racially Antagonistic films, Passing films, Genre films, and Achievement films. These categories are developed in order to discuss the major themes in Micheaux's silent features—in many cases a particular film may fit several categories. In addition, I will also attempt to answer why he went from an inter- and intraracially confrontational cinematic style to one that was more genre-driven and less provocative in the issues, portrayals, and sensibilities it created.

Oscar Micheaux was born in Metropolis, Illinois, in 1884. He was one of the first generation of African Americans born into freedom. His parents had migrated to Illinois after the Civil War. His father owned his farm and his mother was a schoolteacher. They implanted three ideas in the young boy's mind that would be valuable messages of his own—the importance of owning land, respect for farming as a profession, and the value of education.[21]

In his hometown, Micheaux had frequent conversations with black Pullman porters who worked on the Illinois Central Railroad. They persuaded him that the big city was where he wanted to go.[22] The lure of the city, with its criminal element, tempting women, and excitement would prove to be common themes in his writing and filmmaking. Micheaux left for Chicago in 1900, a generation ahead of most other African Americans who migrated to the city. He worked as a Pullman porter in the early years of the century. This position, one of the most respected jobs available to African-American men at the time, exposed him to the great social, economic, and cultural diversity of the nation.[23]

By 1904, he had saved enough money working as a porter to become a property owner and farmer like his father. He purchased land near the Rosebud Indian Reservation near Gregory, South Dakota. Over the next few years, the ever thrifty and industrious Micheaux was able to purchase adjoining land and develop a successful homestead. He hoped to sell the land for a profit as the railroads expanded westward.[24] He was respected and well liked by most of his white neighbors. Convinced that other African Americans should follow his example, he made several trips to Chicago, unsuccessfully trying to convince relatives and friends to join him. In 1910, Oscar married Orlean McCracken. As Bowser and Spence claim, the marriage had more to do with Micheaux's legal ability to obtain more land under the lottery system than with any semblance of love or romance.[25] The marriage was doomed almost from the beginning; a child's death, Orlean's loneliness on the homestead, and economic problems led to a permanent separation. Orlean's minister father eventually brought her back to Chicago.[26] Thus, Micheaux not only lost a wife but an additional homestead.

In 1913 Micheaux wrote and published a novel, *The Conquest*. Having a limited education, Oscar taught himself how to write. According to Henry T. Sampson, Micheaux began writing as a form of therapy.[27] His homesteading venture became a financial disaster and his marriage was a failure. Though described as fictional, the book was largely autobiographical, covering the first twenty-nine years of Micheaux's life. The protagonist of *The Conquest* is Oscar Devereaux (no mistaking who this volume was about). There are many similarities between the two men's lives—both come from large families, have fathers from Kentucky who become farmers, and lose brothers in the Spanish-American War. The book also covers Oscar's years as a Pullman porter and as a farmer. J. Ronald Green claims that the "biographical and historical accuracy of the book should not be underemphasized."[28] *The Conquest* is an important stepping-stone in understanding Micheaux's filmmaking because it contains many of the basic premises that are critical to his films. In the novel, Micheaux wanted to give the reader a model for success (even though his own farming endeavors led to economic and personal disaster). He wanted to create a character that other African-American men could emulate—a man who was strong, educated, practical, and courageous.[29] As Bowser and Spence comment, "His silent pictures and early novels not only reveal the details of one man's experience and his personal pursuit of success, but offer a particular point of view and commentary on the upward movement of a people."[30]

With the publication of his first book, Micheaux immediately switched careers, believing he could earn a living as a novelist. He published two more books before his filmmaking debut: *The Forged Note* (1915) and *The Homesteader* (1917). Both books drew heavily upon his experiences in Chicago and on the farm in South Dakota. Many of the characters whom he met in real life would eventually come to inhabit his films. The novels are a manipulation of his life experiences; he rewrote his biography to illustrate his philosophies on manhood and race. I heartily agree with Pearl Bowser and Louise Spence's concept of Micheaux's "biographical legend." He made extensive use of his life experiences in his creative work. Thus, as they have argued, it "gave credibility to and validated the racial experiences of his audiences."[31] Micheaux subscribed to the political and racial philosophies of Booker T. Washington more than W. E. B. DuBois's in his novels; his "radicalism" would develop only after his filmmaking career began.[32]

The popularity of Micheaux's novel *The Homesteader* eventually drew the attention of George P. Johnson, booking manager of the Lincoln Motion Picture Company. The Lincoln Company expressed interest in filming the novel and Micheaux traveled to Omaha, Nebraska, for discussions. The contract was negotiated and drawn up, but at the last moment Micheaux insisted that he should supervise the motion picture production in Los Angeles. He wanted to expand the format from the standard three-reel Lincoln production to a six-reel feature. This was not acceptable to the Lincoln Company or financially possible and the project fell through.[33] Micheaux's topics for cinematic exploration were certainly not conducive to the relatively safe dramas of racial uplift that the Lincoln Motion Picture Company specialized in. Interracial romance (one of the themes of *The Homesteader*) was not a topic the Johnson brothers regularly included in their features. This desire to have his novel made into a motion picture on his own terms led to the formation of the Micheaux Film and Book Company.[34] Micheaux was affected dramatically by his experiences in South Dakota. He believed that the trek of southern African Americans northward to cities like Chicago was unnecessary. Instead, he believed African Americans should buy property and work hard to succeed.[35] During the 1920s, hundreds of thousands of African Americans were escaping poverty, limited economic opportunity, and the system of Jim Crow by moving north. Through his films, Micheaux offered an alternative—the West. In his novel *The Homesteader,* he claimed

that "there is something about a new country [the West] an air of hopeful-
ness that is contagious . . . here in this new land come the best from everywhere . . . with them there is no 'negro problem,' . . . [their] world was too
busy to bother with such."[36] He believed that the West offered African
Americans new opportunities and the possibility of escaping racism and prejudice. Micheaux's first silent feature, *The Homesteader,* was a Western. During the silent era, Micheaux did not change his philosophy regarding the
opportunities the West might bring.[37] In 1918, Micheaux's energies
switched from writing books to film production. He spent nine months
transforming *The Homesteader* into a screenplay. His film and book company
had offices in Chicago (the major black metropolis of the era and
Micheaux's urban home) and Sioux City, Iowa. To finance the film, he sold
stock in his company to midwestern white farmers at prices ranging from
$75 to $100 per share.[38] He eventually obtained over $15,000 in capital
(demonstrating his strength as a businessman) and began shooting an eight-
reel film at the old Selig Studios in Chicago. Many of the rural exteriors were
shot around Sioux City and near Gregory, South Dakota.[39]

The Homesteader was highly autobiographical, drawing from pivotal incidents in Micheaux's life. A reworking of his third novel, Micheaux's heroic
male figure in the book and film was Jean-Baptiste. The name is symbolic;
it draws upon the legacy of Jean-Baptiste Point du Sable, a black French
frontiersman and the founder of Chicago, Micheaux's adopted home. It also
draws on John the Baptist, the saintly yet tortured follower of Christ. *The
Homesteader* is simply a highly objectified viewing of the events of
Micheaux's life and he uses the hero as a soapbox through which he espouses many of his racial and political beliefs.

The Homesteader is no longer available for viewing, but the film historian
can construct an outline of it based on novel and film reviews of the period.
Micheaux's production was unique in several respects. Released in 1919, *The
Homesteader* was one of the first films to use established black stage talent.
Charles Lucas, Evelyn Preer, and Iris Hall, the stars of the film, were re-
spected actors who were members of the Lafayette Players Dramatic Stock
Company of New York City. The Lafayette Players regularly went on tour so
Micheaux was presenting actors and actresses with whom the African-Amer-
ican urban community was already familiar. Second, the film was nearly three
hours long (eight reels), by far the longest film yet produced by an African
American.[40]

In his promotional advertising, Micheaux argued that his film was different. Released four years after *The Birth of a Nation, The Homesteader* was

"destined to mark a new epoch in the achievements of the Darker Race."[41] Micheaux presented African Americans as the leading characters in the film. He claimed,

> The Black Man and Woman [have had] almost no opportunity to display their skills or qualities, every Race man and woman should cast aside their skepticism regarding the Negro's ability as a motion picture star, and go and see, not only for the absorbing interest obtained therein, but as an appreciation of those finer arts which no race can ignore and hope to obtain a higher plane of thought and action.[42]

> Another feature to the advantage of *The Homesteader* is that aside from the general public, whom themselves, having never seen a picture in which the Negro race and Negro hero is so portrayed and therefore, be expected to appreciate the photoplay as a diversion . . . 12 million Negro people will have their first opportunity to see their race in stellar roles.[43]

Tony Langston, entertainment editor of the *Chicago Defender,* agreed:

> There have been many of our people who have had chances to 'strut their stuff' across the screen; some of them have shown a certain amount of ability while others have been indifferent, poor and worse impressions. . . . The folks who have been used in the making of *The Homesteader* [are different] . . . now we 'have it in us' to make good in the silent drama.[44]

In the cinematic version of Micheaux's life, Jean-Baptiste purchases land in South Dakota. From the beginning of the story the reader/moviegoer is persuaded to identify with the character. He is described as "young—the Homesteader—is just past 22—[is] vigorous, strong, healthy and courageous."[45] Charles Lucas, as the Homesteader, was a very light-skinned, handsome leading man with "good" hair and a strong physique. In a promotional photo he is depicted strongly upright and determined, with the leading lady Evelyn Preer feeling his manly bicep. Jean-Baptiste has the character traits and physical features to make him a potentially successful homesteader. He is also clearly independent, a self-made man. In the novel, Micheaux explains, "His father had given him only the French name that was his, for his father had been poor—his heritage then had been indefati-

The Homesteader used the heroic protagonist as a soapbox through which Oscar Micheaux was able to espouse his own racial and political beliefs. (Schomburg Center for Research in Black Culture)

gable as well; his firm determination to make his way, his great desire to make good."[46]

In both the novel and film, the Homesteader is depicted as a solitary figure. He is "far off in the Dakotas," away from the trappings of civilization. Jean-Baptiste is also alone because he is the only African American for hundreds of miles. Racially and geographically, the man of "strength, courage and conviction" was alone in the wilderness.[47] But Jean-Baptiste does not plan on spending the rest of his life by himself. He had "a great hope for the future of this bitter empire."[48] This great hope was to find a "great love," his "dream girl." Jean-Baptiste regularly daydreams about his future love.[49]

At this point in the novel and film, Jack Stewart, a Scotchman, and his daughter Agnes wander into the Dakotas. Agnes is described as a beautiful, captivating woman who not only sweeps Jean-Baptiste off his feet but saves his life twice. Agnes and Jean-Baptiste are desperately in love with each other. A reviewer in the *Chicago Defender* describes this relationship as "the most appealing and idealistic ever created."[50] But the couple could never be married or consummate their love because Agnes is white and Jean-Baptiste is black. Micheaux explained that "according to the custom of the country and its laws, she could never be anything to him."[51] If marriage did take place, he argued that "it would create a chasm so deep socially that bridging [it] was impossible."[52] The film and novel go to great lengths to explain the racial and social disaster such a marriage might bring. The narrator gives an example of another black man who married interracially and lost his children, who decided to "pass" as white. As Bowser and Spence argue, "For Micheaux, the problem of miscegenation is not the mixing of the races but the denial of racial identity and disloyalty that comes from trying to hide one's race."[53]

The most telling racial observations and commentary in the film and book are the lovers' reaction to their predicament. Agnes questions, "I have wondered so often since meeting him, how it feels to be a Negro."[54] As immigrants to this country, Agnes and her father attempt to understand the geographic distinctions in racism and segregation. Agnes explains, "I understand that there is a sort of prejudice against the race in the country; that in the South they are held down and badly treated; that in the North, even, they are not fairly treated."[55] Agnes and her father attempt to understand the nature of prejudice. Her father states, "We cannot understand why one should be disliked because his skin is dark; or because his ancestors were slaves."[56] Then in a shattering critique of race and the southern justification for racial violence, Agnes comments, "It is said that some of the race are very ignorant and vicious; that they very often commit the unspeakable crime [rape of a white woman], I suppose that is possible."[57] Micheaux is problematic in this section. Reiterating the worst racist thoughts of many Americans, he then, through Agnes, clearly points out that Jean-Baptiste is "different." She insists, "Take that Jean-Baptiste, for instance, an educated man and what a gentleman."[58] In one final slap at white racial bigotry and the nonrecognition of reality, Agnes explains, "But Papa, he says that only about half the colored people in this country are full blood; that in the days of slavery and since, the white man who is very often ready to abuse the black man, has been the cause of this mixture . . . I should think their consciences would disturb them."[59] In this brief scene, Micheaux, the novelist and filmmaker, exploded the polite confines of African-American filmmaking. He comments on racial identification, the nature of prejudice, interracial rape, and southern bigotry, topics not touched by other black filmmakers. No African-American filmmaker dared to make such direct and painfully true observations as Micheaux does in *The Homesteader*. Although the Johnson brothers and Richard Maurice may have presented alternative versions of black masculinity, Micheaux was vigorously displaying the racial and social patterns of real life. As Bowser and Spence claim, "He envisioned himself as an instructive voice and an empowering interpreter of Black life for the community."[60]

Jean-Baptiste does not propose marriage to Agnes because it would mean both personal disaster and lack of commitment to his race. He makes moral decisions for purposes larger than himself. "It is not that I care so much for the fruits of my labor; but if I could actually succeed, it would mean so much to the credit of a multitude of others—Others who need the example."[61] There is little separation between the narrator's thoughts and those of Jean-Baptiste. The novel continues: "The individual here did not count so much; it was the cause. His race needed examples, they needed instances of success to overcome the effects of ignorance and an animal viciousness that were prevalent among them."[62] Jean-Baptiste throws away his one true love because of the racial dictates of the era. He justifies his actions and pain on the basis of loyalty to the race and example.

Jean-Baptiste eventually travels to Chicago to obtain an African-American wife. He settles on his third choice, Orlean. She is described in the novel as "timid and weak-willed."[63] She is actually controlled by Ethel, her sister, and the Reverend N. Justin McCarthy, her father (Micheaux's real father-in-law was named McCracken). According to Micheaux, the male McCarthy was the prime example of everything wrong with the African-American man. Two of the chapters in the novel are titled "The Evil Genius" and "The Preacher's Evil Influence." Both novel and film are vicious attempts to get back at his despised ex-father-in-law. McCarthy may have been a man of the cloth but Micheaux depicts him as anything but moral. From the outset of his appearance in the novel and film he is described as a "vain" man who "had a way of making his faults and shortcomings appear to be those of others."[64]

The real conflict in the story is not between husband and wife but between son-in-law and father-in-law, each representing the flip side of black manhood. Reverend McCarthy is an urban Negro, corrupted by immoral influences so prevalent in the wicked big city. He is only interested in marrying off Orlean for the potential financial gain it might bring to the family. He is totally opposed to his daughter going to live in the West but the prospect of obtaining valuable farmland persuades him to give away his daughter. Jean-Baptiste works hard and saves his money; the Reverend steals at least $1,000 a year from the church.[65] Jean-Baptiste is educated and proficient. The Reverend is neither informed nor a practical man; he can barely read the newspaper, let alone the Bible.[66] Jean-Baptiste is a humble man whereas the Reverend "hated any member of his household who dared disagree with him. Of course, his 'Majesty' did not see it that way."[67] If Jean-Baptiste was strong, courageous, practical, and intelligent, the Reverend was "narrow, impractical, hypocritical, envious, spiteful," and materialistic.[68] As J. Ronald Green points out, for an individual who was suspicious of all ministers and preachers, Micheaux did his fair share of preaching.[69]

Eventually, Orlean's unhappiness on the farm, her loneliness, perpetual interference by her sister and father, and the death of the young couple's child destroys the marriage. While Jean-Baptiste is busy trying to keep his farm afloat, Agnes gives birth and the child dies. This is unforgivable to the Reverend McCarthy. (Of course, the novel and film also present the fact that he was not present at the birth of either of his daughters.) The Reverend goes to South Dakota, takes his daughter back to Chicago, and promptly persuades her to divorce and take her share of the property. Jean-Baptiste is distraught and deeply disturbed. "In his life, there were certain things he held sacred. Chief among them were the marriage vow."[70] Even though he never truly loved Orlean, divorce was out of the question. He had made a commitment for life. Equally disturbing was the possible loss of his land. His goal was to own one thousand acres of land before he was thirty. McCarthy's attempt to strip him of his hard work would be psychologically and economically devastating.

But fate intervenes and saves Jean-Baptiste. The death of her child and being ripped away from her husband cause Orlean to go mad. In a rage of fury, she kills her father and commits suicide. Jean-Baptiste is saved from the possibility of divorce and losing his land. Quite conveniently, it is discovered that Agnes, his true love, had a mother who was a West Indian. Therefore, being of mixed racial ancestry made marriage to Jean-Baptiste socially acceptable. As the *Chicago Defender* explained, "The story has a beautiful ending after a life of storm and misery."[71]

Two of Micheaux's first three novels were of the Western genre. They were reworked portraits of a lone man struggling against the environment and his own solitary isolation. But he also fought against a culture and a society in which he did not fit in. Bowser and Spence argue that under Micheaux's system of individualism, the "burden of race" was that individual acts impacted the entire racial group. They claim, "By setting himself up as a model of one who had risen above the prevalent notion of the Negro as 'inferior' he was inadvertently reinforcing the very attitude he imagined he was overcoming."[72] As the *Chicago Defender* observed, "*The Homesteader* is not a sensational picture or story as western stories go, but it is the story of the west as it is."[73]

Migration from the east to the west or from the small town to the big city was a theme in a number of Micheaux's features. The motivations to migrate in the early twentieth century were numerous—to escape from lynching and racial violence, for economic opportunity, or for the ability to vote. In *Symbol of the Unconquered* (1920), a black woman goes West. In *Deceit* (1921), a couple move from the small town to the big city. In *Birthright* (1924), a man travels from the North to the South. What Micheaux was reflecting was the reality of African-American life. Lives were displaced and morals changed as hundreds of thousands of African Americans participated in the Great Migration of the 1910s and 1920s. This migration was a flight from lynching, peonage, economic exploitation, and political disenfranchisement. Micheaux's solution—the West—may not have been attractive to African Americans at the time but during the World War II years, thousands of African Americans did make the journey westward, looking for well-paying military and industrial jobs.[74] Micheaux saw the West as a place where one could realize one's own destiny. Race theaters regularly featured Westerns in the late 1910s and throughout the 1920s. As a "mythic space of moral drama," Westerns offered unbridled opportunities to display unrestricted black manhood.[75]

The Homesteader also belongs to the genre of what I consider Racially Antagonistic films. This refers to films that challenged the dominant racial ideology of white America or that challenged morals, values, or ideals within the African-American community. J. Ronald Green brilliantly refers to this as the "cutting gaze." As a foundational tool, Micheaux's focus on criticism of negative imagery "contributed to uplift by criticizing the obstacles to uplift."[76] This applied to criticism of both the black and white communities.

Micheaux apparently had trouble getting *The Homesteader* passed by the Chicago Board of Censors (one of the first municipal censorship boards in the country). The obvious problem was the hint of interracial romance that was so dominant in the first half of the film. Another major problem concerned Micheaux's depiction of Reverend McCarthy.[77] The filmmaker used the controversy over censorship of the film to sell his own product. One of his advertisements for *The Homesteader* read: "Passed by the Censor Board Despite the Protests of Three Chicago Ministers who claimed it was based upon the supposed hypocritical actions of a prominent colored preacher of this city [Chicago]."[78] Apparently, it was necessary for the filmmaker to gather a committee of prominent African Americans to persuade the Board of Censors to pass the film. This committee included Oscar De Priest, Ida B. Wells Barnett, George W. Ellis, and Tony Langston and N. Fields of the

Chicago Defender.[79] Despite its controversial hint of interracial romance and exposure of religious hypocrisy, *The Homesteader* played in theaters throughout the South, including black theaters in Tennessee, Alabama, Georgia, Florida, and Louisiana.[80]

Within Our Gates (1920) was a powerful indictment of the American racial system and its indignities. It was a turning point in the history of African-American cinema in its bold and frank presentation of race relations in the United States. The film addressed vigilante violence, lynching, rape, economic exploitation, black education, and a multitude of subjects of integral importance to the African-American community. It is perhaps the most important black-directed film in the silent era and for this reason it will be addressed in depth in the next chapter. The film was also a landmark production for its complex and diverse portrayals of African-American manhood.

Within Our Gates had an obvious impact on Micheaux's conscience and artistry. He could not leave the film alone in regard to its topical nature or its commercial possibilities. Micheaux constantly recycled ideas throughout his cinematic and literary career and *Within Our Gates* could not simply be dismissed. *The Gunsaulus Mystery* (1921) was Micheaux's second attempt to show the horrible nature of lynching. Censorship troubles and criticism from the black press and white press over *Within Our Gates* did not deter him from continuing to extrapolate on the subject. *The Gunsaulus Mystery* was based on the infamous Leo Frank murder case. Frank, a Jew, was accused of killing a young white girl in Marietta, Georgia, in 1915. He was later lynched by a southern mob. The case was widely covered by the press, and Micheaux used this publicity to produce a film with a similar theme. The eight-reel film was billed as a "mystery-drama" that demonstrated "the progressiveness of the race."[81] In the film, the Leo Frank character is replaced by two African-American men, both falsely accused of murdering a young girl. The interchangeability of anti-Semitism for racism toward African Americans was a plot device that liberal Hollywood writers would attempt to use in the late 1940s in films like *Home of the Brave* and *Lost Boundaries*. Once again, Micheaux demonstrated the American judicial system's readiness to accuse a black man of a crime.[82]

The topic was also explored by Micheaux in *Jasper Landry's Will* (1923). The film was either a recut version or a sequel to *Within Our Gates*. In any case, the major theme of the film was the lynching of Jasper Landry, one of the major characters in *Within Our Gates*.[83]

Micheaux's filmmaking was a type of balancing act that caused him to make some deliberate but unusual choices in screen material. Micheaux cre-

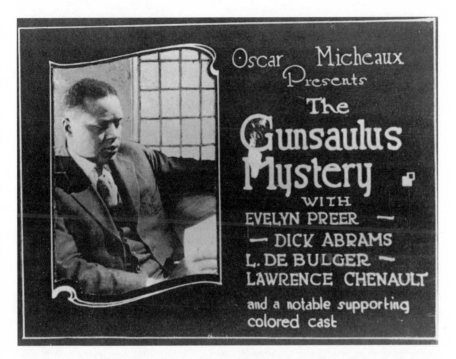

Advertisement for *The Gunsaulus Mystery* (1921). This Oscar Micheaux film was based on the infamous Leo Frank lynching, with two African-American men substituting for the Frank character. (Schomburg Center for Research in Black Culture)

ated films for an exclusively black audience but the films had to be approved by white censors.[84] He also had to be careful not to offend too many powerful groups (the religious community, prominent politicians) within the African-American community with his intraracial criticism. Finally, he had to make a commercial product, one that would not only placate the censors but appeal to the mainstream black urban audience. For such a maverick filmmaker as Micheaux, this was a cumbersome task.

The Brute (1920), Micheaux's third feature film, demonstrated this complex mix of motives. The film was taken from a production by the Lafayette Players, a popular black theatrical group. Because it starred Evelyn Preer and Lawrence Chenault, two of the best-known black actors in the nation, it had strong commercial possibilities. Its appeal was enhanced by the use of Sam Langford, a well-known black prizefighter. *The Brute* was powerful social commentary that examined "the problem of the brute in the household." The film concerned the precarious economic position of African-American women. Mildred Carson's guardian, Aunt Clara, has "blind ambitions to see the girl do well in the matrimonial field" so she marries her off to Bull McGee, "a shrewd gambler and boss of the underworld."[85] McGee's creed is "to make a woman love you, knock her down."[86] After months of physical abuse, her ex-fiancé (played by Chenault) suddenly reappears and emancipates Mildred. The two lovers are free to marry by the end of the film. *The Brute* was an obvious condemnation of the physical abuse of women; McGee dies in the end. In *Fire and Desire,* Jane Gaines documents Micheaux's use of exploitive advertising and ballyhoo to promote *The Brute.* A quintessential showman, Micheaux's copy cut both ways—by drawing curious audiences to its provocative material and dealing with a serious social issue.[87]

Micheaux had an extra hook to attract the black audience to the film. Sam Langford, of course, boxed in the film. One ad promoted a seventeen-round championship match in the film (which obviously was edited).[88] What is important about the boxing scenes was that Langford successfully defeated a white opponent. Micheaux displayed racial pride through boxing, which had existed since Jack Johnson had successfully become heavyweight champion of the world in 1908. Micheaux was displaying a heroic, powerful black man. Because of this, the white censorship board of Chicago ordered aggressive cuts that Micheaux had to implement to exhibit the film. Most of these cuts concerned the display of McGee's criminal tendencies, but the Chicago Municipal Censorship Board also demanded that the filmmaker cut the scene in which Langford knocked out his white opponent.[89] Censorship boards and African-American filmmakers contested issues of black and white masculinity on the screen. Black filmmakers such as Micheaux were attempting to reflect reality, but white censorship boards limited threatening portrayals of black manhood.

Some African-American critics were not happy with *The Brute* either. A critic for the *New York Age* argued, "As I look at the picture I was reminded of the attitudes of the daily press which magnifies the vices and minimizes our virtues."[90] This reviewer was most concerned with positive portrayals of African-American men. He argued that "a determined effort must be made so . . . that the Negro is given high ideals and types which he can emulate and of which he can feel justly proud."[91] Micheaux had no problem in displaying the sordid side of African-American life. If it produced a "dynamic, throbbing, sensationalistic" story, told a moral, and packed in the audiences, Micheaux was more than willing to use any plot device he could.[92]

Micheaux's seven-reel production *Son of Satan* (1924) was also highly controversial within the African-American community for showing the seamier side of black life. The film was probably Micheaux's most stereotype-filled regarding its portrayals of African-American men. "Scenes of drinking, carousing . . . and playing craps" by African-American men were included.[93] Despite the numerous negative portrayals of black men in the film, not everyone was opposed to these depictions. D. Ireland Thomas of the *Chicago Defender* claimed that "some may not like the production because it shows some of our Race in their true colors. They might also protest against the language used . . . but I must admit it is true to nature. We have got to hand it to Oscar Micheaux when it comes to giving us the real stuff."[94]

Micheaux had no problem with displaying the reality of African-American manhood, even when it meant validating some of the stereotypical behaviors of African Americans that were in a multitude of white-produced films. But Micheaux would also prove to be racially provocative to white America. In *Son of Satan,* the leader of a "hooded organization" is killed. Micheaux delivers an uncomplimentary, vindictive portrayal of the Ku Klux Klan when they were at their absolute height of power in the United States in the early 1920s, which resulted in numerous problems with censorship boards. Micheaux was unabashedly defiant to both white and black America.[95]

Micheaux's *Body and Soul* (1924) is a significant film for a number of reasons. It was Paul Robeson's first starring film. It fits into the genre of being a Racially Antagonistic film but its provocation is focused on religious hypocrisy in the African-American community.[96]

Body and Soul is a difficult film to analyze. Thomas Cripps argues that there are at least two alternative versions of the film.[97] He claims that the original version is Micheaux's intended product. The second version is Micheaux's reedited version after the original had been rejected by the New York Censor Board. J. Ronald Green has argued that Cripps's analysis is unverified and that there may have been multiple versions of *Body and Soul.*[98] Whatever the situation, *Body and Soul* is a prime example of how the black cinematic vision was affected by the hegemonic white community through motion picture censorship. As Jane Gaines has argued, "One can hypothesize that all race movies had to pass a special white test before they could be exhibited."[99] Even a defiant filmmaker like Micheaux, who relied on his own source of capital to finance films, was affected by the dominant white culture in manufacturing his film product.[100]

Body and Soul was Micheaux's quintessential effort to get back at his father-in-law and all "bootleg" preachers whom he considered immoral or corrupt. This was controversial on Micheaux's part, considering the importance of the church in the African-American community.[101] The film focuses

on the Right Reverend Isaiah T. Jenkins, alias "Jenkins the Deliverer," a criminal who poses as a man of God. From the opening shots of the film there is
no question in the viewer's mind but that Jenkins is a notoriously corrupt
man. He meets an African-American bootlegger and openly begins drinking.
He then blackmails the bootlegger to make a "contribution" to his ministry.
In the 1920s and 1930s, the black press was full of scandalous stories about
such improprieties among ministers.

After concluding a service, Jenkins is introduced to Isabelle and her mother
Martha Jane. The bootlegger wants to use the young woman for his Cotton
Blossom Shoulder Shakers and Jenkins personally wants to exploit Isabelle
sexually. Martha desperately wants her daughter to marry the preacher; she is
the symbol of the black community's blind loyalty and admiration for ministers. Jenkins's pastoral black outfit and large brim hat provide him a cover for
his immoral activities. Whenever the women of the congregation meet Jenkins
they treat him like a saint. Isabelle can see beyond Jenkins's false exterior. She
refuses to be romantically involved or even consider marriage to the man.
Desperate, she is forced to leave home and goes to live in poverty in Atlanta.
Her mother eventually finds the sickly child whom she had assumed had run
off with her nest egg. Isabelle admits that she did not steal the hardworking
woman's money; Jenkins confiscated the money and raped the poor girl. Isabelle eventually dies of starvation, privation, and grief, and her mother confronts the minister in front of the congregation. They turn on their preacher
and he runs for his life, chased by bloodhounds. One can only imagine that
death is his fate in the end.

According to Cripps, this was the version of the film that the New York
Board of Censors refused to be allowed to be exhibited.[102] The Reverend
Jenkins, brought to life by the skilled acting ability of Paul Robeson, is a
monster. He truly is the epitome of evil, one of the few male characters
Micheaux created without a redeeming bone in his body. Robeson's charis-
matic screen presence makes this portrayal even more disturbing. But
Micheaux's screenwriting and plot devices help to create this awful creature.
In a brilliant rape scene, all Micheaux shows in successive shots are Robeson's
shoes, the opening of a door, Isabelle's naked shoulder and frightened look,
and Robeson's broad malicious grin. It is a cleverly scripted series of shots.

In an alternative version of Micheaux's film, Robeson plays two brothers—the Reverend Jenkins and his timid, sweet brother Sylvester. Sylvester
really wants to marry Isabelle and save her from her fate, even after she has
been raped. In a contrived plot twist, Martha Jane wakes at the end to find
it all a dream. The Reverend is a detective trying to uncover a ring of crim-

inals. Sylvester and Isabelle are married and have newfound wealth, due to a scientific discovery by the groom.[103]

Body and Soul is a brilliant example of how Micheaux recut his films to save his product. What was lost in artistic ingenuity was made up for by Micheaux's skill in pacifying a number of white censorship boards, each with different demands. Micheaux, of course, also had to charm working- and middle-class African-American audiences to see his film. *Body and Soul* was exhibited in New York at the same time that Robeson was appearing in Eugene O'Neill's *The Emperor Jones*. Robeson was already considered the "world's greatest actor of his race."[104]

Micheaux's Racially Antagonistic films were the most daring in African-American silent cinema. They challenged the system of racial discrimination and segregation in both the North and the South. They questioned values and morals within the African-American community such as blind obedience to religious authorities and false materialism. They also challenged hypermasculine attributes such as the physical and sexual abuse of women. Within Micheaux's Racially Antagonistic films, a multitude of diverse African-American men were portrayed. These depictions included negative imagery that sometimes mirrored stereotypes of African-American men found in mainstream Hollywood productions (gambling, drinking, and criminal behavior). Micheaux fought with the African-American press during much of his career over the demand to show only positive portrayals of African Americans.[105] But Micheaux insisted on depicting "real" African-American life in such films. He argued, "I am too much imbued with the spirit of Booker T. Washington to ingraft false virtues upon ourselves, to make ourselves that which we are not. Nothing could be a greater blow to our own progress. The recognition of our true situation will react in itself as a stimulus for self-advancement."[106]

The third major theme or categorization of the Micheaux silent oeuvre are his Passing films, which were linked to interracial romance. "Passing" referred to individuals with black African ancestry, even a minimal amount, who attempted to "pass" as full-blooded white Americans. This theme often got him into trouble with censors. At least five of Micheaux's silent features concerned interracial romance. Bowser and Spence claim that these films were a reworking of the melodramatic genre from a black point of view.[107] A number of these films were later remade as sound productions in the 1930s and 1940s. They include *The Homesteader,* which has already been discussed, *The Symbol of the Unconquered* (1920), *Virgin of the Seminole* (1922), *The House Behind the Cedars* (1924), and *Thirty Years Later* (1928). The themes of these films will be discussed chronologically. Micheaux's perennial use of the Passing theme was rehashed and crystallized as his film-making career progressed.

The Symbol of the Unconquered, Micheaux's fourth feature film, was his first blatant attack on the Ku Klux Klan. Along with *Within Our Gates* and *The Brute, The Symbol of the Unconquered* demonstrated the radical edge to Micheaux's filmmaking in the early years of his career. The film combined generic attributes of Micheaux's style—it was a Western melodrama that was racially antagonistic and included interracial romance. In this film, Evan Mason, a beautiful light-skinned woman from the South, is willed a mine by her grandfather. She travels to the Northwest to claim her land and is rescued by Hugh Van Allan, an African-American adventurer. Hugh falls in love with Evan but he cannot express it; he assumes she is white because of her skin color. (Micheaux's heroes always seem to fall in love with very light-skinned women.) Hugh becomes wealthy after an oil strike and this gives rise to the envy of Tom Cutchall, a white southern racist, and Jefferson Driscoll, a black man passing for white. The pair use the Klan to run Hugh off his claim so they can become rich. Instead, Evan and Hugh outsmart the Klan, discover Evan's true racial identity, and get married.[108]

The Symbol of the Unconquered both strained the boundaries of realism and dealt with the contemporary African-American problem with the Klan. First, it can be seen as wish fulfillment of the idea that the black couple could defeat the Klan. It was certainly a form of dreamscape. One reviewer commented on the timeliness of this project "in view of the present attempt to organize night riders in this country for the express purpose of holding back the advance of the Negro."[109] Second, some moviegoers had a tough time accepting the passing motif. One critic argued that "as in nine cases out of ten, Negroes instinctively recognize one of their own, some are apt to wonder why he [Hugh] did not recognize the truth sooner."[110]

The Symbol of the Unconquered was a dramatic rebuttal to Griffith's *The Birth of a Nation* and a telling form of black escapism. Rather than depicting the Klan as heroic freedom fighters, Micheaux portrayed them as vicious intimidators, willing to use violence for material gain.[111] The black couple's defeat of the Klan (with bricks) certainly brought applause in black theaters. But the film also sent out contradictory messages on passing that have long disturbed the filmmaker's critics. Jefferson Driscoll, the black man who passes for white and works with the Klan, is castigated by Micheaux as a "man who hates his race."[112] As Jane Gaines points out, Driscoll is acting like a white bigot.[113] Driscoll is looked upon as the worst sort of black man. He is one of the few African-American male characters in Micheaux's oeuvre who is vile, through and through—truly, a one-dimensional character.[114] Within the context of racial identification, Micheaux adhered to a "one drop theory"—any African-American ancestry makes you a black man. Micheaux also adhered to a binary construction of masculinity. Any black blood makes you a black man; therefore, you must accept your fate and be loyal to your race. This belief becomes a clever plot device in *Symbol of the Unconquered*. Since Driscoll's racial identity is established early in the film, this whips up the African-American audience's rejection of his character.[115]

Not surprisingly, *Symbol of the Unconquered* met with censorship problems. In Chicago, the retaliation against the Klan and the interracial romance disturbed censors. Chicago had one black film censor on the board whose responsibility was to review films for black audiences. The man, A. J. Bowling, was a Methodist minister and a former student at Harvard University, a product of the black bourgeoisie.[116] The *Chicago Defender* claimed that "no picture which has a Negro theme can be passed by the censor board until it has been seen by Rev. Bowling."[117] The board forced Micheaux to make substantial cuts in the film concerning the objectionable retaliatory scene against the Klan and other racial references.

Bowling is one of the few censors in film history to have a film made in his honor. Micheaux, never a man to hide his emotions, took out his cinematic wrath on Bowling, much as he did on his ex–father-in-law. Micheaux's feature *Deceit* (1921) was a slap at Bowling and meddling ministers who disturbed the production and exhibition of his films. Micheaux's alter ego in the film was Alfred Dubois (identification with W. E. B. DuBois, no doubt). He produces a film entitled *The Hypocrite* but runs up against a delegation of preachers and their censor representative, Christian Bentley. They attempt to stop the film and Dubois appeals his case, taking it to an audience for approval. The film has been lost but there can be little question it came out in Dubois/Micheaux's favor.[118]

Micheaux carried out his interracial infatuation with *Virgin of the Seminole*. In this Western, a black man becomes a member of the Royal Canadian Mounted Police and a successful rancher. Micheaux gets around his infatuation with white women by making the love interest a Seminole Indian.[119]

The House Behind the Cedars is based on African-American author Charles W. Chestnutt's novel of the same title. This film also confronts the problems that occur when an African American manages to pass for white. The story concerns a mulatto attorney and his sister Rowena, who both pass for white. Rowena is courted by George Tyron, an aristocratic white gentleman, and Frank Fowler, a politically and financially powerful black man. She eventually ends up with Fowler, who is portrayed as the only man to have the proper devotion to her.[120]

What troubled southern censors was that Tyron continued to romance Rowena even after he found out that she was a mulatto. This places an interesting twist on Micheaux's emphasis on the light-skinned/white woman. The Virginia Board of Censors claimed that the film should not be displayed in the state because it might "cause friction between the races and might therefore incite to crime."[121] The board of censors went further by arguing that *The House Behind the Cedars* "indirectly contravenes the spirit of the recently enacted anti-miscegenation law."[122] Micheaux went on the defensive, claiming that the only film that had ever incited the black race to riot was *The Birth of a Nation*.[123] He also asked the board of censors if they had any "representative colored citizens" on their panel. Micheaux clearly wanted his film passed for purely economic reasons but his questioning of the hegemonic restraints placed on black filmmakers by white institutional apparatuses made him far more daring than other black filmmakers and foreshadowed arguments of the future civil rights movement of the 1950s and 1960s.[124]

Micheaux's final silent Passing film was *Thirty Years Later,* which again concerned mistaken racial identity and the revelation of racial truth that leads to a united couple. This film emphasized the idea that being a mulatto was not an embarrassment; black ancestry was something to be proud of.

What is one to make of Micheaux's Passing films and how they relate to masculinity? First, all Passing films required a heterosexual marriage between people of color at the end. Second, the emphasis on mulatto females displayed Micheaux's concept of womanly beauty and desirability among African-American men. This proves Micheaux's color-consciousness. But a message underlies Micheaux's Passing films that his critics disregard—racial pride. Although "passing for white" seemed to be a theme that filmmakers were obsessed with for over forty years (*Imitation of Life* [1934, 1959], *Pinky* [1949]), it reflected a reality in African-American lives—the perception that it was easier to be white. Claiming one's black manhood meant choosing a more difficult path in life but it also meant being true to one's self. Rowena, the character in *The House Behind the Cedars,* tells Frank, her black boyfriend, "I am miserable" (regarding the nonrecognition of her racial heritage). Bowser and Spence, in *Writing Himself into History,* discuss how Micheaux significantly expanded the role of Frank in *The House Behind the Cedars,* rendering him a model hero in the context of the narrative.[125] Racial pride and manliness went hand-in-hand, according to the filmmaker.

Micheaux also created a number of "Genre" films during the 1920s. He took a well-established Hollywood genre, such as the Western, the detective story, or the mystery and placed African-American characters in them. This began in the silent era and would prove to be his staple form of filmmaking in his sound films of the 1930s and 1940s.

A genre can be defined as "a system of codes, conventions and visual styles which enables an audience to determine rapidly and with some complexity the kind of narrative they are viewing."[126] The Genre film appealed to African-American audiences on two levels. First, it created a standard cinematic product that the filmmaker was comfortable with and could easily identify. Second, it appealed to a racial sensibility. African-American audiences were literally seeing themselves on the screen. This sense of racial identification took place between the filmgoer and the film they were watching and within the moviegoing audience. If one considers filmgoing an event, then African Americans were surrounded by people who were racially similar. The meaning of a film was, therefore, dictated by the individual filmgoer's perceptions and the reaction of an audience as a whole.

Micheaux's Genre films were either mystery melodramas or action-adventure stories. *The Shadow* (1921) and *The Ghost of Tolston's Manor* (1922/1923) are examples of the mystery film. *The Dungeon* (1922), *The Conjure Woman* (1925), another adaptation of a Charles W. Chestnutt novel, and *Easy Street* (1928) were action/adventure films.

Of the Genre films, more information is available regarding *The Dungeon* because of its trouble with various boards of censorship. *The Dungeon* was an example of how Micheaux could take a conventional melodrama and concisely critique contemporary society. Micheaux's Genre films were, therefore, not simply adoptions of Hollywood filmmaking techniques; they were adaptations of such genres infused with a black sensibility. In *The Dungeon*, Micheaux went after hypocritical, corrupt politicians. In the film, Gyp Lassiter, a congressional candidate, agrees to accept financially lucrative campaign contributions from white sources in return for an agreement that he would accept permanent residential segregation, forcing African Americans out of the desirable parts of town. Thus, *The Dungeon* was a Racially Antagonistic film masked as an action/adventure story. *The Dungeon* ran into censorship problems regarding its portrayal of sexually promiscuous women, a physical assault on a woman, drug abuse, and violence. These may have been realities in the black community but white censors were not going to allow them on the screen.[127]

The final theme category of Micheaux's body of work are his "Achievement" films. In these films, as with his novels, Micheaux attempts to outline a plan by which African-American men can become successful. J. Ronald Green argues, "In Micheaux's narrative trope . . . manhood is not to be proven by rescue, it is to be reconstructed in some other way, or simply recognized for what it already is."[128] Micheaux frequently commented on the requirements he believed were necessary for black male success. According to Bowser and Spence, Micheaux saw himself as a self-help hero. They claim that in both his business successes and his semiautobiographical film narratives, Micheaux attempted to lay out a system of values that would inspire accomplishment and self-confidence in African-American men.[129] I differentiate Micheaux's concept of "success" in regard to gender because of the differing attributes he placed on men and women. As in *Within Our Gates*, the typical prescription for female success was simply to marry a good man. Although J. Ronald Green argues that Micheaux's ideal woman is extremely intelligent, competent, and enterprising, I argue that this dependence upon and need for a man is equally integral in Micheaux's gender expectations.[130] For the filmmaker, the masculine attributes necessary for achievement include education *(Within Our Gates)*, industriousness *(Within Our Gates)*, athletic prowess *(The Brute)*, and courage *(Son of Satan, Symbol of the Unconquered)*. Several of Micheaux's films were geared specifically around the idea of African-American male success. These films include *Birthright* (1924), *Marcus Garland* (1925), and *The Millionaire* (1927).[131] *Birthright* is Micheaux's quintessential feature in which he offers suggestions on how African-American men can survive in the real world.[132] The film was based on a popular novel by T. B. Stribling. The protagonist of the film is Peter Siner, a graduate of Harvard University. Siner is determined to go home to the South and establish a school for African-American youth. From the opening shots, the film presented what one critic considered a "true story of conditions that have handicapped the harmony between the races."[133] The first example of this is Siner's arrival in Cairo, Illinois. Upon crossing the Ohio River, he is forced to get out of the Pullman car and go to a Jim Crow car, a humiliation that thousands of African Americans had to face on a daily basis. On the train, Peter meets Peck, a "lively outspoken" African American who is a military veteran recently returned from World War I. Although Peck receives a hearty welcome home, he is almost immediately arrested for shooting craps (is this an attack on the gambling habits of African-American men or a presentation of the lack of respect for black veterans?).

Within the film, Micheaux paints a portrayal of "a small southern town. . . . All the ignorance, prejudice and . . . crimes of both races in the town are graphically depicted."[134] Peter has to fight a number of obstacles

The Wages of Sin (1928) was an example of Micheaux's use of the cinema for revenge. (Schomburg Center for Research in Black Culture)

to achieve his goal. He has to face the indiscriminate arm of southern justice, an attempt to legally bind him to a segregation clause in a school property deed, a brutal beating, and dishonest colleagues. Within the film, Micheaux preaches perseverance. He depicts a southern white community that vehemently opposes black education and a segment of the African-American community that is willing to devote more energy to gambling and drinking than to uplifting the race. Peter Siner is a Race Man; he is a realistic model for Micheaux because even though a series of racial and legal obstacles are placed in his way, he can still persevere.[135]

The Millionaire was Micheaux's misogynistic warning to hardworking, energetic African-American men to not be trapped by conniving women. Phelam Guitry is a soldier of fortune who becomes a successful rancher in South America. Guitry is a man "who as a youth possessed great initiative and definite obstacles."[136] He was known as the Wild Bull of the Pampas.[137] But Celia Welling, a "beautiful, dazzling, unworthy concubine" attempts to marry Guitry only to steal his fortune."[138] Sexual temptation is an element of danger in Micheaux's films, both interracially and financially.

Undoubtedly, Oscar Micheaux is the most prolific and influential black director of the silent era. His films handled topics such as lynching, rape, color
caste, racism, economic crimes, Jim Crow, residential segregation, disenfranchisement, and educational inequality that neither Euro-American nor
African-American directors were willing to address. He also worked out
questions of his own manhood on the screen while trying to create examples of African-American masculinity that he considered desirable. As
Bowser and Spence rightfully argue, "In his desire to have his life serve as an
example for others, Micheaux played up certain aspects of his life, made
artistic uses of his personal history and dramatized particular motifs."[139]
Micheaux clearly used cinema as revenge; censors, preachers, his brother,
and his father-in-law all became targets. If cinema can be considered a tool
of patriarchal control, then Micheaux is guilty. He accepted the contemporary attitude that women were economically and socially dependent on men.
But he also believed in female education and condemned emotional and
physical brutality toward women. As bell hooks argues, "He was not concerned with a simple reduction of black representation to a positive
image."[140] All of the dirty laundry of African-American masculinity was
aired in Micheaux's cinema—gambling, drugs, passing for white, conspiring
with white men for selfish advancement, and criminality. J. Ronald Green
has argued that stereotypes and caricatures were chronic hindrances to promoting racial uplift in Micheaux's career. By directly dealing with these hindrances in his films he was able to rise above them.[141] Jane Gaines argues
that Micheaux used two strategies in creating his racial ideal. The first
"Mechanism of Hypocrisy" was one in which Micheaux criticized African-
American men who hindered the progress of the race. This was often a two-
faced or Uncle Tom character. The second "Melodramatic" strategy
explored the yearning for betterment, the reunification of the family, and the
fulfillment of opportunity.[142]

Oscar Micheaux went beyond the idealization of black manhood that was
so prevalent among other African-American filmmakers. He called upon
African-American men to examine their own activities and manhood, warts
and all. This makes him a unique filmmaker during the silent era.

It is true that Micheaux's political and racial ideology on the screen di-
gressed in the sound era. His silent films simply "said more" than his sound
films.[143] His pictures became less confrontational and more exploitive in his
portrayals of black criminality and sexuality. A litany of black stereotypes
often mirrored mainstream white films. His movies became more generic
and more haphazardly thrown together; quite frequently in his sound pro-

ductions a musical number is slapped into a scene for no reason other than filler. Perhaps Micheaux made a transition later in his career from seeing motion pictures as an artistic and political weapon to that of a commercial product. Monetary gain from filmmaking was always a priority for Micheaux. In February 1928, at the end of the silent era, he was forced to file for bankruptcy. He reorganized in 1929 under the title The Micheaux Film Corporation with an infusion of white capital.

Micheaux faced a number of institutional problems in the late 1920s and early 1930s. Not only was it more expensive to make sound films, but independent theaters (where most race films were exhibited) were being swallowed up by motion picture chains and African-American talent was going to Hollywood where black actors, musicians, and performers were suddenly the rage. In 1931 he reincorporated again with new economic help from Frank Schiffman and Leo Brecher, two white men.[144] Perhaps his Euro-American partners influenced him to bank on safe, marketable, noncontroversial films. But it cannot be denied that Oscar Micheaux's silent features are the most provocative, confrontational, thought-provoking films regarding African-American men and their place in American society in the post–World War I era.

7

WITHIN OUR GATES

Throughout the silent era, Oscar Micheaux created significantly different cinematic portrayals of African-American manhood. White film companies portrayed black men largely as humorous objects—dim-witted, slow-moving, shiftless caricatures who were nonthreatening to the mainstream white audience. Most black-owned film companies of the era depicted African-American men in stark contrasts of good and evil. In sharp melodramatic fashion, these black men were either epitomes of virtue or dastardly. In Micheaux's films it was not difficult to figure out who symbolized the "good" or "bad" examples of black manhood. He attempted to demonstrate the qualities that were needed to be a successful man, but he also explored the motivation behind the negative characteristics of some African-American men. Two themes—the exposure of racial hostility and prejudice toward African Americans and alternative depictions of black manhood—were most prominent in his second film, *Within Our Gates* (1920).

Within Our Gates was one of his most scandalous and controversial films. Criticized by segments of both the black and white communities, the film had numerous censorship problems. It was certainly Micheaux at his most provocative. The filmmaker was illustrating racial violence and bigotry on the screen, topics that were featured in almost every issue of the *Chicago Defender*. The film was released shortly after a summer of race riots in 1919 and the timeliness of the film, in regard to racial sensitivity, played into Micheaux's problems with its exhibition.[1]

A single surviving print of the film was found in Spain in the 1980s, retitled *La Negra*. The original English intertitles were lost, except in four cases. The film has been restored by the Library of Congress but the intertitles on the restoration only approximate Micheaux's originals. The titles were originally in English, translated into Spanish, and then back into English; thus,

African-American syntax and slang were often lost.[2] The discovery of *Within Our Gates* was significant because it remains the oldest surviving example of African-American feature filmmaking. It also is critical to Micheaux's oeuvre because of his direct confrontation with numerous censorship boards concerning the film and because he reworked the movie so many times in other ways (often cutting out controversial scenes or butchering the original product).[3]

The print of *Within Our Gates* now available to the viewer is not the original film that Micheaux screened for film audiences in January 1920. Jane Gaines has argued that the video release of the film is perhaps the skeletal remains of Micheaux's original intended product.[4] But even the surviving print is remarkably radical in consideration of contemporary cinematic discourse among African-American filmmakers of the era. Gaines explains that the problem *The Birth of a Nation* had with censorship was that it told a completely fabricated version of American history. *Within Our Gates,* on the other hand, was critiqued and censored because it told too much truth.[5] J. Ronald Green claims that "because a response to *The Birth of a Nation* was high on the African-American agenda, *Within Our Gates* may reasonably be accepted as a direct rebuttal to Griffith's politics and sensibility."[6] A detailed analysis of the film is in order. The summation is extensive, but it is necessary to establish the numerous ways in which Micheaux commented on black manhood in the film.

From the opening title, Micheaux makes it clear that this film will deal with a topic completely avoided by contemporary African-American and white filmmakers—lynching. Mark Reid claims that Micheaux himself witnessed the horrible lynching of Leo Frank—thus, he had personal experience with the horrible crime.[7] Micheaux's title reads: "At the opening of our drama, we find our characters in the North, where the prejudice and hatreds of the South do not exist—although this does not prevent the occasional lynching of a Negro."

The film centers on a heroine, Sylvia Landry, a schoolteacher from the South, "typical of the intelligent Negro of our times." Even though Sylvia is the protagonist, a wide variety of male figures surround her, giving the filmmaker numerous opportunities to construct varying portrayals of African-American manhood.

The first half of the film centers on Piney Woods, "far from all civilizations and in the depths of the forests of the south where ignorance and the lynch law reign supreme, [where] we find . . . the school for Negroes."[8] Micheaux points out the geographic distinctions in racial prejudice in the United

States. Although Micheaux encouraged African Americans to migrate to the West rather than to the North, he clearly illustrated the racial hostility blacks faced in the South. The viewer is introduced to Reverend Wilson Jacobs, the founder of the school and an "apostle of education for the black race."

Micheaux demonstrates the lack of educational opportunities available to African-American children in the South. Sylvia arrives in Piney Woods and a title explains that so do "others . . . who could not read." A dark-skinned farmer and his two small children walk into Reverend Jacob's office. He explains that boll weevils have eaten up his cotton crop (a very real problem in the 1910s) and since he could not pay his rent, his mule was taken away. He explains, "I hears 'bout your school 'n so we walked from my place, aways off, cause my children don't do nothin' but say 'Pape without schoolin' we c'n never mount to nothing. So her I is, ready to work day n' night so's my children can go to school." The use of dialect is not meant to be derogatory. It is realistic in the context of its portrayal of a poor uneducated sharecropper and his willingness to go to extreme measures to give his children a future. Whereas other African-American filmmakers ridiculed the poor black southerner, Micheaux held him up as a model, a poor man who was sacrificing for the future of his family. His desire is for his children to be educated so that they will have a better life than he does—the American dream. Many white Americans believed African Americans were too lazy or stupid to want an education. This type of scene never appeared in mainstream white productions of the period.

Wilson explains to Sylvia that the school is just about out of money. New students have to be turned away every day because of the lack of funds. Sylvia decides that she must raise money for the school. With her bags packed, she explains to Wilson, "It is my duty and the duty of each member of our race to destroy ignorance and superstition." The film then introduces Dr. V. Vivian (Charles D. Lucas—the Homesteader), who is "passionately engaged in social questions." The doctor is reading a *Literary Digest*. As Pearl Bowser and Louise Spence argue, Vivian is "the antithesis of any image African Americans would have seen in white-made movies playing in the same theatres."[9] The camera shows the passage he is reading. This is critical because several times throughout the film, Micheaux shows us what Dr. Vivian is studying; this serves as a mouthpiece for Micheaux's point of view. The copy says that "Reverend Thurston has begun an active campaign for the education of the black race. He asks that the federal government contribute significantly, so that Negro children in all of the U.S. can receive proper instruction." Thus, Micheaux addresses a serious contemporary problem that virtually all filmmakers of the period, both black and white, ignored. Dr. Vivian then meets Sylvia while rescuing her from a thief.

Micheaux was one of the few black independent filmmakers to use a multiracial cast. This is a critical subject in race films because, as Jane Gaines argues, "one could watch hours of race movies without seeing a white face."[10] Micheaux's films, therefore, must have been received differently by African-American audiences than all-black race films, which made up the majority of the genre. Micheaux was depicting the reality of American life, not a world in which there were no white people. J. Ronald Green claims that although African Americans remain the central actors at every point in the narrative, Micheaux includes the full range of whites in the film—those with good qualities and those with bad qualities—much like his black characters.[11]

In the film, Micheaux introduces Mrs. Geraldine Stratton, a rich southern woman passing through Boston.[12] She is the embodiment of southern prejudice. She opposes female suffrage because she fears black women will get the right to vote. She reads a newspaper column, "Law Proposed to Stop Negroes of Vote." It explains that Mississippi senator James K. Vardaman has proposed a bill to negate the Fifteenth Amendment. His justification is that "from the soles of their flat feet to the crown of their head, Negroes are undoubtedly inferior beings, therefore, how can we in conscience permit them to vote?" This is a clever device employed by Micheaux: such a blatant racial attack guarantees the unification of the black audience.[13]

Sylvia has little luck raising funds until quite accidentally, she meets a wealthy white philanthropist, Mrs. Elena Warwick, who hits her with her automobile. Sylvia explains the Piney Woods school financial crisis. Mrs. Warwick then approaches Geraldine for advice about the matter, and she espouses a litany of reasons why it would be foolish for Mrs. Warwick to donate money for black education. She argues that black men are nothing more than "lumberjacks and field hands" and claims that "thinking would only give them a headache." This white bigot represents traditional racist arguments that support discrimination and prejudice. Micheaux is quite subversive here by making Geraldine the point of ridicule. She justifies her argument by claiming that all black men want to do is "belong to a dozen lodges, consume religion without restraint . . . and go straight to heaven." As a symbol of southern bigotry, she is the "irregular" member of the cast. Geraldine suggests to Mrs. Warwick that rather than spend $5,000 on black education, she should give $100 to Old Ned, "the best colored preacher in the world."

Micheaux includes three highly negative portrayals of African-American manhood in *Within Our Gates*—Larry, the criminal; Old Ned, the preacher;

and Ephrem, the servant. It seemed almost impossible for Micheaux not to include a negative portrayal of black preachers in his films. He viewed traditional black religiosity (and specifically the men involved) as dangerous to African-American freedom and advancement. Geraldine explains, "Old Ned will do more to keep Negroes in their place than all your schools put together."

The film then begins a five-minute segment criticizing Old Ned and the black religious community. Members of black churches complained bitterly about these depictions. Old Ned is clearly an Uncle Tom but he is not an evil man. In fact, Micheaux goes to great lengths to make him a tragic figure trapped by the racial system in which he exists.

Old Ned preaches to his congregation that "white folks with all their schooling, all their wealth, will most all fall into the everlasting inferno, while our race, lacking these vices and whose souls are more pure, most all will ascend into heaven." Old Ned justifies the present racial system as God's ordained plan. Being poor and uneducated are attributes that will lead African Americans into heaven.

On Monday, Old Ned meets his white friends. They ask him, "What do you make of this? It's about the negroes' right to vote. We are all in favor of your people but we ain't be havin' negroes voting." Being a "good old colored man," Ned answers, "Y'all know what I always preach. This is a land for the white man and black folk got to know their place." The two middle-aged men clap and Old Ned begins an emotional sermon. He argues that he does not need politics or wealth—all he needs is Jesus. The white men clap again. Even though Old Ned argues that the majority of white people will go straight to hell and most black people will go to heaven, the white men openly support his religious views. They do not challenge him because they understand that this black religious doctrine justifies the current racial and social system. Black religion, therefore, is a means of control—a way of keeping the black man in his place. In a humiliating move, one of the white men kicks Ned in the rear end and makes a fool of him as he responds, "Yess'm. White folks is mighty fine."

One of the most poignant scenes of the film takes place as Old Ned closes the door. He goes from a smiling, grinning buffoon to a disgusted black man. It has all been a performance. Old Ned says to the camera, "Again, I've sold my birthright. All for a miserable mess of pottage." Despondent and frustrated, he argues, "Negroes and Whites—all are equal. As for me, miserable sinner, hell is my destiny." This is a remarkably provocative scene. Uncle Tom characters were a staple in white mainstream films and some black independent productions, but a director had never attempted to explain the psychology behind such a man. As Old Ned chastises himself, Micheaux demonstrates to the viewer that this character is less than a man. Any individual who denigrates his own race, who uses religion to keep his people down while boosting his own meager privilege is not only unmanly but certainly will be condemned in the eyes of God. This is powerful commentary and was rare in films of any kind. As Lawrence Levine argues in *Black Culture and Black Consciousness,* the self that African Americans portrayed to whites was seldom who they actually conceived of themselves as. Levine reflects this psychology in a song sung by generations of African Americans:

> Got one mind for white folks to see,
> 'Nother for what I know is me:
> He don't know, he don't know my mind.[14]

The film then proceeds along a second story line—a lengthy flashback. This was the way for Micheaux to work in the lynching angle—it also became the most action-packed and racially confrontational part of the film.

Sylvia is the adopted daughter of the Landrys. Jasper Landry, a workman, is described as "typical of the thousands of poor Negro laborers in the Great Delta, lacking education and the vote, but in whose heart burned an eternal hope." Jasper is a middle-aged, dark-complected man who lives with his family in a metal hut. A typical southern sharecropper, he is elevated by Micheaux. Jasper's "eternal hope" is a "home for [his] family, a few acres of land, a church to attend and an education for their children." The importance of education in self-improvement is stressed throughout the film. Of any of the African-American male characters in the film, Jasper Landry was perhaps most similar to the male audience members watching the film. Many of the spectators were recent migrants, each having many of the same dreams as Landry. He is a proud man, a loving father, and a dutiful husband. His stepdaughter is now well educated because of his hard work. Jasper has been successful enough to be able to send his son Emil to school. This is a totally different cinematic view of African-American masculinity. It is indeed radical. If African-American men have the same hopes, dreams, and feelings as white men then it is very difficult to justify racism, lynching, and segregation.

Jasper works the land of Philip Gridlestone. Described as a "modern Nero, feared by the Negroes [and] envied and hated by the white farmers," Gridlestone has been stealing from his sharecroppers for years. Their lack of education has allowed him to juggle the books to his financial advantage. Gridlestone is assisted by Ephrem, his gossipy servant. In many ways, Eph is the most despicable of the African-American male characters. He frequently drinks his "master's liquor." Described as an "incorrigible" tattletale, his only "pleasure was to take from one place to another" any gossip he could obtain.

Sylvia is determined that she will no longer allow her father to be robbed by Gridlestone so she carefully manages her father's accounts so he can settle with Gridlestone without argument. That afternoon, Jasper enters the back door of Gridlestone's house and goes into his office. Gridlestone looks upon Jasper with disgust while Eph, the spy, is snooping outside the window. Gridlestone warned Jasper, "You're getting mighty smart, eh. I'm on to you. And remember the white man makes the law in this country."[15] At that point, a poor white man comes to the window with a gun. The title reads, "Yes, Gridlestone has cheated him also and when he called him to terms had laughed in his face, calling him Poor White Trash—and no better than a Negro" (this, of course, being the ultimate insult to a white man).

Gridlestone explains that he has always treated colored people well, but he remembers the example set by his slave-owning father—the only way to keep black men in line is to whack them once in a while. He then knocks Jasper to the ground. Eph laughs at the scene and chuckles himself down to the ground. The white man shoots Gridlestone through another window. Eph, startled, believes naturally that Jasper has done it. Jasper grabs his head in frustration, realizing the horrible dilemma he is in, alone with a dead white body.

Eph gleefully rushes to spread the news, going to all the white shops in town explaining that Jasper has killed Mastah Gridlestone. For this reason, the film argues, he was known as the white man's friend.

White men start to gather on the city sidewalks to discuss the matter. Landry gets his family, their belongings, and his gun, and they run off to the swamps. They attempt to escape through a terrific rainstorm. Mobs of men and boys set out on foot to capture the family. The manhunt continues for more than a week. Micheaux goes to great lengths to portray this mob as being made up of poor white men. He truly evokes a mob mentality when the real killer of Gridlestone is accidentally killed by some of the searchers—a victim of circumstances.

Eph is in his full glory. "Tain't no doubt 'bout it—da whi' folks love me," he says to himself. All around him, though, white people are growing impatient. "He I is 'mung da whit folk while dem other niggahs hide in da woods," he thinks. Suddenly, Eph looks around nervously. "While we's wait'n what ya say we grab this boy," says one of the white men, referring to Eph. "But you know me mastah John—I's the one who tells you." It makes no difference. Eph is taken away—and lynched.

Later in the film, a newspaper account describes Eph as being a "recent victim of accidental death at unknown hands." For moviegoers all too familiar with a racialized southern code of justice, Eph's lynching is not shocking; it is simply a way of life. The audacity of Micheaux to show mob injustice and incitement to violence, leading to the lynching of an innocent black man who is simply in the wrong place at the wrong time is overwhelming. No director, African American or Euro-American, dared to deal with this all too real subject matter.

The same newspaper account gives a distorted view of the scene between Landry and Gridlestone. Reenacting the false newspaper account, Landry is shown chasing Gridlestone around the room while the white man, wounded, begs him for mercy. He falls to the ground and then the "savage Negro" beats him. Micheaux intricately demonstrates how the press, the system of law and order, and those in economic power all worked together to trap black men. He also illustrates how the lynching of black men had become part of consumer culture; a spectacle to be regarded as entertainment, news, and racial justification by the white public.

Jasper Landry, his wife, and son are finally captured. The "Committee," a crazed vigilante group of white citizens, march the family to their place of execution on Sunday, the Lord's day. With clubs in their hands, the barbaric mob takes Mrs. Landry and beats her, while one man strips off her dress. Landry tries to choke the white man who humiliates his wife. What follows is a superbly chilling succession of shots in which Micheaux shows the fate of the Landry family. Jane Gaines calls this "lynching as sensational spectacle." Rather than as a public spectacle in which African Americans are taught to stay in their place, Micheaux displays the gruesome event to cause horror and indignation in his audience.[16] A shot-by-shot analysis is necessary to demonstrate the unsettling artistry that Micheaux uses to shock his audience.

Shot 1 is a telling scene of the lynching rope swinging in the breeze.

Shot 2 shows Mrs. Landry grabbing her boy, trying to protect him.

Shot 3, the single most damning of the entire film, shows the mob placing a noose around ten-year-old Emil's neck. It is a remarkable indictment of southern justice.

Shot 4 shows a noose being placed around Jasper Landry's neck.

Shot 5 shows the boy running away as the mob attends to his father. The men shoot at Emil and he falls, wounded and prostrate on the ground.[17]

Shot 6, in a relieving moment, demonstrates that the boy has faked his death. He runs away and steals a horse while the crowd continues to shoot at him.

Shot 7 shows both man and wife with ropes around their necks.

Shot 8 displays the white men pulling the ropes.

The final shot shows these same men placing kindling around the lynching posts.

These series of shots remain the most remarkable in African-American silent film. They are well edited and graphic, heightening the tension and frustration of the audience. Micheaux told potential viewers in his advertisements, "It will hold you spellbound. Full of details that will make you grit your teeth in silent indignation."[18] Historian Grace Elizabeth Hale claims, "Their [African Americans] knowledge of all these extralegal killings remained paradoxically distant and perhaps fantastic. Even as their very effective networks of communication publicized the brutality that struck close at hand."[19] The *Chicago Defender* and other black newspapers regularly gave gruesome accounts of white southern racial violence. Micheaux's film clearly illustrated visually what African Americans already knew—the brutality against and barbaric treatment of innocent African Americans.

Micheaux then crosscuts the film, alternating the lynching scene with an attempted rape of Sylvia. As Bowser and Spence succinctly argue, "By crosscutting the defilement of the black woman and the lynching of the black male for reasons that have nothing really to do with crimes against white women, Micheaux demystifies pervasive racist myths."[20] Jane Gaines claims that the crosscutting of these two events demonstrates the connecting roots of race, gender, and sexuality.[21]

Sylvia is trapped in a house with Armand Gridlestone, Philip's brother. A title reads: "Still not satisfied with the poor victims in the bonfire, Gridlestone goes looking for Sylvia." Micheaux interweaves scenes of the demise of the Landry family with the molestation of Sylvia, implying that they are happening at the same time. The scenes read as follows:

Scene 1—Gridlestone chases Sylvia around the room.

Scene 2—The mob cuts down the lynching ropes.

Scene 3—Gridlestone rips off Sylvia's coat.

Scene 4—The mob starts burning the lynched bodies.
Scene 5—Sylvia grabs a knife and frantically fights for her life.
Scene 6—A huge burning bonfire in the night consumes the Landrys' remains.
Scene 7—Sylvia gives up after a terrific fight.

The only thing that saves Sylvia from being raped is Armand Gridlestone's recognition of a scar on Sylvia's chest—identification that this was his mulatto daughter.[22] He never reveals to Sylvia that she is his daughter but he stops attacking her. Thus, incest, interracial desire, and rape are combined in one explosive scene.

Jane Gaines argues that using crosscutting techniques in the melodramatic form has special meaning for the disenfranchised spectator because of the ways the device is used to inscribe power relations. The lynching of the Landry family and the possible rape of Sylvia placed the contemporary African-American spectator in a totally hopeless position, made all too painful because of the recognition that these things happened in the real world. But Gaines argues that this editing technique ultimately empowers the minority spectator by awarding them moral superiority, demonstrating that they recognize the injustice and cruelty evident on the screen.[23] This dramatic scene is structured remarkably like the final climax of Griffith's *The Birth of a Nation*. In *The Birth of a Nation* it is a mob of black soldiers that threaten the white leading characters the audience is supposed to identify with. In *Within Our Gates*, it is a lynch mob of whites that threaten the major black figures.

In true melodramatic fashion, there must be a happy ending. Sylvia and Dr. Vivian reunite to spend the rest of their lives together. But the epilogue of the story is one of the most startling changes in political sympathies evident in cinema. The spectator has just witnessed the brutal crimes of lynching and attempted rape. Dr. Vivian, after just reliving the horrifying anguish of the Landry family as told by another character in the film, seems to apologize it all away. "Be proud of our country, Sylvia. We should never forget what our people did in Cuba under Roosevelt's command. And in Carrazel in Mexico. And later in France from Bruges to Chateau Thierry. We were never immigrants. Be proud of our country always." Coming immediately after the American victory in World War I and the wide participation of African Americans in the war, this sentiment might be excused.

But he continues, "And you, Sylvia, have been thinking deeply about this I know, but unfortunately your thoughts have been warped. In spite of all your misfortunes you will always be a patriot and a wife." The film then ends with a title explaining that Sylvia realized later that Dr. Vivian was right after all.

How in the world can the viewer explain this 360-degree turn in political attitudes? How could all of these crimes against Sylvia's family be excused? Why was Micheaux trying to sweep under the rug the problems he had so clearly laid out for the viewer?

There are two obvious answers. Micheaux may have simply been an apologist for white America. He may have been the epitome of bourgeois black values, ignoring the realities of poor black southerners. But this explanation completely contradicts the content of the entire film. Why would Micheaux choose to be so painfully provocative, only to cloak racial injustice with patriotism and war victory?

Micheaux may have also added the final scene in the film after censorship problems. The film was initially turned down by the Chicago Board of Censors for its graphic display of lynching. According to the Associated Negro Press, the Chicago Board of Censors initially banned the film in its entirety.[24] Micheaux provided a frank discussion of some of the racial and sexual problems in American society; certainly other filmmakers would have encountered censorship problems with the same material. Or, Micheaux may have added this final scene as a way to avoid problems with the multitude of state and municipal motion picture censorship boards that were operating at the time. Micheaux often had to compromise his work; he could either cooperate with the censorship boards or fail as an independent filmmaker.[25]

There may have been a third reason for the final scene. The film was clearly a product of its times. Produced during the "Red Summer" of 1919, *Within Our Gates* was a powerful indictment of the immense racial tension that existed in the postwar era. The epilogue may have been a call for peace and an end to violence, of which African Americans were the principal victims.

Chicago, where the film premiered, had been wracked by a terrible race riot the previous summer. In addition, between April and October 1919, over twenty-five race riots had taken place in towns and cities across the United States, in both southern and northern locations.[26] Many white urban dwellers resented the burgeoning black community. As Micheaux accurately reports in his opening title, racial violence was no longer unique to the South. *Within Our Gates,* therefore, drew from the moment, demonstrating the tumultuous racial anxieties of the postwar years.

Micheaux walked a tightrope. Through his films he attempted to graphically demonstrate the injustices that African-American people had to experi-

This photo, taken shortly after the Chicago Race Riot of 1919, illustrates the nexus of the end of World War I, growing urban racial conflict, and popular entertainment. (Chicago Historical Society)

ence on a daily basis—the threat of rape, economic exploitation, an indifferent criminal system, a manipulated press, mob brutality and violence, a lack of educational opportunity, propagandized messages of black inferiority, and even death through lynching. Yet at the same time, Micheaux attempted to defuse the racial flame by reminding African Americans of their duty and loyalty to their nation (as proven by African-American participation in World War I) and to the uplift of the race. Micheaux has been roundly criticized for these disparate themes but his critics often embody a "presentist view" when making such remarks. They forget the social dislocation and the fresh wounds still evident from one of the bloodiest summers the nation had ever experienced.

So what did this have to do with Micheaux's "manhood" and his portrayal of African-American masculinity on the screen? Micheaux, quite simply, laid his manhood on the line by even making such a film. Micheaux admitted that the film was a bit "radical."[27] He released the film in the very week that the NAACP announced that at least nine African-American veterans had been lynched in 1919, many while still in uniform. This was a bold move.[28] But *Within Our Gates* is more significant for the diversity of the presentations of African-American men that Micheaux included on the screen. While Dr. Vivian and Conrad Drebert (a character who appears early in the film) fit the mold for standard Micheaux heroic figures—light-skinned, muscular, paternalistic, well educated, professional, concerned for their race— Micheaux also includes examples of black manhood that were more representational of the majority of audience members. Certainly, Jasper Landry and the unnamed sharecropper are atypical characters in the vocabulary of African-American filmmaking of the period. Urban African-American men at the time may have been portrayed as corrupt or open to the vices of the wicked city, but at least they were urban and worldly. In numerous black-directed films of the silent era, the poor rural African-American sharecropper was usually seen as an uneducated country rube, a man who simply tried to live day to day with little concern for the future. Micheaux's two rural farmers were quite the opposite. Realizing the value of education for their children, disciplined and hardworking, these men were willing to make sacrifices for the future of their family.

Micheaux included three negative portrayals of black manhood—Larry, Old Ned, and Eph. They were not simply described as "evil" or "bad" characters, though. Micheaux attempted to impart a lesson with each male character. Larry, the urban con man, was a man who chose crime rather than work and was willing to exploit members of his own race to meet his needs. Larry discovers crime simply did not pay and his eventual fate is death. Old Ned, the preacher, was a tortured man. Ready to warp traditional Christian practices "to get him a bit of the pottage," Old Ned was also aware of the results of his actions. A tragic figure, he represented the humiliation that black men endured when they stooped for the white man and "yes sahed" their way into submission. Eph was a variation of the Uncle Tom character. More dangerous than Old Ned, Eph was ready to willingly sacrifice members of his own race to the gallows to gain acceptance from the white community. Eph was completely devoid of racial loyalty and eventually became the victim of his displaced allegiances. Committed to the white man, he found the relationship was not mutual. The terror in his eyes was more evident when the pitiful figure realized he would be the next black male victim to be sacrificed at the altar of white male barbarism. J. Ronald Green argues that Micheaux presented caricatures for the purpose of criticizing them.[29] I would argue that these negative portrayals in *Within Our Gates* went beyond caricature because of their exploratory and explanatory factors. In his novel *The Wind from Nowhere*, Micheaux claimed, "My race's greatest enemies are not white people who even despise and hate us, but Negroes who want to be white and who hate and despise us."[30]

Within Our Gates was a powerful indictment of the American racial system and its indignities. It was a turning point in the history of African-American cinema in its bold and frank presentation and for its complex and diverse portrayals of African-American manhood. Micheaux did not temper his criticism of America's race relations for the rest of the silent era. This placed him in a unique category of African-American directors. Not only was he the most provocative African-American film director, he was the most successful. Obviously, African-American audiences were clamoring for visual representations that embodied a black point of view and Micheaux delivered.

8

BLACKFACE, WHITE INDEPENDENT ALL-BLACK PRODUCTIONS, AND THE COMING OF SOUND: THE LATE SILENT ERA, 1915–1931

Throughout black silent filmmaking (1913–1931), African Americans created films that reflected black imagery of race and gender in contemporary society. During the same period, mainstream Hollywood studios and white independent companies also produced films with African-American male portrayals. This chapter will examine racialized masculinity by white filmmakers and will compare these portrayals with African-American cinematic imagery of race and masculinity. The concept of a "black cinematic aesthetic" will be discussed as it relates to the ideological position of the filmmaker and the racial makeup of the production team's cast and crew. Finally, a discussion of the introduction of sound film and the pivotal role that "voice" gave to African-American men on film will be included. This "transition to sound" not only fundamentally changed the aesthetics and technology of filmmaking but it significantly altered the cultural dynamics and racialized positioning of American filmmakers.

First, a discussion of African-American male portrayals in mainstream Hollywood productions is in order. Since these were the films viewed by the largest audience, in some respects they are the most pivotal in terms of their influence.[1]

Hollywood's vision of African-American men in the late silent era comes in two modes—African-American men acting as members of their own race or white men in blackface. Blackface, as a form of popular entertainment, dwindled in popularity in the postwar era when it began to be viewed as a relic of the past. But a nostalgic twist on blackface later added to a reinvented appeal. Although the majority of screen portrayals of African-American men in the prewar period were of white men in blackface, this became less common in Hollywood productions in the postwar era. Nevertheless, a binary construction of black men/white men began slowly to dissolve as black men began to portray themselves on the screen. This became even more apparent as light-skinned character actors like Noble Johnson began to portray a wide variety of ethnic types (Native American, Polynesian, African). Thus, a "difference of opposites" may have been created within the early silent framework of racial typology but it slowly unraveled as white and black men crossed racial and ethnic lines in their character portrayals. When one factors in black independent films in which light-skinned men attempted to pass as white, the racialized structure becomes more digressive.[2]

The majority of blackface portrayals in the late silent era took place between 1915 and 1917.[3] A number of factors may have contributed to the decline, though not the extinction, of the racialized ritual of blackface. First, there was fallout from *The Birth of a Nation*. Racially sensitive progressives condemned Griffith's most popular film for its highly negative black portrayals. This heightened the sensitivity of studios, persuading them to not film racially antagonistic productions. Second, motion pictures went from their vaudevillian roots to a more "classic" film style. This style was based on the technical possibilities of the new medium. In the postwar era, there was a quest by filmmakers for realism, and blackface entertainment was simply not realistic. If African-American men were to be portrayed, it only made sense to feature real black men. This indicates a growing sophistication in the viewer's ability to "read" a film. Third, as the film studios attempted to appeal to a mass middle-class audience, the working-class roots of blackface entertainment hurt the quality the studios were trying to project. Movie mogul Adolph Zukor was typical of those in the industry in wanting to remove "the slum tradition in the movies."[4] Fourth, African-American male participation in World War I and the organization of African Americans into pressure groups like the NAACP may have made studios more sensitive to the derogatory nature of blackface entertainment. Clyde Taylor argues that "mainstream filmmaking in the United States never again fashioned a portrait of Blacks massed in menace against white society."[5] This became even more critical following the race riots of 1919. Racially controversial material was avoided, particularly during a period in which Hollywood was threatened with government censorship. The process of getting films passed by municipal and state censorship boards was cumbersome, and a racially provocative film might take a lengthy and expensive road to release.

But there is no simple explanation for the gradual decline of blackface in films. World War I and the postwar era was not free of racism and prejudice. Madison Grant published his popular and influential *The Passing of the Great Race* in 1916. Xenophobic literature warned of racial mixing with immigrants, or even worse, African Americans.[6] Racial zealotry seemed to reach a fever pitch with the resurgence of the Ku Klux Klan in the early 1920s. However, an examination of blackface themes in films of the late 1910s reveals the increasingly restrictive nature of the performance. In *Wurra Wurra* (Kalem, 1916), blackface performers imitate cannibals. *Conning the Cannibal* (unknown, 1917) uses blackface again in the context of cannibals—the ultimate Other. In *The Jungle Outcasts* (Centaur, 1916), Samuel Bigelow portrays Waji, an African soldier. *Mixed Kids* (Universal, 1914) and *Minding the Baby* (Cub, 1917) both use the time-worn plot device of misplaced children of different races. *Dark and Cloudy* (1919) uses blackface as comic pretext.[7]

In the late 1910s, blackface in the cinema was relegated to use as a comic device or as a way to mock or dramatize the excesses of animalistic cannibals far removed from normal civilized society. Blackface entertainment died a lingering death in the context of American film in the 1920s, only to be revived with the release of *The Jazz Singer* in 1927.[8] *The Jazz Singer* is canonized in American screen history for demonstrating the financial possibilities of sound in film. But *The Jazz Singer* should also be remembered as the film that revived the use of blackface entertainment in film and relegated it to the genre in which it would exist for the next fifteen years—the movie musical.[9] *The Jazz Singer* was not about African Americans in an obvious sense; there were no black performers in the film. But the movie's widespread popularity, its sheer technological novelty, and the star power of Al Jolson universalized blackface entertainment and sent it around the world, teaching the rest of the world about the peculiar American nexus of race, gender, and burnt cork.

The Jazz Singer was based on a popular Broadway play by Samuel Raphaelson. The film opens with a title: "In every living soul, a spirit cries for expression. Perhaps the plaintive wailing song of jazz, after all, is the misunderstood utterance of prayer." Throughout the play and film, there is a call for assimilation and acceptance. Expression, as related by Jolson's musical style, was integral to jazz as a form of music. The linkage of the spiritual, emotive power of the music with religious tradition is a critical theme of the film. *The Jazz Singer* borrowed early-twentieth-century African-American musical styles and created a new brand of blackface. Although the film used blackface as an assimilationist tool it also romanticized the practice as part of "traditional" American theater.

The opening shots show a young Jakie Rabinowitz singing popular songs in a local café. His cantor father drags him out of the establishment, determined he will sing only hymns of Jewish spiritual tradition. At this point, the film creates a world of dichotomies. Cantor Rabinowitz is traditional, orthodox, paternalistic, nonassimilationist, and Old World. Young Jakie is fully American, modern, filled with spirit, and secular. Rabinowitz would have never known his son was singing secular songs if a fellow Jew, Yudelson, had not informed the cantor of his "raggy time songs." The original shooting script called them "nigger songs."[10] Jakie is beaten for disobeying his father; therefore, he runs away from home.

Years later, Jakie Rabinowitz anglicizes his name to Jack Robin. He is a talented and aspiring jazz singer. The original number in which we hear Jolson is "Dirty Hands, Dirty Face." The song is about the love a father has for his child, but the symbolic link with blackface (dirtiness) is obvious. After completing a song, Jolson issues his famous dictum: "Wait a minute. Wait a minute. You ain't heard nothing, yet."

And the audience had not. For the first time in film, a mass audience witnesses the emotive, passionate musical stylings of Al Jolson—the Jazz Singer. The love interest in the film, a young dancer named Mary Dale, tells Jack, "There are lots of jazz singers, but you have a tear in your voice." The tear Mary is speaking of is the authentic voice that Jolson brings to his music; he feels as he sings.

At no point in the film does the text argue that jazz began in the African-American community. There are no African-American artists, musicians, or singers in the movie. Jack Robin, therefore, must gain his authenticity as a jazz singer by blacking up—by taking on an imitative, expressive style of singing, mimicking African-American performers of the period. The "tear" Jack Robin possesses is his ability to personally relate to the music. He does not just sing a song, he lives it.

In a letter that Jack sends to his mother, Mary is revealed as a *shiksa,* a Gentile. The assimilationist tendencies of Jack Robin's figure continue; he is interested in and might possibly marry a woman outside of his "race." Therefore, miscegenation occurs at various levels in the film; musical miscegenation with the young Jewish singer borrowing African-American melodies and lyrics and sexual miscegenation with the two lovers admiring each other's artistry.

In true melodramatic form, Jack Robin gets his big break on Broadway. On his opening night, which coincides with the Jewish Day of Atonement, his father lies dying in bed. The congregation and his mother ask Jack to take over his father's cantor position and this creates the ultimate moral dilemma for the young jazz singer. Should he sacrifice his career by canceling on opening night? Or does he turn his back on his parents and the Jewish community?

Theater promotion for *The Jazz Singer*. In this film from 1927, Al Jolson/Jack Robin is the ultimate assimilationist, an obvious link between the African-American and white races. (Museum of Modern Art)

The first time that Jolson applies blackface in his dressing room he is getting ready for his final dress rehearsal. He tells Mary about the evening's performance, "I'm going to put everything I got into my songs." After
finishing the blackface application, Jolson bursts into a big close-up smile—
the authenticity of the performer is now complete; his smile replicates the
performing coon of the late nineteenth century. As he touches up his
makeup he looks at a picture of his mother and says, "I'd love to sing for my
people, maybe it's the call of the ages, the cry of my race." Jazz and religious
music are therefore embodied with instinctual urges primitively inbred in
the racial group.

Al Jolson/Jack Robin is the ultimate assimilationist because he straddles several different worlds of social activity. He is a Jew working in the Gentile world
of popular entertainment. He is also a link between the African-American and
white races. He can sing like no other white man can—emotionally, spiritually,
thoughtfully. As Jack Robin applies his standard blackface makeup, the area
around his mouth is kept white in traditional style. He is, therefore, "black,"
but also "is not." Jolson is performing as ventriloquist, a Jew mouthing the
words and thoughts of the African American.

Sara Rabinowitz comes into the dressing room to see her son. She does
not recognize him in blackface. "Jakie, this ain't you," she says. "He talks
like Jakie but he looks like his shadow." If blackface is racial cross-dressing,
what purpose does it serve in this film?[11] What role does it play in the film's
thematic structure?

In *The Jazz Singer*, blackface is used as a tool of assimilation. Assimilating
into a dominant national culture involves accepting the most traditional
conservative mores of the society. If Jolson was a newfangled jazz singer, his
theatrical usage of blackface linked him to a popular culture with deep roots
in the American past. As Jolson mugs for the camera as the "sad Negro," as
he sings "Mammy" in the film's finale, he is playing into a national tradition
that embraces the racism of the past. As Michael Rogin has argued, blackface takes on nostalgic value with no consideration of the blatantly racist
connotations of its usage.[12] Throughout the 1930s and 1940s, Hollywood
would use blackface as a nostalgic tool, usually in the context of a musical
production number. Examples include the films *Babes in Arms* (1939), *Holiday Inn* (1942), and *Dixie* (1943). *The Jazz Singer* fully "Americanized"
the theatrical practice. As part of the history of American popular entertainment, it was now fully screened before the world.

Between 1916 and 1929, the major Hollywood studios employed
African-American men in a number of secondary roles. The studios appeared

to be much more careful in not allowing blatantly racist portrayals of African-American men (chicken stealing, watermelon eating) like those that existed in the prewar years. One of the ways this progression can be traced is in the decline of the career of D. W. Griffith. Griffith's faltering career coincided with the mobilization of African-American organizations and newspapers against derogatory portrayals of people of color. The nation was moving forward while Griffith's racial messages seemed to have been stuck in the past. The Ku Klux Klan may have been growing in numbers during the early 1920s but motion picture audiences were staying away from Griffith's features in droves. His racial beliefs were only one factor in his rapidly declining career. Three cinematic examples of his nineteenth-century racial sentiment include *One Exciting Night* (1922), *The White Rose* (1923), and *His Darker Self* (1924). In each of these films, Griffith used white men in blackface to portray African-American men. His stories were ultimately about white male masculinity—their divine and natural right to judge and punish everyone. In the filmmaker's narrative system, dominance over non-whites is required to maintain the hegemony of white men.[13]

One Exciting Night is Griffith's litany of black male racial types—the faithful servant, the black brute, and the coon. Sam, the Kaffir, in a confounding and plot-disturbing twist, plays two types—the faithful servant and the brute. Griffith's muddled story line helps to explain part of the film's lack of appeal. As the faithful servant, Sam is willing to sacrifice his life and his future for a white woman (as in the films *His Trust* and *His Trust Fulfilled*). He remains as a vestige of Griffith's Civil War genre films. Black Sam is the quintessential black brute—menacing, criminal, untrusting, brutal, and a potential rapist. Griffith literally turns Black Sam into the Kaffir in the film, playing on the racial fear of every white audience member with the implication that any black man can be dangerous. In a black filmmaker's hands, this message of the evil brute turning out to be a lifesaver could be considered subversive, but in Griffith's film it is a plot device that plays on white fear.

In *One Exciting Night*, Romeo Washington is the southern coon. Frightened of ghosts, a liar, lazy, and driven by sexual lust, Romeo is a black man who needs control. Romeo's energy (or lack of it) can be transformed only in a positive manner as a servile member of a white household. Although Griffith elevates the romantic relationship between the white leading character, Agnes, and her lover as being that of true love, he mocks the relationship between Romeo and a black maid as being sexual or frivolous. The fact that both of these black men were portrayed by white men in blackface, coupled with Griffith's racialized gender portrayals, demonstrates little actual growth in his racial ideology, despite the controversy over *The Birth of a Nation.*

The White Rose demonstrates that Griffith's conceptualization of the South and its racial system was more a pre–Civil War mentality rather than that of the post–World War I era.[14] Griffith again refused to allow black actors to portray black men. The basic plot revolves around Joseph Beauregard, a wealthy young southerner studying for the ministry, and Bessie Williams, a naïve grocery clerk who is infatuated with the young man. Joseph is accompanied by Apollo, an African American, whom Joseph "in a weak moment, promoted from the cornfield." We first see Apollo playing craps.[15]

Throughout the film, Griffith contrasts the romantic relationship of Joseph and Bessie with that of Apollo and Auntie Easter. The black romance is consistently mocked and ridiculed. At one point in the film, Apollo goes up to Auntie Easter and explains, "I does love you sure til I look down. From the waist up you're honey and molasses—but them bow legs. They are poison ivy." Griffith compares the femininity of white women with that of black women. Auntie Easter is a full-figured, ample black woman. She is deliberately meant to be the opposite of the blonde waifs that Griffith romanticized. Griffith demonstrates the segregation of southern life; as Bessie and Joseph dance in a hall, Apollo and Auntie Easter dance in another room. The white couple dance romantically; the black couple dance comically. When Auntie Easter and Apollo go for an afternoon stroll, it is described as "Lovers Lane in Darktown."

Bessie ends up pregnant. She obviously cannot marry Joseph because of his higher social standing. This leaves her alone with the child. She loses her job and wanders aimlessly; no one will hire a woman with an illegitimate child. Auntie Easter and Apollo eventually find her and give her a place to stay in their quarters. Auntie Easter looks at Apollo in a harsh way and says, "All you!" This, in a sense, implies that her gender loyalty is stronger than her racial loyalty. In the film's finale, Joseph discovers Bessie's fate, severs his ties with the church, leaves his fiancée, and joins his true love. The focus of *The White Rose,* like *One Exciting Night,* is on the white romantic couple. African-American romance or coupling is simply an instrument of comic plot device or satirical comparison.

His Darker Self completed Griffith's triumvirate of early twenties' racialized feature films. Within each of the films, two dominant plots were used—a romantic adventure using white characters and satiric comedy, usually in ridicule, of the African-American characters. The main African-American male character in *His Darker Self* is Uncle Eph, a bumbling Uncle Tom character who assumes he is hauling crates of bananas daily, when he is really carting away cases of contraband liquor. Uncle Eph is manipulated by Bill Jackson, another dark brute type. One day when Jackson's dance hall is raided by Prohibition officers, Jackson assumes Eph has turned him in. As a result, Jackson frames Uncle Eph for murder. His savior is Charles Sappington, a white man. He goes undercover to prove Eph's innocence by donning blackface and working as a busboy in Jackson's establishment. Sappington saves Eph from hanging in the nick of time and captures Jackson and makes him plead his guilt.[16]

Griffith ridiculed black romantic love and set up a rigid binary of African-American cinematic manhood. Black men were either murdering black brutes (Black Sam in *One Exciting Night*, Bill Jackson in *His Darker Self*) or bumbling southern coons (Romeo Washington in *One Exciting Night*, Apollo in *The White Rose*, and Uncle Eph in *His Darker Self*). In the film *One Exciting Night*, both character types were present in the same African-American male character.

The antebellum southern film genre fell out of favor with the motion picture studios during the late 1910s and throughout the 1920s. Griffith may have updated his films with more modern elements (bootlegging in *His Darker Self*, flappers in *The White Rose*, safari adventures in *One Exciting Night*), but his stock black male characters were reminiscent of the types he established with *The Birth of a Nation* and his Civil War films. Griffith's films simply did not reflect the modernity of the 1920s, as seen in his continued use of the blackface tradition.

Blackface became much less common in mainstream Hollywood films. African-American actors like Sam Baker, George Godfrey, Benny Ayers, and Noble Johnson began getting work regularly in secondary roles in mainstream feature films. Although the racism of these portrayals was much less overt, Hollywood typecast African-American men in a limited number of specific characterizations. Throughout the 1920s, African-American men continued to play servants or faithful retainers to the white hero/protagonist. Throughout the decade, the African-American man was a signifier of servility. African-American men were to cater to the interests of the white man or woman. *Picturegoer* magazine claimed, "The Negro is so much a part of the daily life of America that he is seen in at least fifty percent of these films in his natural capacity as lift-man, railway guard, boot black etc."[17] In King Vidor's major MGM production *The Big Parade* (1925), Rex Ingram portrayed a faithful southern servant. African-American men were always carrying bags or some large item for white folks. Douglas Carter was a porter in *Love Is an Awful Thing* (1922). George Reed served the same role in Clarence Badger's *Red Lights* (1923). The career of Martin Turner, an African-American character actor of the twenties, shows this typecasting. He was a servant named Cellar in *They're Off* (1923), Snowball, the valet, in *Knockout Kid* (1925), another valet in *Super Speed* (1925), and yet another valet named Ivory in *Silent Sheldon* (1925). His only divergent role appeared to be that of a cook (Barbeque Sam) in *Rainbow Rangers* (1925). One can argue that the portrayal of African-American men as cooks, servants, baggage handlers, porters, and valets was simply a reflection of the limited economic roles they held in contemporary American life. But the marginalization of these characters is more evident in the names they were given. Certainly, neither Snowball nor Ivory were names that African Americans would give themselves.[18] The power of naming, therefore, lies with the white director or screenwriter. The power to name is the power to define. The white hero/protagonist limited the role of the African-American male character by naming him dependent on the activities and actions with which he was involved. The action revolved around the white male protagonist. He defined the activities, role, actions, and personae of the African-American characters. This was a dependent relationship that involved even naming the black man.

The popularity of the servile role led to the resurrection of Uncle Tom. In 1922 *Variety* proclaimed, "The generation is ready for a new Uncle Tom."[19] The quintessential servile African-American male character, canonized in the halls of American literature and theater, was revived in the 1920s by mainstream studios. The question is, "Why?" Certainly, several generations were well versed in the popular abolitionist tract and its various melodramatic stage productions. Perhaps the studios felt that audiences would flock to a dramatic production they were already familiar with. *Uncle Tom's Cabin* may have been revived as a cinematic topic because of its cross-racial appeal. White audiences would flock to see the self-sacrificing "good Negro" and African-American audiences would clamor to see black actors and actresses on the stage in a major Hollywood production.

Uncle Tom and his incarnations served as a valuable ideological tool in Hollywood's racial repertoire—as pacifier. The major studios seemed to completely thematically ignore the growing exodus of African Americans from the South to northern cities. The urban cinematic Negro, when portrayed, was usually nothing more than a prop. As a valet or baggage handler he had as much weight in the film as a vase on the table. Instead, Hollywood focused on African Americans in southern rural settings or as exotic black Others. The return of Uncle Tom as cinematic device was wish fulfillment by Hollywood. The wish was that the new urban black and the racial tension he brought with him would simply go away. Uncle Tom was a soothing pacifier in an age of frustrating cross-racial urban anxiety.

This was not a return to the antebellum, southern, faithful servant genre. Instead, *Uncle Tom's Cabin* was comedically reworked in a number of fashions. *Little Eva Ascends* (1922), *Uncle Tom's Gal* (1925), and *Uncle Tom's Uncle* (1926) were all examples. By far the most publicized of the adaptations were the 1927 features *Topsy and Eva* and *Uncle Tom's Cabin*.

Topsy and Eva was based on a popular vaudeville show starring the Duncan sisters. Vivian Duncan played Eva St. Claire and her sister Rosetta played Topsy, in blackface. The screen adaptation of the play starred Noble Johnson as Uncle Tom. The film was a racist joke from beginning to end. Eva, the white character, is born on St. Valentine's Day. Topsy is born on April Fool's Day. Eva is born on a beautiful southern night, delivered by a doctor. Topsy is dropped by a black stork in a trash can. Noble Johnson's acting skills were completely wasted. *Variety* claimed, "Noble Johnson, as Uncle Tom, had little choice to shine either. He played in the meek fashion of the play."[20] The film went through three directors, the last being D. W. Griffith, who was brought in during the last ten days of production. If the intentional targets of ridicule in *Topsy and Eva* were African-American women, the sanctimonious demeanor of Noble Johnson's Uncle Tom was equally frustrating to African-American audiences.[21]

Uncle Tom's Cabin was one of Universal's major releases of 1927. Originally, the title character was to be played by Charles Gilpin, arguably the best-known black stage actor of his generation. Gilpin originated the title character in Eugene O'Neill's *Emperor Jones*. Apparently, Gilpin's overly aggressive reading of the script, his refusal to submit to the total authority of the director, and his drinking caused the studio to fire him. He was replaced by James B. Lowe, who had previously served as a sidekick in a Universal Western serial, *Blue Streak*.[22]

James B. Lowe, as Uncle Tom, was the linchpin of the film. A Universal press release on Lowe is a revealing example of how studio heads viewed the black actor, one of the first to star in a major Hollywood production:

James B. Lowe made history. A history that only reflects credit to the Negro race, not only because he has given the "Uncle Tom" character a new slant, but because of his exemplary conduct with the Universal Company. They look upon Lowe at the Universal Studios as being a black god. Of the directors, writers, artists and actors who have seen James Lowe work at the studio there are none who will not say he is the most suited of all men for the part of "Tom." Those who are religious say that a heavenly power brought him to Universal and all predict a most marvelous future and a worldwide reputation for James B. Lowe.[23]

Lowe never made another motion picture for Universal after *Uncle Tom's Cabin*. In fact, he never made another film. Universal's dedication to Lowe lasted only until the film was successfully completed. For the producer, Lowe's race was the critical factor, defining and limiting his acting abilities. He is indeed a credit to the Negro race and a living black god. The producers, perhaps because of their experience with Gilpin, refer to the actor in childlike terms. He displayed "exemplary conduct" and was most suited to the role of Uncle Tom because he was pliable. Universal Studios needed an actor who would sacrifice himself for the financial gain of the company.[24]

If the dominant cinematic role for black actors in the silent era was servility, there was another opportunity to display their acting ability—as a primitive or foreign exotic. Noble Johnson, perhaps the most regularly employed black actor in Hollywood during the silent era, made a career out of playing foreign exotic types. His light skin, large muscular build, and ability to disguise himself in makeup and costumes made him an actor in great demand for secondary roles.[25] By far the majority of exotics that African-American men portrayed were African. They were "natives" (usually cannibals) who confronted European or American invaders. They were non-European Others whose interaction with the white invader usually resulted in violence and bloodshed. By the finale of the film, the white master had achieved hegemony over the conquered territory and its people.[26]

If cinema was a medium in which white men attempted to maintain their control and reassert their manhood, then race provided them with a powerful tool. In the silent cinema, those in power habitually passed themselves off as normal as opposed to the inferiority of the Other. In their elevation of "whiteness," Hollywood directors, screenwriters, and studio personnel appealed to an audience that they presumed was white. This was considered commonsense marketing by studio heads since the majority of motion picture audiences were Euro-American in origin.

James Lowe in Universal's *Uncle Tom's Cabin* (1927). The studio praised Lowe, star of the film, for his "exemplary conduct." (Museum of Modern Art)

In action-adventure films set in Africa or other foreign locations, heroic figures were inscribed with instinctual values and loyalties concretely based on race and gender. This is most provocatively demonstrated in the wildly popular *Tarzan of the Apes* (1919).[27] As a child, Tarzan is raised by apes after his shipwrecked English parents die in the jungles of Africa. Kala, Tarzan's ape mother, raises him as her child. She is killed by an African tribesman and Tarzan seeks revenge by sneaking up and strangling his ape-mother's killer. The murderer was the chief of the neighboring native village. A title reads: "In superstitious awe of the strange white man who killed their chief, the natives brought offerings for days." They are implied to be the embodiment of the primitive.

An English search crew looks for the lost boy (who is now a man, played by Elmo Lincoln). He leaves the white invaders a note that reads, "This is the house of Tarzan, killer of beasts. Touch not what belongs to Tarzan. Tarzan watches." This warning is symbolic because it reflects the racial message of the film. Up to this point in the movie, Tarzan has killed no animals; he has killed only the black man. It is implied that the black man must be a beast; he is more animal-like than human. This becomes even more apparent when a black native in war paint captures Jane. Her helpless effeminate English fiancé provides no help, so Tarzan comes to the rescue. The African native is portrayed by a real black man, not a white man in blackface. The black native and Tarzan wrestle ferociously while Jane screams and hysterically faints. Naturally, Tarzan instinctively fights for the white woman even though he has never seen one since infanthood.[28] Racial loyalty and female protection are, therefore, instinctual, within the genetic code of every white man.

The white search crew travel peacefully to the native village. The natives react in fear, afraid that the white settlers are going to attack them (based on European imperialistic adventures between 1885 and 1914, they had a reason to be afraid). They are described as "Negroes" (an American term) who are "whipped into a frenzy." The irrational nature of the African primitives is stressed over the rationality of their "enemies." Instinctually, Tarzan fights on the side of the white search party. Racial solidarity and paternalistic protection of women is emphasized, since it was only "natural" that "the strong guard the weak."

In *Tarzan of the Apes*, whiteness and blackness dominate the narrative framework. Tarzan, despite having been brought up in the wilds of Africa by an ape, is the instinctual white man. He educates himself (he teaches himself to read through books left by his parents), he seeks revenge on those who harm his family, he protects the weak (women), and he boldly proclaims domination over his surroundings. Elmo Lincoln, as Tarzan, regularly beats his manly chest (and large gut), declaring his rule and power over his environment. According to the film, black men are irrational, prone to unprovoked violence, potential rapists, superstitious, and losers in combat.

Throughout the silent film era of the late 1910s and 1920s, there was an attempt to establish the "normalcy" of white male control over whatever environment he may inhabit. For example, *Tarzan of the Apes* provides a remarkable discourse on social Darwinism and heredity.[29] The film justifies white settlement and control over the African continent and serves as a white power fantasy of the "natural" superiority of the white man over the black man.

The establishment of hegemony over the natural environment and the people who inhabit it remains a fundamental premise of male-dominated genres such as action/adventure, Western, detective, and gangster genres. Using a Godamerian argument, "the viewer could always foray into foreign territory [the exotic locale] because he knew he was secretly at home"— comfortable with the understanding that a white male-dominated world would exist by the conclusion of the film."[30]

Throughout the action/adventure genre of the 1920s the integrity of the race is defined primarily as the moral rectitude of its menfolk. The failure to establish a patriarchal system of domination and control through the rule of white men would eventually lead to disaster. Using this premise, it was necessary to establish a black Other as far removed from the gender and racial characteristics of the white man as possible. The primary black African male character became the cannibal—the consumer of human flesh. The cinematic use of cannibal themes in this period was quite common. Noble Johnson played cannibal chieftains regularly. One such example was the feature *Love Aflame* (1917). In this five-reel feature, African natives are cannibals and they worship a volcano. A reviewer for *Moving Picture World* considered the film's premise "preposterous" but the cannibal theme was a staple of the weekly serials.[31]

In 1920s adventure yarns, the cannibal motif was employed to evoke a dark, menacing environment. This was provocatively true in the gritty MGM adult drama *West of Zanzibar* (1928).[32] This cynical Tod Browning feature starred Lon Chaney as a former vaudevillian magician who loses his wife and legs at the same time. She runs away with another man and he becomes obsessed with seeking revenge. He moves to the frontier of civilization and lives in a hut in Zanzibar with the daughter whom his wife conceived with the other man. Flint (Chaney) is waited on regularly by black natives. The first appearance of a black man in the film is that of a coal-black, bald man, drenched in sweat, who bows to Flint. Flint is able to manipulate local tribesmen with simple feats of Western technology. The locals immediately assume he is some type of god. One replies, "Fire! Only . . . thing . . . great . . . Evil Spirit . . . fear! White master . . . greater . . . than . . . all . . . Evil Spirits! He . . . fears . . . nothing!" Throughout this dark film, the appearance of numerous Africans is supposed to give the film a sense of foreboding. Flint sells his daughter into prostitution in retaliation for her illegitimacy. He makes her eat on the floor and wear half-ripped clothing. Crocodiles, slithering snakes, and ferocious beasts all contribute to the threatening atmosphere of the film. Coal-black natives and their voodoo magic are used for the same effect.[33]

Ethnographic films of the postwar years maintained an obsession with the concept of masculine racial "difference." *The Gorilla Hunt* (1926) argued that the friendship of African male pygmies could be bought with nothing more than salt and safety pins. *The Bushman* (1927) portrayed the principal activities of African people as hunting (wildness) and dancing (playfulness). The linking of cultural stereotypes of African Americans with those of African natives is pointed. In the 1920s, documentary filmmakers were far from objective. In *The Bushman* the director played a phonograph recording of an Al Jolson song that included the word "pickaninny." The global pattern of white male domination and superiority over the racial/ethnic/female Other is a pivotal theme in the cinematic discourse on colonialism.

Black actors not only portrayed Africans in African settings, they could also be placed anywhere in which exotic representations of masculinity were needed. Douglas Fairbanks's *The Thief of Baghdad* (1924) managed to incorporate two dominant roles of black male representation into one theme. Throughout the film, scantily clad black men regularly transport items throughout the Middle Eastern city. In the film, Fairbanks narrowly misses contact with a huge, muscular, half-naked black bodyguard (Sam Baker) carrying a large, gleaming sword. The camera focuses on his massive bronzed body. Throughout the period, African men or black men of other nations were portrayed as unclothed. The iconography of the naked black savage implied a sexualized male. In *Tarzan of the Apes,* the young white child steals clothes from two African women to cover his nakedness. Being clothed is an important symbol of being civilized. In these action-adventure and documentary films the preoccupation with the naked black male body is not necessarily homosexual desire for the racialized Other but an obsession with black male sexuality. In *The Thief of Baghdad,* the huge black bodyguard carries a massive sword that is threatening to the white hero Fairbanks. The fetishization of this black male menace is both life-threatening (the character is attempting to break into the room of a princess) and sexual (the black guard controls the entrance to the same bedroom). The oversize sword is the embodiment of a phallic symbol in the muscle-bound protector. He is both a sexual and a physical threat. Sexuality is the most salient mark of Otherness.[34]

Yet in films in which black men portray African-American characters they are almost always fully clothed—usually in the uniform of a butler, servant, or porter. The sexuality of these men is controlled by a dominant white society; therefore, they are fully clothed with the racial markings of a black man and the economic uniform of a low-paid service worker. Certainly, many African-American male sharecroppers and farmers in the hot Delta worked without a shirt but this was never displayed. It was too close to home. The visual representation of the hypermasculine, oversexed black man would rarely be portrayed in films with African-American male characters. The black man as "Negro beast"—violent, sex-obsessed, irresponsible, and stupid—was too dangerous to envision in a migratory and racially mixed society. This stereotype was transferred to the wilds of Africa or to exotic imaginary locales where the phantasia of black male sexuality could be played out safely.[35]

Edward Said quite accurately has argued:

> It is recognizably true that the chain of stereotypical signification is curiously mixed and split, polymorphous and perverse, an articulation of multiple belief. The Black is both savage [cannibal] and yet the most obedient and dignified of servants [the bearer of food]; he is the embodiment of rampant sexuality and yet innocent as a child; he is mystical, primitive, simple-minded and yet the most worldly and accomplished liar and manipulator of social forces.[36]

Despite the limiting framework of black masculinity that the dominant cinema portrayed, some mainstream studio filmmakers of the 1920s pushed the boundaries of "acceptable" roles of black actors. Two films that stand out for their humanistic, inclusive approach to African-American men include *Beggars of Life* (1928) and *Old Ironsides* (1923).

Beggars of Life was an adult drama of a sexually harassed teenage girl and a male transient. The film explored the lives of those on the bottom rung of

American society. As "The Girl" and "The Boy" flee from the law they encounter a hobo encampment in the woods. Included in this group of men is one African American—Mose (Edgar Washington Blue). Throughout the film, Mose plays nursemaid to one of his fellow white transients. Although this may be interpreted as another servile role, the compassion and friendship between Mose and his sick friend is apparent. They define each other in racialized terms. "Lay still, white boy, you gonna be OK," Mose says to the patient. As the black hobo goes foraging for food, the invalid white man grows fearful as he realizes that death is near. In one of the most poignant scenes in American silent film, the dying man reaches his hands out and moans, "Hey Black Man, Where's your hand? I'm afraid." The man dies alone.

In *Old Ironsides,* former boxer George Godfrey plays "The Cook" of a late-eighteenth-century sailing frigate. Although he is engaged in a classic black profession, Godfrey asserts his masculinity and participates as an equal in a way that was unparalleled in contemporary films. The Cook has character traits that are inherent in other stereotyped black cinematic portrayals such as speaking in dialect and being superstitious but he shines when the real action of the picture begins.

Four shipmates are captured by Barbary pirates and forced to work in a North African prison. Chains link the four men together. The Cook is the instigator of the plan to break them out of prison. He first battles the pirates and keeps the group cohesive. When they are stranded in a rowboat in the middle of the ocean without fresh water, it is the Cook who keeps spirits up.

Both African Americans and Euro-Americans worked outside the studio system to produce films specifically for African-American audiences throughout the silent period. All-black production companies were discussed in Chapters 5 and 6. But varying degrees of collaboration took place between Euro-Americans and African Americans in jointly producing films in independent studios not wholly owned or controlled by African Americans. The resulting cinematic product of these joint efforts ran the gamut of political and racial sensibilities. Some films were strong indictments of racism in American society whereas others were critiques of African-American color consciousness. Some were black achievement films, others were blatantly racist productions that even mainstream studios would be afraid to produce for fear of racial repercussions.

Such independent filmmaking leads to critical theoretical problems when attempting to define a black cinematic epistemology. In traditional film criticism, "black film" has been defined as movies that have a significant number of black characters.[37] Mark A. Reid defines black independent film as "a film which focuses on the black community and is written, directed, produced, and distributed by individuals who have some ancestral link to black Africa."[38] Gladstone Yearwood argues that "black cinema must be based on a demythification and demystification of institutionalized cinema."[39] Reid, therefore, would define black independent film by who produces the cinematic product, regardless of its content, whereas Yearwood would focus on the content of the film and not the racial makeup of the filmmaker.

With these contradictory definitions, can the white-owned and -financed film companies of the late 1910s and the 1920s be considered creators of black independent cinema? Were they critical in developing African-American portrayals that redefined masculinity in a counterhegemonic fashion? Were white independent filmmakers also using the popular medium of film to redefine black manhood? The apparent answer is—it depends. Some white-owned movie companies were instrumental in delivering portrayals of black masculinity that countered the stereotypical images in the films of the major studios. Included in this group would be Fife Productions, Reol Productions, the Norman Film Manufacturing Company, North State Film Corporation, Southern Motion Picture Corporation, Democracy Film Corporation, Dunbar Film Corporation, and the Colored Players Film Corporation. Companies that delivered blatantly racist or stereotypical productions included the Ebony Film Corporation, Historical Feature Films, and the Harris Dickson Film Company.[40] The purveyors of racist imagery will be discussed first.

Historical Feature Films / Ebony Film Corporation

There was a strong connection between Historical Feature Films and Ebony Film Corporation. Historical Feature Films was formed in 1915 and produced four films—*A Natural Born Shooter* (1915), *Money Talks in Darktown* (1915), *Aladdin Jones* (1915), and *Two Knights of Vaudeville* (1916). The four films were bought by the Ebony Company before they were released. They were subsequently billed as Ebony Comedies.[41]

Aladdin Jones (1915) depicts a henpecked husband and his overbearing wife. The film is a strong representation of the black matriarchal household. *Aladdin Jones* presented its pivotal African-American male character, Jonesy, as "dusky," "shiftless," and a drunkard. In a long dream sequence the viewer sees Jonesy's fantasies, which include beer, money, a tantalizing woman, and a "shack to sleep in."[42]

Money Talks in Darktown (1915) claimed that black romantic love was financially oriented. The film argues that African-American women are attracted only to light-skinned men or sugar daddies. One potential suitor uses skin bleacher and hair straightener to change his appearance for the woman he loves. It so destroys his looks that he becomes a freak in a sideshow. It does not matter to his girlfriend Flossie, who argues, "it's the color of his money that talks." The film implies that African-American women are superficial and money-grubbing, only after men who are good-looking or financially secure. Romantic love is never implied.[43]

Two Knights of Vaudeville (1916) establishes that African-American men are illiterate, uncouth, and unrestrained. The irony of the film is that Eubie Blake and Noble Sissle, two of the preeminent figures of black Broadway, starred in the production. The co-opting or active participation of African-American men in their own denigration is a topic that needs to be further explored. Perhaps these popular performers believed that this film would be their entrée into bigger and better things in film. Maybe their vaudevillian roots made them simply accept the ridicule of the black man.[44]

The Ebony Film Corporation's purchase and release of these films was a public relations disaster. One such example concerned the Phoenix Theater in Chicago. Manager Al Gaines booked *A Natural Born Shooter* for an exhibition in May 1917, not realizing that it was "one of the low degrading comedies which was made two years ago."[45] The film was immediately canceled. The *Chicago Defender* went on the attack against the company, claiming that "at no time has the Defender been asleep on this comedy proposition; the exploitation of films which exhibited the depraved ideas which a certain set of cheap scenario writers have regarding the moral nature of our people will not go unchallenged."[46] The *Defender* made sure that its readers knew that a white man contacted Gaines about booking the film and that "the sooner that these detractors discover that the Defender is in the fight against their rotten stuff the better."[47]

Because black theater owners and audiences did not realize that the four Historical Feature Films were not original Ebony Productions, they assumed that this was the type of product the company would regularly release. A boycott of Ebony films eventually forced the company to go out of business in 1919.[48]

The Ebony Film Corporation had been formed in 1917 with an all-white management staff with one exception—L. J. Pollard, an African-American director. The company produced twenty-one two-reel black-cast comedies with a stock company of forty African-American actors. Ebony comedies were different from many of the other all-black independent films developed by white sources of capital in that they were booked in both black and white theaters. Black comedies were accepted in white theaters but all-black dramas were not. The association of the African-American man with laughter was a cinematic theme that would continue well to the end of the century. An advertisement in *Motion Picture World* proclaimed, "Colored people are funny. If colored people weren't funny, there would be no plantation melodies, no banjoes, no cake walk, no buck and wing dance, no minstrel show and no black-face vaudeville."[49]

Henry Sampson in *Blacks in Black and White* argues that the Ebony Company was destroyed because of the release of the Historical Feature Film's body of work. He claims Ebony Comedies "were free of racial stereotypes."[50] The reality was that Ebony's films were as racially insulting to African Americans as the Historical Feature Films.

A Reckless Rover (1918) managed to insult both African-American and Chinese-American men. The opening title shows a cartoon pictorial of an ape-like African-American man on his knees, stealing clothes from a Chinese laundry. A highly caricatured Chinese man is ready to hit him in the rear with a hot iron. Both men are in blackface and have big bug eyes. The opening title claims that "compared to Rastus Jones, a South American sloth is a human dynamo of energy." The film dissolves to Rastus, a middle-aged African-American man in bed. A landlady comes into his apartment and asks, "Where's my last 18 weeks board money?" Rastus simply turns over and goes back to sleep. She proceeds to get a black policeman. Through a series of slapstick antics, the policeman attempts to break into the apartment. Rastus tries to keep the cop out, pleading, "Can't you let a guy sleep?" The title cards used in the film include a caricature of Rastus looking exactly like a primate.[51]

Rastus's character traits include laziness, thievery, lying, sexual harassment, and drug use. Although the African-American policeman may be considered an alternative portrayal of black masculinity, he is pictured as a bumbling fool.

The major African-American character in *Spying the Spy* (1918) is Sambo Sam. Made in the heat of World War I, the film ridicules African-American participation in defense of their country. Sambo Sam imagines he is a top-notch spy and wants to infiltrate German espionage activities. He attempts to infiltrate a supposed spy ring, which is really a black fraternal lodge. He becomes a victim of their elaborate initiation rite, only to display typical cinematic attributes of African-American masculinity—fear and terror.[52]

The Comeback of Barnacle Bill (1918) contrasts two portrayals of African-American manhood—Sam, a bumbling hayseed, and Hector, a well-educated, urbane golf enthusiast. Sam eventually gets the girl because he is able to save her father from a foreclosure on his farm.[53]

Reviews of Ebony comedies confirm the lowbrow humor of the films and their attempts to marginalize African-American manhood. One critic argued that "the comedies depict without affection the happy-go-lucky characteristics of the colored race."[54] Another reviewer claimed that the films were "light and inconsequential to fit the mood of some who do not want to think [African-American audiences]."[55] He later described African-American moviegoers as "the rougher audience."[56]

The African-American community protested loudly against Ebony comedies. Tony Langston, entertainment editor of the *Chicago Defender*, was among those who fought back. He proclaimed: "The moving picture business can no longer be considered in its infancy and the policies of the modern houses should not be subjected to the humiliating experience of seeing things which lower the Race in the estimation of its own people as well as in the eyes of whatever members of the 'other' race who may happen to be in attendance."[57]

A female reader of the *Defender* also protested the content of Ebony films: "I consider it my duty, as a member of the respectable class of theatre patrons, to protest against a certain class of pictures which have been and are being shown at the theatres in this district. I refer to the . . . Ebony Film Company . . . which make an exaggerated display of the disgraceful action of the lowest element of the race. It was with abject humiliation that myself and many of my friends sat through the scenes of degradation on the screen."[58]

African Americans did help produce these negative images. The African-American community also protested and boycotted these films because they were slanderous. Over two-thirds of the black actors used in Ebony comedies were men. This meant that the majority of the derogatory, humiliating portrayals on the screen were gendered, slanting toward African-American men. The construction of black masculinity through the cinema involved black production and black critical reception. African Americans protested such films through economic and journalistic means.

Harris Dickson Company

A similar critical response took place when the Harris Dickson Company produced *The Custard Nine* (1921). The film was adapted from a series of stories that appeared in the *Saturday Evening Post* by Harris Dickson, a white southerner. Dickson, a self-acknowledged "expert" on the southern Negro, wrote stories that were heavy in dialect and incendiary toward African-American men. *The Custard Nine* received such negative press in the black media that its exhibition was limited to white southern theaters. Lester Walton, a columnist in the *New York Age,* wrote, "The trouble with Mr. Dickson is that he fails to take us seriously. He looks upon all of us out of humorous eyes. He seems utterly unconscious of the fact that there are thousands of us who possess dignity, education and refinement. We, too, have in our race planters, lawyers, doctors and soldiers [all traditional male professions] as he says his people have been for many generations."[59]

A number of white-owned independent film companies challenged these independent companies' and mainstream studios' portrayals of African-American masculinity. The companies will be addressed individually in the approximate chronological order in which they began manufacturing films. Their entire body of work will be reviewed to analyze what messages regarding African-American manhood each company produced. Common themes will emerge in the companies' repertoires; these themes will address issues for both the African-American and the Euro-American communities.

Southern Motion Picture Company

The Southern Motion Picture Company is an example of many film companies that produced only one film between 1914 and 1929. Their only feature, *When True Love Wins* (1915), offers some revealing commentary on the gendering of race pictures and the cooperation of African Americans and Euro-Americans in making such films.

When True Love Wins was written by Isaac Fisher, an African-American essayist from Tuskegee Institute. He was approached by D. B. Griswood, the white manager of the company, to write a screenplay showing "the better side of the race."[60] Griswood explained, "I am very proud of the reception accorded our play, but it only verifies our belief in the race pride of our colored people. I have long since been convinced that the better class of the colored people would soon get tired of always seeing their race shown on the screen either in a scrap or in a crap game."[61] Issues of class and race were critical in the production of the film. Griswood was aware of the African-American community's growing frustration regarding derogatory cinematic depictions of their race. In attempting to appeal to the "better class" of African Americans, he created a bourgeois production, similar in theme and intent to the productions of the Lincoln Motion Picture Company, an all-black firm.

The film's plot is "woven around the love affairs of Thelma Dayton."[62] She is interested in three young men, each of whom has a "hidden strength" that appeals to her. On the surface, it appears as if the protagonist of the film is female. But according to a reviewer of *When True Love Wins*, the film focused on "the hero who has to choose between the opportunity to win Thelma and do his duty for his country."[63] This romantic drama makes the hero choose between patriotism and romance. The hero finds he can have it all; his dedication to his country and willingness to take up arms to defend it makes him irresistible to Thelma. The film can be examined from two perspectives. Either *When True Love Wins* demonstrates that patriotism is a major virtue of the middle-class African-American community or it can be interpreted that a white-owned motion picture company used its cinematic skills to convince African-American men to enlist in the military during the Mexican crisis. Being a racially cooperative effort, it is debatable which proposition is true, regarding who "controlled" the final product.

Quality Amusement Company / Reol Productions

Robert Levy, an important Jewish-American figure in African-American entertainment, was a key figure in the formation of two independent motion picture companies. He began his career as general manager of the Quality Amusement Company, which operated the Lafayette Players, the most respected African-American dramatic stock company in the nation. The Quality Amusement Company produced one film, *Eyes of Youth* (1920), that had a story line almost identical to that of *When True Love Wins*. In the film, an African-American woman (Abbie Mitchell) has to choose between several suitors. A medium tells her of her eventual future with each of the possible choices. A comparative analysis of African-American masculinity was once again the major theme of a film.[64]

In 1920, Levy formed Reol Productions, which made ten films between 1920 and 1924. As in his feature *Eyes of Youth*, Levy depended on actors and actresses in the Lafayette Players to be the talent pool of his films. Levy is an example of how difficult it is to understand the motivation of white Americans involved in the production of all-black feature films. Levy advertised regularly in major black newspapers, informing theater owners and managers that he would provide them with a "regular monthly release of super-features."[65] One of the major complaints of owners of all-black houses was the irregular distribution of all-black productions. But in prominent boldface letters, Levy also announced twice in the same ad, "WE HAVE NO

SHARES TO SELL."⁶⁶ Was this ad to convince theater owners that Reol Productions was not a fly-by-night operation like dozens of film companies that had stolen money from African-American investors? Or was it a sign that Levy's motivation was strictly economic; that he had no intention in sharing profits with the African-American community?⁶⁷

The Burden of Race (1921) featured the star of many Micheaux productions, Lawrence Chenault. The film was thematically similar to *The Homesteader* or a number of other Micheaux features in which an African-American male character is in love with a white female. The all-American hero of the film was educated at a university where he "excelled both in academic achievement and as an athlete."⁶⁸ At college he falls in love with a white woman. There was "no hope of love's fruition" but she was his "inspiration." He "stood at the pinnacle of success and fame" but between them was a "mighty chasm."⁶⁹ Micheaux's films consistently concluded that such a romantic entanglement was absolutely impossible, yet *The Burden of Race* toyed with the theme of "race pride vs. love."⁷⁰ An advertisement for the film announced, "It's not creed or color that matters—it's the man that counts."⁷¹ This was a very daring attitude for a 1921 feature film. Miscegenation was outlawed in many states and black romantic or sexual desire for a white woman could lead to lynching.

The Spirit of the Gods (1921) was one of Reol's most publicized features. The screenplay was an adaptation of a story by Paul Laurence Dunbar, considered one of the finest African-American writers. The Reol Corporation prominently featured the film's connections with Dunbar, showing a picture of him, rather than any of the stars in the film, and calling the author "the Shakespeare of the Race."⁷²

The film attempted to deal with some realistic features of contemporary African-American life. The *California Eagle* argued that the film "showed the relationship between the two Races from a southern viewpoint."⁷³ This viewpoint was an indication of two contemporary features of African-American life—the Great Migration and the unlawful imprisonment of innocent African-American men. The film involved an African-American man who is innocently imprisoned in Virginia for a crime he did not commit. Rather than stay in the South, his family moves to New York City, "that vast desert of humanity," the center of "that great monsoon of human struggle."⁷⁴ His close family is torn apart by the move. The son becomes involved in underworld activity, the daughter sings in a cabaret/brothel, and the wife, who considers her husband's imprisonment a divorce, is ready to marry another man who simply wants to steal her money.⁷⁵ The family is eventually reunited but only after a powerful indictment of the evils of the big city and a call for the protection of the patriarchal nuclear family. The film reversed the common cinematic ridicule of southern African-American life. Instead, the film implies that northern migration is only destructive to the black family.

Two Reol features, *Easy Money* (1921) and *Secret Sorrow* (1921) construct a binary formula of African-American male identity. *Easy Money* involves a romantic triangle: A woman is pursued by a wealthy admirer and a poor man. The poor man ends up being the virtuous one, exposing the motives of the wealthy man by the end of the film.[76] *Secret Sorrow* concerned two fatherless sons. One son, Arthur, is adopted by a prominent doctor and ends up being assistant district attorney of New York (an improbable job for a black man in 1921). The other brother, Joe, becomes a gangster and is eventually indicted on a murder charge. Conveniently, the plot has Arthur prosecuting Joe on the murder rap, neither one aware they are siblings. The film concludes with a reunited family. *Secret Sorrow* demonstrates the importance of environment in shaping the destiny of a man.

Like *Secret Sorrow,* a number of the Reol productions placed African-American men in career positions that were usually not available in the real world.[77] *The Call of His People* (1922) focused on Nelson Holmes, general manager of the Brazilian-American Coffee Syndicate. A "passing" picture, Holmes's true racial identity, that of African American, is revealed to all at the end of the picture. Perhaps serving as wish fulfillment, the company owner tells Holmes that it is the man and not the color that counts for the job. *The Schemers* (1922) has as its protagonist a brilliant but struggling young chemist. In *Spitfire* (1922), a young bourgeois African-American novelist is told by his publicist that he has not lived among the lowly people of his race, so his writing lacks authenticity. In order to gain the "flavor" of the lower class, he goes to live among poor rural folk.

Reol films were certainly remarkable for their positive portrayals of African-American men shown in a wide variety of professions. Performed by members of the Lafayette Players, the films included the finest African-American theatrical artists of the period. Levy geared his achievement stories and romances to the black bourgeoisie. Yet by 1924 he was forced to abandon the company. He explained to the *Baltimore Afro-American,* "Negro amusement buyers are fickle and possessed of a peculiar psychic complex, and they prefer to patronize the galleries of white theaters rather than theirs."[78] This highly enlightening commentary helps explain Levy's double intention in making all-black films. He wanted to provide uplifting melodramas to encourage African Americans but he was also after economic profit. His commentary also reveals a great deal about African-American spectatorship. African Americans may have been attracted to white movie houses because they provided a higher quality product or a more comfortable or appealing environment. Like the film producers of many all-black features, Levy learned that an all-black cast would not guarantee a packed African-American theater. African-American identification with all-white pictures was a crucial economic factor in the world of all-black theaters and a topic that needs to be more fully explored.

Fife Productions

Fife Productions of Chicago produced only one film. Their feature *A Modern Cain* (1921) demonstrated that producers were willing to mine biblical stories, familiar to African-American audiences, for cinematic material. Billed as a "Sensationalistic Melodrama Full of Gripping Situations," the film presented a struggle of "Brother vs. Brother in a Fight for Right, Fame and Fortune and [of course] the Love of a Trusting, Faithful Woman."[79] Like all good melodramas, the bad brother dies in the end and the good brother gets the girl. *A Modern Cain,* like so many other all-black features, delivered a binary construction of African-American manhood. One has to question whether the repeated use of the theme among white producers of all-black pictures was simply a variation of the racist Bad Nigger/Good Negro dichotomy of African-American manhood or a simple morality tale.

North State Film Corporation

The North State Film Corporation focused their attention on the racial and social responsibilities of the African-American man more than any other white independent film company of the early 1920s. Their first feature, *A Giant of His Race* (1921), traced the African ancestry of black Americans. The film begins in Africa, tracing the ancestral slave roots of Munga, a young man. He works his way through medical school and "decides to devote his life to the uplift of his people."[80] An epidemic known as "yellow fever" sweeps through the African-American community and Munga dedicates his life to finding a cure for the killer disease. In the end, Munga not only finds an antidote but he is rewarded with a good woman and financial gain. *The Devil's Match* (1923), another North State feature, finds an African-American man facing an insurmountable obstacle. A young minister attempts to build a church in a dangerous section of town run by a mobster known as "The Devil." *His Great Chance* (1922) dwells on children's duty to their parents. Two brothers succeed as professional dancers and forget their rural parents. In the end, they recognize their mistakes and join their folks at Christmas.

North State features received favorable reviews from the African-American community. Leigh Whipper, an African-American director and writer for *Billboard,* claimed that "after seeing the production, I can say it *[A Giant of His Race]* is the best Negro picture I have witnessed."[81] Regarding *His Great Chance,* he said, "The cast is the best-balanced one I have seen in any production."[82] North State features focused on the responsibility of African-American men and the difficulty of overcoming immoral influences.

Norman Film Manufacturing Company

The Norman Film Manufacturing Company was one of the most prolific of the white independent companies.[83] It continued production for a much longer period of time than most firms—from 1916 to 1928. Like many other independent film companies, the Norman Company was regionally based outside of the studio system of Hollywood—in northern Florida. The entrepreneur behind the company was Richard Edward Norman, who entered film production in 1912. His early films were made on demand; churches, schools, and other organizations would have him film important events. In 1916, he made his first commercial feature film with an all-white cast. In 1919, he remade the same film, *The Green Eyed Monster,* with an all-black cast. It was not successful, so he re-edited the film, retitled it *The Love Bug,* and found himself with a hit.[84] From this point on, Norman focused on producing all-black pictures. *The Green Eyed Monster/Love Bug* concerned a romantic triangle and economic rivalry between the two leading men. But Norman, more racially sensitive than most white producers, stressed that "the characterizations in this spectacular production were enacted by colored people from many walks of life. The lawyer, doctor, banker, and finished actor and actresses portray this story in a subtle way which suggests the advancements of the colored race along educational and financial lines."[85] Norman stressed not only the diversity of African-American men but also the progress of the race. The majority of Norman's all-black films were action-adventures that proved to be profitable at the box office. After the success of *The Love Bug,* a number of prominent African-American actors and actresses inquired about being in his next feature.[86]

The Bulldogger (1921) was one of the first all-black Westerns. It starred

Anita Bush, a well-known dramatic actress, and Bill Pickett, a black rodeo star and cowboy. The film was shot in Boley, Oklahoma, an all-black town. A number of local black cowboys were used as extras. The advertising for the film stressed the "death-defying feats of Courage and Skill" of the Bulldogger, Pickett.[87] His championship rodeo and horsemanship skills were the features of the film. The Norman press book claimed, "It proves conclusively that the black cowboy is capable of doing anything the white cowboy does."[88]

Norman shot enough footage at Boley that he was able to create a second film, *The Crimson Skull* (1921). The film starred Bush and the dean of contemporary black film actors, Lawrence Chenault. Norman also shot extra footage of Pickett's bulldogging skills to round out the film. Bush's correspondence with Norman regarding the possible hiring of Chenault as a leading man reveals the qualifications for black screen heroes in the 1920s. In recommending Chenault, she claimed, "He is light, and nice looking."[89] As Gloria J. Gibson-Hudson reports in *Black Film Review*, there were numerous mentions of Chenault's light complexion, reflecting the color-conscious casting of contemporary filmmakers.[90]

The appeal of *The Crimson Skull* and *The Bulldogger*, which were released almost simultaneously, was in their portrayal of African-American cowboys. Many urban and southern African Americans had never heard of such a phenomenon and the black press played up the angle. The films were released during a period in which Westerns were the most popular genre among male audiences, so a racialized portrayal only added to the appeal for black moviegoers. The *Cleveland Gazette* claimed, "No expense was spared to make it a typical picture of the old swash-buckling west, with the added attraction of a cast composed of our actors and actresses who could ride and shoot in true western style. . . . Real Afro-American cowboys were secured in Boley. . . . Their dare-devil riding and handling of the six-gun proved them excelled by none."[91] J. A. Jackson announced in *Billboard*, "A feature of the production will be the number of bona fide Negro cowboys who will appear in the picture. Many of our race, and even many of the general public, are unaware that some of the most proficient riders and ropers of the range are colored men."[92]

Norman's *Regeneration* (1923) was a variation on the Robinson Crusoe tale in which Norman continued his color-coded good/bad casting scheme. Light-skinned actors Stella Mayo and Cary Brooks played the protagonists. The villain was played by Alfred Norcom, a dark-skinned actor. In several promotional posters, Hurley is poised over Mayo's half-naked body with a knife, not only indicating danger but possible rape. The dark-skinned beast was alive in Norman's films.[93]

The last surviving Norman film is *The Flying Ace* (1926) which focused on the aeronautic exploits of Captain Billy Stokes. Stokes was played by Lawrence Criner, one of the original Lafayette Players. Stokes is an all-American hero. He is a decorated World War I veteran, a pilot, and a detective in the Intelligence Division of a major railroad. In the course of the film he breaks up an elaborate attempt to swindle thousands of dollars from his former railroad employer. *The Flying Ace* is interesting for a number of reasons. African-American men perform in a number of professions—general manager of a railroad, paymaster, constable, dentist, aviator, and bootlegger. But in the film, the social prominence of a profession does not correlate with the inability to commit a crime. In the film, the prominent African-American men are guilty of criminal behavior.[94]

The film was also remarkably condescending to women. Ruth, the female lead, is a helpless nitwit. She is always checking her makeup and complaining about her lack of intelligence. After being shown the interior of an airplane she gasps, "Gracious if it's as complicated as all that I fear I can never learn to fly."

Norman's last all-black feature, *Black Gold* (1928), reunited Lawrence Criner and Kathryn Boyd, stars of *The Flying Ace*. Filmed in Tatums, another all-black Oklahoma town, the story was set in oil country. Richard Norman guaranteed, "*Black Gold* is authentic from every chilling detail, and aside from its thrills, is a true portrayal of the Romance of Oil towards which no one can point a finger of criticism."[95] The film concerned Matt Ashton, a ranch owner, who sinks all of his money into oil drilling, only to be taken advantage of by a large company.

Norman Film Corporation's pictures were standard action-adventure fare. Each starred a light-skinned man who was respected and reputable and who faced a formidable challenge. Set in locations that were exotic for African-American audiences (the Wild West, the South Pacific, in the air), the film showed heroics of African-American men and gave audiences a racial role model they could cheer for. Built into the Norman formula was the helplessness of the African-American woman; only the strong black warrior could ever save her. Also included in the Norman standard was the dark-skinned villain, conforming to the color-coded assessment of African-American character traits.

Democracy Film Corporation

The Democracy Film Corporation originated in Los Angeles, California, in 1919. It was white-owned but heavily publicized in the black press. The company focused on current social and racial problems, placed in narrative form. The company's first release, *Injustice* (1919), claimed to be an answer to *The Birth of a Nation*. Both a passing picture and a commentary on African-American participation and heroism in World War I, the film premiered shortly after the Chicago Race Riot. The promotional literature for the film claimed:

> This picture INJUSTICE will be endorsed by leading People of all races and will be shown all over the CIVILIZED WORLD. We will be a direct answer to The WORLD that the COLORED AMERICANS as a UNIT WAS THE MOST LOYAL of all participants in The WORLD'S war for RIGHT and JUSTICE, and still is the only RACE that must suffer INJUSTICE. THINK what this will mean to the CHILDHOOD of our Race.
> *GET UP LIKE A MAN . . . AND DO YOUR DUTY*[96]

The film unnerved members of the white community. A white journalist reported that the film was a "frank appeal to the emotions of colored folk to revolt against the social handicaps which have been imposed upon them. Surely no good purpose can be served by such an appeal at the present time."[97] George P. Johnson of the Lincoln Motion Picture Company did not have a problem with the content of *Injustice* but with the business practices of the Democracy Company. He claimed, "It is a reproduction of the same old story of a white man making a fool of a bunch of Negroes who thought they were wise on a business that they knew absolutely nothing about."[98] Johnson was commenting on the dozens of stock-swindling schemes that then existed in the African-American community. So-called motion picture companies tried to raise money for film production, but would never produce a single feature.

The company's second film (reorganized under the name Loyalty Film Company) was *Reformation* (1920). The film's central figure was Carter Spencer, a wild, dissolute man who spends most of his time flirting, gambling, and drinking despite the fact that his mother is a devout church member. He falls in love with Clarice Penlow, who will not marry Carter because of his wild ways. When Prohibition goes into effect, she influences Spencer to apply for a position as a secret service agent to help enforce the ban on alcohol. His love for Clarice makes him change his ways.[99]

Colored Players Film Corporation

The Colored Players Film Corporation, located in Philadelphia, produced a number of high-quality films with well-respected actors. The company produced four films during 1926–1927. The film was led by David Starkman, a Philadelphia businessman with interests in theaters that served a black clientele. His business partner, Sherman H. Dudley, was an African-American vaudevillian comedian and was listed as producer of a number of the Colored Player films, even though the financial interests in the corporation strictly belonged to Starkman.[100] Starkman's daughter's commentary on her father's decision to make all-black films summarized what I argue was the basic motivation of many of the white producers. She claims, "My father was a crusader. Nobody played the black people as heroes and heroines. This fit in with his ethics. He felt that black people shouldn't be stepped on, that at the same time he was making money, he could glorify their position."[101] Starkman, therefore, was concerned with racial justice but also was willing to profit from filling the need for better films in the African-American community. Thomas Cripps has argued that Starkman attempted to appeal to middle-class black audiences with his high-quality productions. His attempt to reach this audience is similar to earlier attempts by theater owners between 1910 and 1920 to appeal to middle-class white audiences.[102]

The four features produced by the Colored Players Film Corporation were social dramas. Melodramatic in tone, the films attempted to reflect real problems in African-American lives. Contemporary critics argue that the melodramatic form translates ideological dilemmas into private predicaments.[103] These "dilemmas" often translated into competing interests within the African-American community or social problems that African Americans faced. Only in the features of Micheaux does the larger, more omnipresent dilemma of white racism play in the melodramatic narrative. But within the subtext of the Colored Players films, the African-American characters are haunted by economic, social, and political barriers placed on them by white society as well as African-American society.

All three of the Colored Players features of 1927 deal with African-American male redemption. In *Children of Fate*, Ross Hampton cannot escape his addiction to gambling. In *A Prince of His Race*, Tom Bueford, a "member of a good family," is imprisoned for five years for manslaughter. His association with evil influences brings him down. This imprisonment disgraces him and his family but it becomes life-shattering when Tom's mother lies on her deathbed and her son cannot comfort her. Luckily, he gets a twenty-four-hour leave of absence to be at her bedside. The moral of the film is the unforeseen consequences that a man may suffer when spending time with the wrong crowd of people. The disgrace of a jail term and the loss of a sweetheart are predicaments Tom must face because of his poor judgment. *Ten Nights in a Bar Room* was based on a classical theatrical tale of the evils of alcoholism. Starkman heightened the commercial appeal of these last two features by hiring well-known theatrical artists and by increasing the budget of his films. *Ten Nights* featured Charles Gilpin, the world's most famous black theatrical actor (and alcoholic) and Lawrence Chenault, the most prolific black screen actor of his generation.[104] Gilpin played Joe Morgan, an alcoholic whose irresponsibility and addiction to drink are so strong that he compromises his family's future. He gets in a drunken fight with Simon Slade (Chenault), the landlord of half of the town, owner of the local saloon, and supplier of his booze. As the two men fight, Slade throws a glass at Joe but it misses him and hits his daughter Mary, who has come to the saloon to beg her father to come home. Mary eventually dies. When the local community hears of the girl's death, they reach the breaking point. They burn down Slade's saloon and chase him to his accidental death. In the conclusion of the film, Morgan is a changed man. The final title reads, "Little Mary's death awakes in Joe Morgan *the manhood* that had so long been submerged beneath Simon Slade's rum."[105]

The filming of *Ten Nights in a Bar Room* was a wise commercial move by Starkman. Based on a widely known novel and theatrical production, the film was an early-twentieth-century standard, much like *Uncle Tom's Cabin*. But Starkman appealed to an African-American clientele that did not regularly patronize motion pictures—the African-American religious community. The film was billed as a "racial novelty . . . which carries a deep moral."[106] Tony Langston of the *Chicago Defender* proclaimed, "Churches are acclaiming the picture. . . . It appears they have agreed to forget their differences and to tell the people to go and see *Ten Nights*."[107]

Ten Nights in a Bar Room also delivered a powerful commentary during Prohibition. During a period in which illegal liquor sales could prove to be one of the most lucrative occupations open to African-American men, *Ten Nights* preached abstinence from contributing to "sin and misery of the world."[108] Simon Slade, the owner of the saloon, meets an untimely death. Harvey Green, a professional gambler and lieutenant of Slade's, dies in the burning saloon. The meaning of the fires of hell is apparent. A title reads: "The Lord works in mysterious ways, His wonders to perform." According to the film, one is not considered a true man unless one lives by the rules of

God. Joe Morgan cannot reclaim his manhood until he gives up alcohol and repents for the sin of neglecting his family. Satan's evil temptation fills Joe's drunken hallucinations. A true man is one who cares for his family and resists the evil ways of the world.

Like the other three Colored Players films, *The Scar of Shame* attempted to define contemporary African-American manhood and the attributes needed for survival. *The Scar of Shame* is considered a classic of silent black cinema, and a surviving print still exists. An in-depth analysis is available in the appendix.[109] The film begins with a lengthy "nature or nurture" opening title:

> Childhood training and companions often is the deciding factor in our early lives—it shapes our destinies and guides our ambition. If early in life, some knowing loving hand, lights the lamp of knowledge and with tender care keeps it burning, then our course will run true 'til the end of our useful time on this earth, but if that lamp should fail through lack of tender care, through lack of loving hands to feed its hungry flame—then will come sorrow and—SHAME!

Although this call for nurture and responsibility for children is apparent, the ambivalent stance of the film calls into question this very theme.

The Scar of Shame examines class differences in the African-American community. Louise, a poor, abused woman, is "saved" by Alvin, a talented bourgeois musician. He rescues her from her stepfather's beatings but is condescending toward her because of her lower-class status. Alvin is afraid to introduce her to his mother. He explains to Louise, "Caste is one of those things Mother is very determined about—and you—don't belong to our set." Both Louise and Alvin become victims of the caste system. Louise's rejection by her adopted family makes her stoop to a life of stealing. Alvin, the symbol of bourgeois responsibility, is abandoned by the wife he protects. But the film claims that Louise is doomed because of her lower-class status. *The Scar of Shame* argues that the African-American community is divided by class but it offers no solutions for bringing the race together. In fact, the upper class and lower elements both fragment the community even further with their selfish actions and behaviors.

The introduction of sound technology to film production in the late 1920s had profound consequences on the motion picture industry. Although many of the social changes within the studio system have been well documented by film historians, the impact of sound on depictions of racial Otherness has been given little attention. In fact, the history of technology in film and the history of the cinematic depictions of African Americans seem to be mutually exclusive categories within film studies. Jesse Rhines has argued that "since its inception, the Hollywood film industry has been greatly influenced by both external and internal structural change and so has the involvement of African Americans within it."[110]

The introduction of sound in films such as Warner Brothers' *Don Juan* (1927) and *The Jazz Singer* (1927) sent shock waves through the motion picture industry. Among those greatly affected were independent producers outside the studio system. Film scholar Alan Williams argues that "the coming of sound . . . reduced diversity and acted against those who would oppose the classical Hollywood cinema with alternatives of their own."[111] The transition of motion pictures from silent to sound had a stultifying effect on independent production of all-black features. Jane Gaines marks 1931 as the end of the silent era in race movies. This was the year in which Oscar Micheaux released *The Exile*.[112] Although 1927 may have been a transitional year for white studios in Hollywood, minority filmmakers did not make the transition to sound films until a later date. Neither independent African-American nor white producers could afford sound film productions. These producers, forever on the edge of bankruptcy, could not raise the capital for the huge financial investment necessary for the technical transition to sound. They also were encumbered because theaters needed to be rewired for sound. In the late 1920s, this was approximately a $20,000 investment for each theater.[113] Because of segregation, most all-black features were exhibited in theaters that were not first-run, or even second-run theaters; they were among the last to be rewired. African-American audiences flocked to theaters with sound film to hear the novelty, abandoning all-black features and the theaters that displayed them. It was impractical to make African-American films if there were no theaters in which they could be exhibited.

This proved to be disastrous for African-American men who wanted to continue to use the cinema as a means to redefine themselves and their race. During the late 1920s, as studios began to consolidate because of financial pressure and the transition to sound, there was a sharp decline in race pictures. The transition to sound was in the hands of the major studios, driving virtually every black and white independent producer of all-black pictures out of business. The major studios consolidated their control of distribution markets and forced many African-American producers into unequal partnerships.[114] Sound technology, therefore, all but killed off a significant form of black creative expression that had proliferated in the late 1910s and throughout the 1920s.[115]

The vast majority of depictions of African-American men in film from 1928 to 1933 were those of the dominant studio culture. This culture had typecast blacks for years. Early sound directors continued this trend by using both typecasting and typage when casting African Americans in film. Typecasting was the act of assigning an actor repeatedly to the same type of part. Typage depended on cultural stereotypes that emphasized the physical eccentricities (racial and otherwise) of actors. Typage was a critical tool that allowed a director to mold a performance. The mythology of racial representation in early sound film was based on the premise that film acting was basically realistic behavior. The shuffling, thievery, or laziness of an African-American male character, in the context of film acting, was simply behaving as an African American would in the "real" world.[116]

I do not accept the overly deterministic model in which the director or production team hegemonically makes meaning. The vococentric quality of sound that privileges the voice, highlighting and setting it off from other sounds, has the ability to go against the deterministic qualities of a director's paradigm.[117] Cultural forms of expression do not have single meanings. People make sense of these meanings in differing ways, according to the subcultural codes made available to them. There are multiple ways in which audiences make sense of images *and* the voices or sounds that accompany them.[118] In the late 1920s, film director Paul Fejos claimed, "The talking picture . . . will in its perfection accomplish the making of the audience a party to the dramatic conflict. . . . in the audible picture . . . there is no line of demarcation between the character and the audience."[119] The audience makes meaning through the visual and aural content that the production team delivers on the screen *and* through the speakers.

African Americans lost control over their ability to make their own pictures, but this does not mean they were absent from the screen. The novelty of sound created a rage for black depictions from the major studios but relegated African Americans almost exclusively to the realms of musicals and comedies. A February 1927 *Picturegoer* article entitled "Black Laughter" put it crudely: "There is something irresistibly contagious about the wide grin of the darkie. Perhaps it is a flash of white teeth against this ebony background which makes it so effective and evokes an immediate ensuing guffaw. Perhaps it is merely tradition associated with so many nigger minstrels of one's youth, but black faces and comedy usually go together on the screen."[120] The demand for the black voice on the screen came almost a decade after a similar demand for a black presence on Broadway and in musical theater.

From 1927 to 1929, a number of the major Hollywood studios produced black two-reelers featuring African-American musical performances that contained comedic overtones. These two-reelers featured the leading black stars of vaudeville, jazz, and the blues. Studio sponsorship of these all-black productions, coupled with the novelty of seeing famous performers actually singing and making music, helped to kill off the independent black silent feature.

The major studios' preoccupation, if not fascination, with African-American musicality demonstrates the profit motivation of the filmmaking establishment. The studios were willing to recognize the musical talents of new jazz artists like Duke Ellington, but only in heavily scripted, formalized two-reel shorts. The filmmakers were also all too willing to appeal to nostalgia for the old-time darkie—the contented happy slave or the sharecropping Negro who knew his place.[121]

Sound in films would prove to create a double-edged sword concerning studio control over African-American performers, though. And *control* was the word. A publicity release for the film *Hallelujah,* an all-black musical, argued, "The task of keeping the natural but undisciplined dramatic instinct of a race [African-American] under control was the most difficult problem encountered by [director] King Vidor."[122]

The major studios relegated African-American actors and actresses almost exclusively to musical or comedic roles in the early years of sound features. The experimental nature of sound and its financial risk forced studios to focus on productions they considered "safe." Like the old-time southern darkie, the white establishment's association of the African American with music or laughter was deeply ingrained in the white American conscience and seemed to be a sure bet to "sell." But by limiting African Americans to such genres, studio production heads were also introducing a potentially subversive element to African-American film presentation. This was the desire and ability to rise above an inferior or racially belittling script with expression, inflection, or nuance—through the voice. In silent films, African-American actors were limited by the material and by a range of voiceless expressions. Highly derogatory titling could sink an underplayed, sophisticated performance. The element of voice, in which African-American artists could speak and display their own emotional register, would serve as a means by which artists could break the confines of restrictive studio content.

Although African-American actors were initially restricted by genre, this newfound ability to claim one's own voice would be a remarkable tool in the construction of African-American masculinity through the next fifty years of film. One only has to consider the powerful vocal qualities of actors such as Sidney Poitier, Denzel Washington, or James Earl Jones to prove this point. The roots of this vocal and aural experiment lay in two of the earliest black sound features, *Hearts in Dixie* and *Hallelujah* (both 1929). These films included stereotypes and racially gendered behavior from the worst recesses of American racism. But both films also contained performances from African-American actors who were able to rise above the limited script and bring dignity to their performances. Twentieth Century Fox *(Hearts in Dixie)* and Metro-Goldwyn-Mayer *(Hallelujah)* each decided to invest millions of dollars in these all-black features.

Hearts in Dixie featured Clarence Muse as Nappus, an elderly African-American farmer. His daughter Chloe (Bernice Pilot) is married to Gummy (Stepin Fetchit) a shiftless, lazy coon character (this was the role that would launch Fetchit's career). They have two children, Chiquapin and Trailia. Chloe and Trailia become ill and instead of sending for a white doctor, a voodoo woman is brought in. Both mother and daughter die and Nappus eventually sells his farm, believing that his grandson Chiquapin must go north and become a doctor so that one day he could return and help his people.[123]

Fox purposefully focused its advertising campaign on the aural and racial features of the film. An advertisement in the 29 April 1929 *Motion Picture Herald* proclaimed: "HEAR THOSE HEARTS BEAT THE CADENCES OF THEIR RACE . . . among the levies and in the cotton fields . . . strumming banjos . . . chanting spirituals . . . where life is infused with an ageless melody throbbing with emotion—epic in its simplicity."[124]

The critical difference between the African-American press and white press reaction to the film was in the consideration of the two male leads. Fetchit was praised overwhelmingly by newspapermen of both races. A critic in the *Chicago Whip*, a black newspaper, claimed, "I . . . loved Stepin Fetchit's every appearance."[125] The *Chicago Defender* agreed: "As a comedian he is next to the late lamented and beloved Bert Williams."[126] White critics also heaped praise upon Fetchit. In *Opportunity*, critic Robert Benchley claimed, "I see no reason for even hesitating in saying that he is the best actor that talking pictures ever produced."[127] George Gerhard of the *New York Evening World* agreed, "Stepin Fetchit—this boy is great. He is the funniest thing imaginable, his dialect recording perfect via movietone."[128] The white critical reaction to Fetchit was so positive that the Fox Corporation began giving the comedian star billing.[129] The identification of Fetchit's shuffling, lazy nature and his slow, uneducated drawl with that of the stereotypical Negro was overwhelmingly present in the words of such white reviewers.

The white critical press all but ignored Clarence Muse's performance and characterization. The African-American press did not. Muse was praised by most black critics for his upright, dignified performance as a poor man willing to sacrifice everything for his family and his people. African-American journalists singled out the one positive African-American male portrayal.[130] Muse's background as one of the Lafayette Players, the premiere New York–based African-American acting troupe, was focused on by a number of black reviewers. The *Chicago Defender* argued, "Muse can act. We know that . . . he made good."[131]

The response of the average African-American spectator is unfortunately not documented. But Muse's performance as the aging grandfather who loved and sacrificed for his grandson and his people has gained more respect as the years have passed. Muse's role was more of a breakthrough than Fetchit's in the advancement of African-American masculinity in cinema. In 1971, Miles Kreuger stated, "Clarence Muse brings to the principal role an aura of wise, quiet strength and dignity that often carries the story through passages that might otherwise seem condescending."[132] Among the more affecting scenes that demonstrated Muse's skill as an actor was one in which he sang the lullaby "Mammy's Gone" as he gently rocked his grandson and granddaughter to sleep. Such a performance would have been impossible without Clarence Muse's vocal talents.

Six months after the release of *Hearts in Dixie* came MGM's *Hallelujah,* a highly publicized film directed by King Vidor. The film focused on the relationship between Zeke (Daniel L. Haynes) and Chick (Nina Mae McKinney). The title of the film is presented over the beating of voodoo drums, suspiciously evoking the "primitivism" of the subject matter. Dramatically, the film is divided into two sections. It begins in the cotton fields of the Delta South as Zeke explains to his Mammy, Pappy, and three young brothers what he will bring them once the cotton is brought to market. The first half of the film is filled with every racist cliché of the first thirty years of American filmmaking. References are made to the family's love of eating chicken, everyone is always dancing, the children are illegitimate, and Zeke, as an African-American man, is unable to control his sexual drive.

Zeke and his younger brother Spunk go to town to sell the family's cotton. An urban temptress, Chick, flirts with Zeke and lures him into a crap game with her partner in crime and lover, Hot Shot. Hot Shot, an overly dressed pompous rogue, cheats the country bumpkin with loaded dice. Realizing that he has left his family penniless, Zeke fights to get his money back. He grabs Hot Shot's gun and accidentally hits his brother, killing him.

Spunk's emotionally charged death scene changes the nature of the film from comic ridicule to a serious portrayal of rural southern black life. At a community mourning ceremony for his dead brother, Zeke undergoes a conversion. Now dedicated to God, his character transforms from a happy-go-lucky uneducated hayseed into an upright man with intensity and seriousness of purpose. The actor literally converts the previous racial clichés into an authentic person. He is no longer a type but a living entity. Daniel Haynes transforms the character of Zeke through posture and voice. He is upright, proud, and dignified. His voice is low and restrained yet powerful and confident. One critic commented, "The sudden illumination or conversion of Zeke the evangelist, following his prayers of agony after his 'sin' represents something more than an emotional storm; and every awakened soul that looks upon that scene recalls something of a vast change in its own nature, a change which takes place when an individual realizes his own weakness."[133]

Zeke begins preaching for a living. His faith is powerful enough to seemingly convert Chick. But the young woman, a symbol of the power of the devil, leads the young man down a path of death and destruction. It is only Chick's own demise and Zeke's subsequent imprisonment that finally saves him for good.

Daniel Haynes took a simple stereotype and gave a complex characterization of a southern African-American man who was torn between family and a temptress, between religious morality and sexual pleasure, between a good woman and a lascivious one. Haynes's ability to vocally and visually express the tension of Zeke's soul was nothing short of remarkable, particularly compared with the simplistic derivative portrayals of African-American masculinity in silent studio productions. Donald Bogle claims that Haynes "had a voice large enough to move an entire theater, and it added depth and texture to his performance."[134]

What makes his accomplishment even more impressive was the frequent displacement of Haynes's voice from his body. Part of the film was shot on a sound stage, but the majority of it was filmed on location in Tennessee and Arkansas. There was no portable studio equipment at the time, so the voices had to be dubbed after filming.[135]

Clarence Muse in *Hearts in Dixie* and Daniel Haynes in *Hallelujah* rose

Daniel Haynes, as Zeke in *Hallelujah,* is an example of an African-American actor who was able to "rise above the material." (Museum of Modern Art)

above the limited, often degrading characterizations they were given in the script. Vidor allowed the actors in *Hallelujah* a broader scope for character development than was previously available to black actors. The real credit for these characterizations has to be attributed to the actors. Rising above the material meant that actors could lend an air of sophistication and realism to their performances. Muse and Haynes embodied this new power. Through vocal characterization and nuance, African-American male actors were able to "rise above the material." They now held a powerful element of control in their possession; in silent film the voice was absent. Titling could transform a performance. Even though African-American actors were still restrained by the words of the screenwriters they now had the ability to add a quality to a film performance that was unavailable in silent film. Donald Bogle claims, "Although the film version was firmly controlled by Vidor, the director had the sense and sensibility to let actors do certain things their own way. Often the actors improvised."[136] Haynes realized the impact that *Hallelujah* would have on the public perception of African Americans. In an interview for a fan magazine during the shooting, he stated, "I think and hope this picture will do much for my people. . . . Our race is rich with talents that have gone unrecognized for centuries. This may be our opportunity to prove ourselves."[137]

A Foucault-like reading of this phenomenon illustrates that the binary system of white male/superior, black male/inferior, as established by studio-produced silent film and enmeshed in American society at large, was collapsing. The advent of voice gave African-American men a tool by which they were able to slowly unravel such oppositions. Thus, a *fixed* binary relationship of racialized gender patterns was never in place during the first thirty years of filmmaking, as evidenced by independent African-American film. Drawing on the theory of Michel Foucault, historically specific discursive relations exist within American film in relationship to the interplay between race and masculinity.[138] Examples of African-American performances that were able to expand the notion of black masculinity in the 1930s include Clarence Brooks in *Arrowsmith* (1931), Clinton Rosamond in *Golden Boy* (1939), and Paul Robeson in his numerous screen performances.

Changes in cinematic technology contributed to the mutable characteristics of cinematic control and experiment. Social meaning through film was produced not only by directors and screenwriters but also by actors. African-American spectators held the power to critically view films and challenge existing power relations. This became even more evident with the black critical reception to the talking pictures *Hearts in Dixie* and *Hallelujah*.

In a preview article on *Hearts in Dixie*, a *New York Times* columnist recognized this new relationship: "The cast of *Hearts in Dixie* even more than its directorial staff shows how the talking picture had produced opportunities for people to whom the whole matter of the cinema is an untrodden field."[139] Although the field was far from "untrodden," the production of independent black-cast films did dwindle in the 1930s and came to a halt in the late 1940s. African-American men, though, through the medium of talking pictures, were given a new device to redefine their manhood by controlling their voice and aspects of their performance.

CONCLUSION

This book has focused on racial imagery and representation through the cinematic medium. The trope of race has been integral to the organization of human thought in the modern world. Race has been a tool used to create a binary we/them construct in American society. In American society, the characteristics of a racial group are often defined by how other racial groups "lack" such characteristics. The very notion of race, therefore, is based on an exclusionary principle.

Race and gender are inextricably intertwined. The silent American cinema created black male and female "types" and white male and female "types." Race and gender have been used as a means of categorizing human beings in highly stereotypical ways. In silent mainstream studio productions (white-owned and -operated), African-American men did not function without the control and discipline of Euro-American men. These films argued that black men needed to be sexually controlled through limited social interaction with white women, forced to labor so they would not descend into their "natural" state of bestiality, and trained to sacrificially offer their lives for their white families. In the majority of all-black productions (with the notable exception of Oscar Micheaux's), African-American men and women lived in a segregated utopian society, apparently free from the domination and control of Euro-Americans.

What is critical about these cinematic racial and gender stereotypes is the assumption that individuals "embody" such characteristics. The majority of Euro-American film production teams assumed that African-American men were, by nature, insolent, stupid, slothful, animalistic, and primitive. Beginning in 1912, African-American filmmakers began to directly contradict these portrayals by arguing that African-American men embodied desirable characteristics. Although the majority of African-American-produced silent films created a dualistic schemata of black manhood, contrasting "good" and "bad" principles of black masculinity, they almost all argued that the negative characteristics that Euro-American filmmakers attributed to African-American men on screen were not inherent in the black male body and spirit. By denying these simplistic racist presumptions, African-American filmmakers were also attacking the Euro-American need for control over the African-American population. By cinematically depicting black men in a variety of professional roles and having them exhibit a number of heroic qualities, African-American filmmakers attacked the system of control that Euro-American society had placed over virtually every aspect of black American life. Filmmaker Oscar Micheaux took this argument one step further by not only portraying alternative versions of black manhood but by directly attacking the system of segregation, violence, and discrimination that inhibited African-American men's lives.

In *White*, Richard Dyer has advanced this argument, demonstrating how whiteness has been implied to mean "normal" in Western society. Dyer argues that race "is something only applied to non-white peoples. As long as white people are not racially seen and normal [the binary construction] they/we functions as a human norm."[1] Thus, skin color operates on two levels—it not only immediately allows the viewer to identify the race of the character on screen but it signifies the true characteristics of such an individual. The black and white bodies are visible, yet the qualities that make up the supposed "true character" of the racial type are invisible. Therefore, the category of whiteness is clearly visible on the screen yet highly unstable. Dyer further argues, "This has provided its strength. Because whiteness carries such rewards and privileges, the sense of a border that might be crossed and a hierarchy that might be climbed has produced a dynamic that has enthralled people who had any chance of participating in it."[2] Certainly, Dyer's argument justifies the large number of passing pictures produced by both African-American and Euro-American directors. The very concept of being able to "pass" for white meant significantly different things for African-American and Euro-American film crews and moviegoers, though. For African Americans, it implied the privilege and acceptability of being part of white American society but it also meant abandoning one's own people. For Euro-American filmmakers, it illustrated the dangers of miscegenation, but it also demonstrated the precarious instability of the dividing line between black and white societies.

Euro-American and African-American filmmaking in the silent era needs to be considered as a discourse. African-American filmmaking was a cinematic rebuttal to the objectified ways in which white filmmakers portrayed black men on the screen. African-American filmmaking was not only a reaction against racial characteristics but also against gendering qualities. African-American filmmaking was an attack on the Euro-American "norm of the text"—on the very assumptions and principles on which black male cinematic depictions were based.

In the twentieth and early twenty-first centuries, we have given primacy to visual images as a source of knowledge through the widespread dissemination of motion pictures and television. The aesthetic technology of the motion picture medium has not been based on a principle of total Euro-American hegemony over the medium, nor has it been based on an ascending linear scheme in which people of color have gradually been able to obtain more power over self-representation in a progressive pattern. Rather, African-American cinematic self-representation needs to be observed as a pattern of alternating waves of increased self-representation and then loss of this self-imagery. African-American self-representation has been influenced by a host of economic, social, and technological factors. Michel Foucault argued, "Truth is a thing of this world; it is produced only by virtue of multiple forms of constraint."[3] Barriers to African-American cinematic self-representation included access to technology, censorship, and limited financial capital. But motion pictures were a critical tool in destroying the myth of black male inferiority. Motion pictures displayed creative ways of organizing African-American society.

In 1998, in the midst of writing this book, I found myself in a hospital emergency ward in Paris. Recovering from my injuries, I was placed next to a Parisian delivery boy for Pizza Hut. When he discovered that I was American, he proceeded to ask me a multitude of questions about the United States. He had never been to the United States before and desperately wanted to visit. The *second* question he asked me was, "Is it true that all black men in the United States carry guns?" The question was a more severe blow than my injuries. It demonstrated, once again, the relentless power of motion pictures and the gross racial and gender distortions that are still perpetuated by the medium around the world.

APPENDIX: TWO SILENT
AFRICAN-AMERICAN FILM SYNOPSES

Synopsis of Eleven P.M. *(Maurice Films)*

Louis Perry, the protagonist of the story, is a light-skinned, handsome man. He is a young athlete and a talented writer. He writes an article on reincarnation for Harry Brown, editor of the *Search Light*. Harry asks Perry if he really believes what he is writing and he explains, "Yes, if there is a progressive stage of existence, there is a declining stage. I believe it is possible for a man by chance of thinking to take refuge in a lower form of material existence, for instance, cats, dogs and other creatures."

The film then introduces Roy Stewart, a mean, cigar-chewing fight promoter and "The Spider," a prizefighter. Perry, the ever-talented man, is also a boxer. Roy explains, "Here's a chance to get even with that high-hatting Perry. We won't even tell him who he is to fight."

Perry's sweetheart June calls. He explains that he will pick her up at 11:00 P.M. Therefore, Perry will finish his newspaper article, box in a match, and take out his sweetheart and her mother in the same evening. At this point, Perry falls asleep.

The movie reverts to a dream sequence that makes up most of the rest of the film but this is not necessarily made clear to the viewer. Roy Stewart becomes a criminal in the dream. He is shot and entrusts his infant son Clyde to Sundaisy, an androgynous mulatto street fiddler (and certainly one of the stranger looking characters in silent film). Roy makes Sundaisy promise that Clyde will get an education. He pleads, "I don't want him to grow up like me. Remember Sundaisy, you promised, you promised Sundaisy."

Ten years go by and Clyde Stewart is just like his dead father. (Thus, this stresses the natural inclination of the child toward criminal behavior as if it was genetically predisposed.) Clyde and his "boys" are already involved in

209

petty crime at the age of twelve. Clyde works in Old Maggie's Soup Joint. June also works there. She is a teenager who is constantly being sexually harassed by the black male customers. One day, Sundaisy defends her honor. Old Maggie, the stepmother of the girl, kicks her out, arguing that she will just have to take the sexual abuse because otherwise she will have no customers. Sundaisy takes Clyde and June away from this crude establishment. He realizes that he cannot control Clyde so he takes him to Reverend Hackett, who runs a boarding school for boys. He now looks for a place for June. Hackett says that he will take her but his intentions seem less than honorable to Sundaisy. Sundaisy explains, "If you take her out of the state you will have the law on your neck for violating the Mann Act." Reverend Hackett explains that there is only one way out of it—he must marry her. He argues that there is no law to interfere with a man taking his wife from one state to another. June does not want this arrangement so Sundaisy realizes he has only one choice—to marry the girl himself.

Reverend Hackett is a crook. He is running an operation in which he trains Clyde to become a criminal. Meanwhile, Sundaisy and June marry and have a child. Twelve years go by. Clyde's apprenticeship under Hackett has made him a "scheming scoundrel." His gang wants him to enter into even more dangerous criminal activities. Meanwhile, Hackett is sent upstate to prison for twenty-five years.

Clyde, now a man, wants to take June away from Sundaisy (she is only a few years older than Clyde). He tries to please the family. Clyde catches June alone one day and tells her, "You are too beautiful, too young to bury yourself in this place. Get wise to yourself kid—come with me and enjoy the bright lights." The temptation of sophisticated urban living versus the simple life with Sundaisy is unsettling for the young woman. "Beautiful women should have beautiful things," he says. "Besides you aren't legally married to Sundaisy. Hackett was only a cheap crook [and not a reverend]." Clyde explains that he is only thinking about her happiness and her hope for the future. June leaves with him, giving up her obligations. When Sundaisy returns, his daughter explains, "My muzzer gone wif devil man." She has taken all of her things and Sundaisy is heartbroken.

Clyde buys June a new outfit. It is sheer and revealing and she is embarrassed when she looks at herself in a mirror. Clyde eventually dumps her and she is an outcast, living a remorseful life in the slums of a big city. Ten years pass. Sundaisy and his daughter Hope make their living as street entertainers. Sundaisy plays his violin while Hope dances and passes the collection plate. Clyde comes by and places money in her hand. He looks at the adolescent girl in a provocative fashion. One of his buddies explains, "This is the little dancing queen I told you about."

Perry (the dreamer) is dating Hope. Clyde concocts a story to trick Hope, saying that Sundaisy has been run over by a car so as to get her back to his place. (He has already deflowered her mother!) He drags her in and attempts to kiss her. Someone tells Perry what has happened and he rushes to Clyde's place, where a fight breaks out. Perry knocks Clyde out cold.

Meanwhile, Sundaisy is heartbroken, walking along the street. He pets a dog and tells the creature how lucky he is. "But maybe you were here before as a man with worries and sorrows and disappointments like Sundaisy, who knows?" Hope and Perry come by and explain to Sundaisy what happened with Clyde. Sundaisy immediately goes to him to comfort him. The gangster scoffs at Sundaisy and the poor man dies heartbroken in Clyde's parlor.

Clyde opens "Blue Heaven," a new cabaret. He wants Hope to dance there. Perry overhears that Hope will be the featured attraction at the new café. A moll, Mae, attempts to convince Hope to dance there. The teenager agrees, dancing provocatively and lifting her skirt high. Clyde is impressed. Perry, who walks in the club to see if the rumor is true, is disgusted.

Perry is knocked out by Clyde's men at the stage door. He wakes up in the hospital bandaged. He has lost his memory. The doctors agree that he is suffering from mental strain.

Clyde begins seeing apparitions of Sundaisy. Clyde is haunted by his death. One day, Sundaisy inhabits a dog's body and attacks Clyde, biting him in the jugular vein and killing him. Perry regains his memory and is reunited with Hope.

The real Perry then wakes up. His girlfriend, her mother, the editor, and the fight promoter all surround him in his office—it is 11:00 P.M. It all has been a dream.

Synopsis of Scar of Shame *(Colored Feature Players)*

Early in the film, viewers are introduced to the three principal male characters. Alvin Hillyard (Harry Henderson) is a light-skinned priggish man described as a "young man of refined tastes, a lover of music and the finer things in life." Eddie Blake (Norman Johnstone), a well-dressed cigar smoker, is a "product of evil environment and whose music is not the same." A pair of dice adorn his introductory title. Spike Howard (William E. Pettus), the heroine's stepfather, is a working-class man and "has his own idea of life."

Louise Howard (Lucia Lynn Moses) is the victim of her alcoholic stepfather, Spike. She has to take care of all of his physical needs and suffers through his beatings and sexual advances. As she scrubs clothes on a washboard, she dreams of having a life of luxury. During one of Spike's many tirades on Louise, Alvin hears her being brutally beaten outside of his boardinghouse room. He jumps out a window to stop her father. Alvin knocks Spike out. Louise swoons and faints into Alvin's arms, whereby he proceeds to take her into the boardinghouse so his landlady can console her.

From the opening shots, a class difference is established between Louise and Alvin. A title informs the viewer: "One half of the world doesn't know how the other half lives." After saving Louise from another beating, Alvin comments, "This is another instance of the injustices some of the women in our race are constantly subjected to, mainly through lack of knowledge of the higher aims of life." Alvin's remarkable commentary condemns the physical abuse of women and at the same time makes Louise responsible for the abuse. This statement confirms Alvin's bourgeois status—blaming the victims for the social problems that they experience.

Alvin looks at Louise with pity. She begs Alvin not to send her back to her stepfather. Lucretia, the landlady, intervenes, and explains that Louise can work and live at the house.

The film delivers a powerful message regarding the peer pressure that African-American men place upon each other. In the next scene, Spike comes upon Eddie and another gentleman in the street. They make fun of his black eye, a sign that he had been beaten in a fight. Rather than admit to the trouncing, Spike explains that he collided with a trolley car. He cannot admit to any weakness according to his masculine code of ethics. Eddie explains that he has plans for Louise. "That baby sure is gettin' to be a swell looker. . . . Why don't you let her work for me 'stead of ruinin' her looks over a tub? I'll git her some rags, learn her to be an entertainer, you won't have to worry 'bout no miss mean cramps." The commercial exploitation of young African-American women is emphasized.

Eddie, Alvin, and Louise all room at the same boardinghouse. Eddie tries to remove her from the establishment so that he can sexually and financially control her. Louise once again has to fight off an attacker and Alvin once again has to intervene. Eddie accuses Alvin "of just tryin' to make her yourself." Alvin threatens, "You dirty dog. I'll teach you to have more respect for our women." Eddie cowardly leaves the house with his bags packed and without a fight. Alvin believes that the only way he can "save" Louise is to marry her. This paternalistic attitude is supported with a smug sense of class superiority. Alvin is complimented and elevated by all of the film's women. "He will be the greatest composer of our race," Lucretia tells Louise. In a letter, his mother, Mrs. Hillyard, attempts to fix him up with an attractive woman, "one of our set."

One of the strengths of *Scar of Shame* is the lack of purely "good" male role models. Eddie is the epitome of evil, but Spike is revealed to have some possibly admirable qualities. Eddie develops a scheme to kidnap Louise and he needs Spike's support. Spike responds, "Lay off her Eddie, I ain't treated her right and all because of that lousy booze of yours." Like Joe Morgan in *Ten Nights in a Bar Room*, Spike is a hopeless alcoholic who can be tantalized and bought off with the mere smell of liquor. Eddie sends a fake telegram to Alvin explaining that his mother is deathly ill. When Alvin leaves, he plans to kidnap the young woman.

The plan works only because Alvin refuses to allow Louise to meet his mother. He has never explained to his mother about his marriage to Louise. He explains to his wife, "Caste is one of the things mother is very determined about—and you—don't belong to our set." At this point, the true loyalties and convictions of his character are revealed. Louise is upset and disgusted. Prior to this announcement, she had been playing with a baby puppet doll. Symbolically, she drops it as Alvin packs his suitcase. She begs him to let her go. Unknowingly, he steps on the head of the doll. All of her hopes and desires have been ruined. She is simply being used by one more man in her life. After Alvin's departure, she explains to her broken doll, "Poor little thing. You too had to be a victim of caste." In a fit of despair and then rage, Louise throws the doll, breaks a mirror, tears up her marriage certificate, and removes her wedding ring. She packs her bags, ready to leave. At this point, Eddie appears. He makes a proposition to Louise to make some real money and she accepts on one condition—that this is strictly business. Alvin realizes he has been duped and returns to the scene. A shootout occurs and Louise is struck in the neck. Alvin is then imprisoned for five years for shooting his wife.

Louise and Eddie earn a living by fleecing gamblers in an illegal upper-class casino. Alvin, meanwhile, escapes from prison and assumes a new identity—Mr. Arthur Jones, professor of music, piano, and voice. His prize student and new love interest is Alice Hathaway. Her father, Ralph Hathaway, is a lawyer, political power, and protector of the club. Conveniently, Louise and Alvin cross paths. Louise has the power to threaten his new relationship, reveal his identity, and send him back to jail. She cannot harm him, though, because she loves him.

Louise finally commits suicide out of love for Alvin. A flickering candle is shown slowly burning and finally extinguished. Alvin reveals his true identity to Alice and in a letter left for Mr. Hathaway, Louise explains her fate. Hathaway, the respected politician and protector of corruption, has the last moralizing words: "A child of environment? If she had the proper training, if she had been taught the finer things in life, the higher aims, the higher hopes, she would not be lying cold in death? Oh! Our people have so much to learn."

The Scar of Shame leaves no tidy conclusions like the vast majority of all-black melodramas. Does Alvin go back to prison? Does he marry Alice? What happens to Eddie? Perhaps the most complex question is why a political racketeer like Hathaway would be the moral voice of the film.

The film attempts to argue that Louise is a tragic mulatta; her lack of loving parental kindness leaves her no choice other than death. Thus, a paradox exists. Why should the black bourgeoisie be held responsible for aiding the lower African-American class when it probably will not lead to any real progress? What, therefore, should be the responsibility of the African-American man?

If the film claims that environment is responsible for one's moral actions, how does one explain the Hathaway character? Is it considered morally proper for Alvin to marry his daughter simply because of his net worth? What about his moral character and how that money is obtained? Why is the overbearing American system of racism and discrimination not discussed? *The Scar of Shame* argues that the African-American community is divided by class but it offers no solutions for bringing the race together. In reality, the upper class (Mother Hillyard) and the lower elements (Eddie) both attempt to fragment the community even further with their selfish actions and behaviors.

NOTES

INTRODUCTION

1. Thomas Cripps, *Slow Fade to Black: The Negro in American Film, 1900–1942* (New York: Oxford University Press, 1977) and *Making Movies Black: The Hollywood Message Movie from World War II to the Civil Rights Era* (New York: Oxford University Press, 1993); Mark A. Reid, *Redefining Black Film* (Berkeley: University of California Press, 1993); Jane M. Gaines, *Fire and Desire: Mixed-Race Movies in the Silent Era* (Chicago: University of Chicago Press, 2001); J. Ronald Green, *Straight Lick: The Cinema of Oscar Micheaux* (Bloomington: Indiana University Press, 2000); Pearl Bowser and Louise Spence, *Writing Himself into History: Oscar Micheaux, His Silent Films, and His Audiences* (New Brunswick, N.J.: Rutgers University Press, 2000).

2. The issue of what terminology to use for people of African descent in this book is a complex one that I gave a great deal of consideration to. The noun "African American" is used whenever possible. It was necessary for me to use the noun "black" in the title and throughout the text because many of the racial depictions in American films were those not only of African Americans but also of African people. In fact, there was a deliberate strategy on the part of many white filmmakers to connect African Americans with the "supposed" primitiveness of Africa. I have also chosen not to capitalize either "black" or "white" throughout the text.

3. Although sound motion pictures were introduced to the American public in the mid-1920s, African Americans did not begin the production of "talking" motion pictures until 1931, when Oscar Micheaux released *The Exile.*

4. Peter Noble, *The Negro in Films* (New York: Arno Press, 1948), 8.

5. Albert Johnson, "Beige, Brown or Black," *Film Quarterly* 13 (fall 1959): 39.

6. Cripps, *Slow Fade to Black,* 8.

7. By "rupture," I am referring to a break with the standard portrayal on the motion picture screen.

8. Charles Musser, *Before the Nickelodeon: Edwin S. Porter and the Edison Manufacturing Company* (Berkeley and Los Angeles: University of California Press, 1991), 530–531.

9. Recent work on the film *The Birth of a Nation* includes Richard Dyer, "Into the Light: The Whiteness of the South in *The Birth of a Nation,*" and Jane Gaines, "*The Birth of a Nation* and *Within Our Gates:* Two Tales of the American South," in *Dixie*

Debates: Perspectives on Southern Cultures, edited by Richard H. King and Helen Taylor (New York: New York University Press, 1996); Vincent F. Rocchio, "The Birth of a (Racist) Nation(al) Cinema" in *Reel Racism* (Boulder, Colo.: Westview Press, 2000); and Russell Merritt, "D. W. Griffith's *The Birth of a Nation:* Going After Little Sister," in *Close Viewings: An Anthology of New Film Criticism,* edited by Peter Lehman (Tallahassee: Florida State University Press, 1990).

10. See William G. Jones, *Black Cinema: Treasures Lost and Found* (Denton: University of North Texas Press, 1991), 184–187.

11. Donald Bogle, *Toms, Coons, Mulattoes, Mammies and Bucks: An Interpretive History of Blacks in American Films* (New York: Continuum, 1989), 4–12.

12. James Murray, *To Find an Image: Black Films from Uncle Tom to Super Fly* (Indianapolis: Bobbs-Merrill Company, 1973); Jim Pines, *Blacks in Films: A Survey of Racial Themes and Images in the American Film* (London: Studio Vista, 1975); James Nesteby, *Black Images in American Films, 1896–1954: The Interplay between Civil Rights and Film Culture* (Washington, D.C.: University Press of America, 1982).

13. Reid, *Redefining Black Film,* 2.

14. I obviously could not view these destroyed films, but I could "reconstruct" their narratives through primary and secondary sources.

15. Henry T. Sampson, *Blacks in Black and White: A Source Book on Black Film* (New York: Scarecrow Press, 1995).

16. Foster formed the Foster Photoplay Company in 1910 but actually produced and directed his first film in 1912.

17. Joel Williamson, *The Crucible of Race: Black and White Relations in the American South since Emancipation* (New York: Oxford University Press, 1984), 5.

18. Ibid., 6.

19. Ibid.

20. Clyde Taylor, "The Re-Birth of the Aesthetic in Cinema," in *The Birth of Whiteness: Race and the Emergence of U.S. Cinema,* edited by Daniel Bernardi (New Brunswick, N.J.: Rutgers University Press, 1996), 31.

21. Williamson, *The Crucible of Race,* 6.

1. RACIALIZED MASCULINITY AND THE POLITICS OF DIFFERENCE

1. Jesse Algeron Rhines, *Black Film/White Money* (New Brunswick, N.J.: Rutgers University Press, 1996), 15.

2. For discussions of turn-of-the-century segregation, see C. Vann Woodward, *The Strange Career of Jim Crow* (New York: Oxford University Press, 1966); Joel Williamson, *The Crucible of Race: Black-White Relations in the American South since Emancipation* (New York: Oxford University Press, 1984); Joel Williamson, ed., *The Origins of Segregation* (Boston: D. C. Heath, 1968); John Dittmer, *Black Georgia in the Progressive Era, 1900–1920* (Urbana: University of Illinois Press, 1977); and Neil McMillen, *Dark Journey: Black Mississippians in the Age of Jim Crow* (Urbana: University of Illinois Press, 1989).

3. See John E. Semonche, *Charting the Future: The Supreme Court Responds to a Changing Society, 1890–1920* (Westport, Conn.: Greenwood Press, 1978); Benno C. Schmidt, Jr., "Principle and Prejudice: The Supreme Court and Race in the Progressive Era: Part 1: The Heydey of Jim Crow," *Columbia Law Review* 82 (1982); Leonard W. Levy and Douglas L. Jones, *Jim Crow in Boston: The Origins of the Separate but Equal Doctrine* (New York: Da Capo Press, 1974); and John William

Graves, "Jim Crow in Arkansas: A Reconsideration of Urban Race Relations in the Post-Reconstruction South," *Journal of Southern History* 55, no. 3 (August 1989): 421–428.

4. See Sean Dennis Cashman, *African Americans and the Quest For Civil Rights, 1900–1990* (New York: New York University Press, 1991), 7–8. See also Edward Ayers, *Southern Crossing: A History of the American South, 1877–1906* (New York: Oxford University Press, 1995).

5. See H. Leon Prather, *We Have Taken a City: Wilmington Racial Massacre and Coup of 1898* (Rutherford, N.J.: Fairleigh Dickinson University Press, 1984); Domenic J. Capeci, Jr., and Jack C. Knight, "Reckoning with Violence: W. E. B. DuBois and the 1906 Atlanta Race Riot," *Journal of Southern History* 62, no. 4 (November 1996): 727–767; Roberta Senechal, *The Sociogenesis of a Race Riot: Springfield, Illinois, in 1908* (Urbana: University of Illinois Press, 1990); Scott Ellsworth, *Death in a Promised Land: The Tulsa Race Riot of 1921* (Baton Rouge: Louisiana State University Press, 1982); Robert V. Haynes, *A Night of Violence: The Houston Riot of 1917* (Baton Rouge: Louisiana State University Press, 1976).

6. W. Fitzhugh Brundage, *Lynching in the New South* (Urbana: University of Illinois Press, 1993), 8. For other lynching statistics, see Edward Ayers, *Vengeance and Justice: Crime and Punishment in the 19th Century American South* (New York: Oxford University Press, 1984); Ida Wells-Barnett, *On Lynchings: Southern Horrors* (New York: Arno Press, 1969).

7. For information on the theatrical nature of lynching, see J. William Harris, "Etiquette, Lynching, and Racial Boundaries in Southern History: A Mississippi Example," *American Historical Review* 100 (April 1995): 387–410; Robert P. Ingalls, "Lynching and Establishment Violence in Tampa, 1858–1935," *Journal of Southern History* 53, no. 4 (November 1987): 613–644.

8. C. Vann Woodward, *Tom Watson: Agrarian Rebel* (New York: Oxford University Press, 1963), 220.

9. Ibid.

10. George M. Frederickson, *The Black Image in the White Mind* (New York: Harper and Row, 1971), 266.

11. Ibid.

12. Thomas F. Gossett, *Race: The History of an Idea in America* (Dallas: Southern Methodist University Press, 1963), 254.

13. Williamson, *The Crucible of Race*, 301.

14. Marion L. Dawson, "The South and the Negro," *North American Review* 172, no. 81 (1901): 280.

15. Thomas Frazier, ed., *Afro-American History: Primary Sources* (New York: Harcourt Brace, 1970), 163.

16. August Meier, *Negro Thought in America, 1880–1915: Racial Ideologies in the Age of Booker T. Washington* (Ann Arbor: University of Michigan Press, 1969), 121–139.

17. See Nancy Weiss, *The National Urban League, 1910–1940* (New York: Oxford University Press, 1974), 3–13.

18. Meier, *Negro Thought in America*, 139–142.

19. Florette Henri, *Black Migration: Movement North, 1900–1920* (Garden City, N.Y.: Anchor Books, 1976), 35.

20. Ibid., 158.

21. Quoted in John Hope Franklin, *From Slavery to Freedom* (New York: Alfred A. Knopf, 1994), 286.

22. Found in Frazier, ed., *Afro-American History*, 234 (my emphasis).

23. Charles Flint Kellogg, *N.A.A.C.P.: A History of the National Association for the Advancement of Colored People*, vol. 1, *1909–1920* (Baltimore: Johns Hopkins University Press, 1967), 149.

24. Cashman, *African Americans and the Quest for Civil Rights, 1900–1990*, 22. By 1913 the *Crisis* was sold in every state of the United States, according to W. E. B. DuBois (Kellogg, *N.A.A.C.P.*, 153).

25. See James R. Grossman, *Land of Hope: Chicago, Black Southerners and the Great Migration* (Chicago: University of Chicago Press, 1989), 141–153.

26. *National Review* (Kansas City, Kans.: 26 April 1913), 2.

27. Gerald Mast, *A Short History of the Movies* (New York: Macmillan, 1986), 43.

28. See Charles Musser, *The Emergence of Cinema: The American Screen to 1907* (New York: Charles Scribner's Sons, 1990).

29. These films will be discussed in the next chapter. For further information see Anthony Slide, *Early American Cinema* (Metuchen, N.J.: Scarecrow Press, 1994); Douglas Gomery, *Shared Pleasures: A History of Movie Presentation in the United States* (Madison: University of Wisconsin Press, 1992).

30. Robert Sklar, *Film: An International History of the Medium* (New York: Harry N. Abrams, 1993), 27.

31. Miriam Hansen, *Babel and Babylon: Spectatorship in American Silent Film* (Cambridge, Mass.: Harvard University Press, 1991), 24.

32. See Charles Musser, *The Emergence of Cinema*, and Thomas Elsaesser, ed., *Early Cinema: Space, Frame, Narrative* (London: British Film Institute, 1990).

33. *Washington Bee*, 9 July 1910, 10.

34. Eric Lott, *Love and Theft: Blackface Minstrelsy and the American Working Class* (Oxford: Oxford University Press, 1993), 1.

35. Robert Toll, *Blacking Up: The Minstrel in Nineteenth Century America* (New York: Oxford University Press, 1974), 67.

36. Jan Nederveen Pieterse, *White on Black: Images of Africa and Blacks in Western Popular Culture* (New Haven, Conn.: Yale University Press, 1992), 133.

37. See Hans Nathan, *Dan Emmett and the Rise of Early Negro Minstrelsy* (Norman: University of Oklahoma Press, 1962); Charles Townsend, *Negro Minstrels* (Upper Saddle, N.J.: New Jersey Literature House, 1969); Jack Haverly, *Negro Minstrels: A Complete Guide* (Upper Saddle, N.J.: New Jersey Literature House, 1969).

38. David Roediger in *The Wages of Whiteness* (London: Verso, 1991) argues that pre–Civil War minstrelsy was geared primarily toward lower-class, male-only audiences. After the Civil War, blackface minstrelsy became more mainstream, playing in respectable theaters to male and female audiences (121).

39. See Eric Lott, "The Seeming Counterfeit: Racial Politics and Early Blackface Minstrelsy," *American Quarterly* 42, no. 2 (June 1991): 223–254.

40. These four books are Robert Toll's *Blacking Up: The Minstrel Show in Nineteenth Century America* (New York: Oxford University Press, 1974); Eric Lott's *Love and Theft*; David Roediger's *The Wages of Whiteness* (London: Verso, 1991); and Michael Rogin's *Blackface, White Noise: Jewish Immigrants in the Melting Pot* (Berkeley: University of California Press, 1996).

41. Stuart Hall has argued, "The central issues of race always appear historically in articulation in a formation with other categories and divisions." Found in Lott, *Love and Theft*, 8.

42. Rogin, *Blackface, White Noise*, 50.

43. Lott, *Love and Theft*, 6–12.

44. *Being White,* produced and directed by Tony Downmunt, Maris Clark, Rooney Martin, and Kobena Mercer, 55 min., Albany Video, London, 1991, videocassette.

45. Lott, *Love and Theft,* 68–69.

46. Kevin Gaines, *Uplifting the Race: Black Leadership, Politics, and Culture in the Twentieth Century* (Chapel Hill: University of North Carolina Press, 1996), 67.

47. Lott, *Love and Theft,* 113.

48. Ibid.

49. Mark Reid, *Redefining Black Film* (Berkeley: University of California Press, 1993), 19–20.

50. See James Hoskins, *Black Dance in America: A History through Its People* (New York: Crowell, 1990).

51. Lott, *Love and Theft,* 148.

52. Blackface minstrelsy could be considered "excessive" because of the extremes the entertainment form used to degrade African Americans. White men could "be black" for a while but African-American minstrels, putting on blackface, could only be the black characters that white audiences imagined.

53. For works on African Americans in blackface see Henry T. Sampson, *Blacks in Blackface: A Source Book on Early Black Minstrel Shows* (Metuchen, N.J.: Scarecrow Press, 1980); Lisa Anderson, "From Blackface to 'Genuine Negroes': Nineteenth Century Minstrelsy and the Icon of the 'Negro,'" *Theatre Research International* 21 (spring 1996): 17–23.

54. Toll, *Blacking Up,* 196. The tragic career of Bert Williams is a prime example of black creative talent limited by racist stereotypes and a lack of opportunity.

55. See Joseph Boskin, *Sambo: The Rise and Demise of an American Jester* (New York: Oxford University Press, 1986).

56. See William J. Mahar, "Black English in Early Blackface Minstrelsy: A New Interpretation of the Sources of Minstrel Show Dialect," *American Quarterly* 37 (summer 1985): 260–285.

57. In the 1990s, comedian Damon Wayans played a variation of the role in the "prisoner sketch" in the popular variety show *In Living Color.*

58. David R. Roediger, "Class, Coons, and Crowds in Antebellum America," in *The Wages of Whiteness,* 95–132.

59. Sam Dennison, *Scandalize My Name: Black Imagery in American Popular Music* (New York: Garland Publishing, 1982), 357.

60. See James Damon, "Shaping the Popular Image of Post-Reconstruction American Blacks: The 'Coon Song' Phenomenon of the Gilded Age," *American Quarterly* 40 (December 1988): 450–471.

61. See Eric Lott, "The Seeming Counterfeit," 450–471.

62. This is similar to the Joel Chandler Harris story of the tortoise and the hare.

63. Michel Foucault, *Language, Counter Memory, Practice: Selected Essays and Interviews* (Ithaca, N.Y.: Cornell University Press, 1977), 161.

2. The Preformed Image

1. *Florida Enchantment* is available at the Library of Congress.

2. In *Vested Interests: Cross-Dressing and Cultural Anxiety,* Marjorie Garber succinctly argues, "The transvestic representations often appear, significantly, within a context that includes 'crossing' (or passing) simultaneously as an element of gender and race. In fact, that overdetermined presence of cross-dressing in so many Western

figurations of black culture suggests some useful ways to interrogate notions of 'stereotype' and 'cliché.'" Many films of the silent era that included cross-dressing as a cinematic device used this tool as a way to subvert or disempower the African-American culture (New York: Routledge, 1992), 268.

3. Bill Nichols, "Sons on the Brink of Manhood," *East-West Film Journal* 4 (1989): 27.

4. Discussions of the use of myth in film include Rita Parks, *The Western Hero in Film and Television: Mass Media Mythology* (Ann Arbor: UMI Research Press, 1982), and Parker Tyler, *Magic and Myth of the Movies* (New York: Simon and Schuster, 1970).

5. Robert Ray, *A Certain Tendency of the Studio System, 1930–1980* (Princeton, N.J.: Princeton University Press, 1985), 26.

6. Richard Dyer, "Entertainment and Utopia," in *The Cultural Studies Reader,* edited by Simon During (London: Routledge, 1993a), 373.

7. Ibid.

8. Ibid.

9. Jane Addams, *The Spirit of Youth and the City Streets* (New York: Macmillan, 1912), 75–106.

10. Dyer, "Entertainment and Utopia," 377.

11. Ibid.

12. Douglas Kellner, "Television, Ideology and Emancipatory Popular Culture," in *Television: The Critical View,* pp. 471–501, edited by Horace Newcomb (New York: Oxford University Press, 1987).

13. Terry Eagleton, *Literary Theory: An Introduction* (London: Blackwell, 1983), 74.

14. For a discussion of the "Other" see Bernard McCrane, *Beyond Anthropology: Society and the Other* (New York: Columbia University Press, 1989).

15. Jane M. Gaines's discussion of the motion picture apparatus as an "othering machine" in *Fire and Desire: Mixed-Race Movies in the Silent Era* contributes significantly to existing theories of spectatorship (Chicago: University of Chicago Press, 2001), 268–269.

16. Thomas Cripps, *Slow Fade to Black: The Negro in American Film, 1900–1942* (New York: Oxford University Press, 1977), 9.

17. Robert C. Allen, *Vaudeville and Film, 1895–1915: A Study in Media Interaction* (New York: Allen Press, 1986).

18. Daniel Bernardi, "The Voice of Whiteness: D. W. Griffith's Biograph Films, 1908–1913," in *The Birth of Whiteness: Race and the Emergence of U.S. Cinema,* edited by Bernardi (New Brunswick, N.J.: Rutgers University Press, 1996), 109.

19. The following film catalogs are located on microfiche in the reading room of the Motion Picture, Broadcasting, and Recorded Sound Division of the Library of Congress.

20. *Minstrels Battling in a Room* and *The Edison Minstrels* are found in the Library of Congress.

21. *Laughing Ben* (Library of Congress); Eric Savada, ed., *American Film Institute Catalog: Film Beginnings, 1893–1910* (Metuchen, N.J.: Scarecrow Press, 1995), 581.

22. *Lubin Film Catalogue* (1907), 17.

23. Joel Williamson, *The Crucible of Race: Black-White Relations in the American South since Emancipation* (New York: Oxford University Press, 1984), 115–116.

24. Jan Nederveen Pieterse, *White on Black: Images of Africa and Blacks in Western Popular Culture* (New Haven, Conn.: Yale University Press, 1982), 152–163.

25. Bill Nichols, *Ideology and the Image: Social Representation in the Cinema and Other Media* (Bloomington: Indiana University Press, 1981), 11.

26. Ibid., 9–11.

27. In *Fire and Desire,* Jane M. Gaines refers to this as "Sambo art" (127).

28. Charles Musser, *Before the Nickelodeon: Edwin S. Porter and the Edison Manufacturing Company* (Berkeley: University of California Press, 1991), 312–314.

29. *Watermelon Eating Contest* (1903) in *Lubin Catalogue Listing* (January 1903), 51.

30. Ibid.

31. *Who Said Watermelon* (1902) in *Lubin Catalogue* (1903), 36.

32. *Watermelon Contest* (1900) in *Edison Catalogue* (1901), 71; *The Watermelon Patch* (1905) in *Edison Film Catalogue* 268 (24 October 1905).

33. *AMB Picture Catalogue* (November 1902), 9.

34. Bernardi, "The Voice of Whiteness," 110.

35. For works on the history of African-American dance, see Edward Thorpe, *Black Dance* (New York: Woodstock, 1990); Katrina Hazzard-Gordon, *Jookin': The Rise of Social Dance Formations in African American Culture* (Philadelphia: Temple University Press, 1990); Jacqui Malone, *Steppin' on the Blues: The Visible Rhythms of African American Dance* (Urbana: University of Illinois Press, 1996).

36. *Buck Dance* (1903) in *Lubin Catalogue,* 69.

37. Eric Lott, *Love and Theft: Blackface Minstrelsy and the American Working Class* (Oxford: Oxford University Press, 1993), 153.

38. Manthia Diawara, "Black Spectatorship: Problems of Identification and Resistance," in *Black American Cinema,* edited by Manthia Diawara (New York: Routledge, 1993), 215.

39. This word is used in countless film catalog descriptions, including *A Darktown Dance, Edison Catalogue* (1900), 28, and *Up to Date Cakewalk, Edison Catalogue* (1900), 36.

40. Pieterse, *White on Black,* 37.

41. See Malone, *Steppin' on the Blues,* 18, and Lynn Fauley Emery, *Black Dance: From 1619 to Today* (Salem, N.H.: Ayer Company Publishers, 1988), 206–214.

42. Langston Hughes, *Black Magic: A Pictorial History of the Negro in American Entertainment* (Englewood Cliffs, N.J.: Prentice-Hall, 1967), 48.

43. Pieterse, *White on Black,* 137.

44. *Cake Walk* (1902), in *Selig Catalogue,* 40.

45. *Cake Walk,* Lubin (1898), in *Lubin Catalogue* (1903), 49.

46. *Up to Date Cake Walk,* Edison (1900), in *Edison Catalogue* (1901), 71.

47. Sam Dennison, *Scandalize My Name: Black Imagery in American Popular Music* (New York: Garland Publishing, 1982), 268.

48. Bernardi, "The Voice of Whiteness," 111.

49. It is considered broad-based because popular songs, films, and cartoon depictions of the era all portrayed the same racist stereotype.

50. Musser, *Before the Nickelodeon,* 101.

51. *Latest Edison Films for Projecting Machines* (June 1897), 45.

52. Ibid.

53. *Chicken Thieves* is in the Library of Congress.

54. *Lubin Catalogue* (1903), 38.

55. *Lubin Catalogue* (1903), 69.

56. Henry T. Sampson, *Blacks in Black and White: A Source Book on Black Film* (New York: Scarecrow Press, 1995), 45.

57. *Biograph Picture Catalogue* (1904), 48–49.
58. *Biograph Bulletin* (1905), 140, 143.
59. Through the viewing of numerous early films, I have come to the conclusion that blackface as a form of characterization did not make a significant impact on the development of the medium until the widespread usage of the story-film in 1903–1904.
60. *Moving Picture World* (6 August 1910), 309.
61. Sampson, *Blacks in Black and White*, 66.
62. Ibid., 44, 84–85, 102–103, 114–115.
63. Ibid., 44.
64. Charles Musser, *The Emergence of Cinema: The American Screen to 1907* (New York: Charles Scribner's Sons, 1990), 360. *A Nigger in the Woodpile* is available in the Library of Congress.
65. Williamson, *The Crucible of Race*, 115–116.
66. Ibid., 6.
67. African Americans in general were considered "childlike." For a discussion of this see Pieterse, *White on Black*, 169–171.
68. *Biograph Production Log* (1905), 62–63. *Everybody Works but Father* is available in the Library of Congress.
69. Promotional advertising for the 1997 television series *Players* showed the rapper Ice T as a crapshooting private detective. Numerous contemporary rap videos incorporate shooting craps.
70. *Edison Catalogue* (1902), 74.
71. *Selig Catalogue* (1903), 24.
72. *Moving Picture World* (8 March 1913), 998.
73. *Lubin Catalogue* (1903), 61.
74. Ibid.
75. In *White on Black*, Pieterse gives a number of examples of the comparison of African Americans with animals in contemporary popular culture (39–44).
76. Quoted in Williamson, *The Crucible of Race*, 122.
77. Nathaniel Shaler quoted in Joel Williamson's *The Crucible of Race*, 120.
78. Joseph Boskin, *Sambo: The Rise and Demise of an American Jester* (New York: Oxford University Press, 1986), 123.
79. Steve Neale and Frank Krutnik, *Popular Film and Television Comedy* (London: Routledge, 1990), 111.
80. For example, J. Ronald Green, *Straight Lick: The Cinema of Oscar Micheaux* (Bloomington: Indiana University Press, 2000).
81. See Williamson, *The Crucible of Race*, 22–24, 121–123.
82. Ibid.
83. For example, see Herbert Shapiro, *White Violence and Black Response: From Reconstruction to Montgomery* (Amherst: University of Massachusetts Press, 1988).
84. *Trick Donkey* and *Trick Donkey No. 2*, Lubin (1903), in *Lubin Picture Catalogue* (1904), 4, 60.
85. Savada, ed., *American Film Institute Catalog*, 320. In "Lester Walton's *Ecriture Noir*: Black Spectatorial Transcodings of 'Cinematic Excess,'" Anna Everette discusses *New York Age* columnist Lester Walton's reaction to a film advertisement that proudly claimed that you could see "JOHN SMITH of PARIS, TEXAS, BURNED at the STAKE. HEAR HIS MOANS AND GROANS." Of course, the victim was an African-American man (*Cinema Journal* 39, no. 3 [spring 2000]): 30–50).

86. *Biograph Picture Catalogue* (November 1902), 37. *How Charlie Lost the Heiress* (1902) and *The Subpoena Server* (1906) are available in the Library of Congress.

87. Sampson, *Blacks in Black and White*, 42–43.

88. Ibid., 60.

89. *Drawing the Color Line, Moving Picture News* (23 January 1909), 93–94.

90. *A Close Call* is available in the Library of Congress.

91. *The Thirteen Club* is available in the Library of Congress.

92. With the threat of the Ku Klux Klan, who can blame them?

93. *Moving Picture World* (16 October 1915), 439.

94. Sampson, *Blacks in Black and White*, 76.

95. *Moving Picture World* (16 October 1915).

96. *Georgia Camp Meeting, Lubin Catalogue* (1903), 43.

97. *Lubin Catalogue* (1903), 36.

98. *Lubin Catalogue* (1903), 52.

99. Sampson, *Blacks in Black and White*, 40, 57, 60.

100. Ibid., 154.

101. *Moving Picture World* (7 August 1909), 196. *Amos n' Andy* is a good example of this.

102. *A Bucktown Romance, Moving Picture World* (6 April 1912), 40.

103. Jacquie Jones, "The Construction of Black Sexuality," in *Black American Film*, edited by Manthia Diawara (New York: Routledge, 1993), 247.

104. Gaines, *Fire and Desire*, 54–55.

105. *Biograph Picture Catalogue* (1904), 28–29.

106. A number of films contain the same theme. Included are *Dark Romance of a Tobacco Can* (1907) and *Under the Old Apple Tree* (1907).

107. See F. James David, *Who Is Black? One Nation's Definition* (University Park: Pennsylvania State University Press, 1991), for statistics on the numbers of individuals of mixed ancestry.

108. The only exceptions to this dichotomy are the characters of Eliza and George in various retellings of *Uncle Tom's Cabin*.

109. The octoroon was desired by white men in films but she was always a tragic character. In *The Octoroon* (Kalem, 1911) and *The Octoroon's Sacrifice* (Republic, 1912), the female octoroon ends up dead by the end of the film. In films like *In Slavery Days* (Rex, 1913), the octoroon was a villainess. The octoroon's "crime" was passing for white and deceiving a decent gentleman into proposing marriage. By the end of the film the true racial nature of the octoroon was revealed and racial stability was preserved.

110. *Dancing Darkies,* American Mutoscope (1896), in *AMB Picture Catalogue* (November 1902), 9.

111. *Dancing Darkey Boy,* Edison (1897), in *Library of Congress Paper Print Collection,* 284.

112. *Watermelon Eating Contest* and *Pickaninnies* are available in the Library of Congress.

113. *The 'Gator and the Pickaninny* (1900) in *AMB Picture Catalogue* (November 1902), 40. This film is available in the Library of Congress.

114. *New York Clipper* (2 October 1908). *The 'Gator and the Pickaninny* is an example of the "child elimination" genre.

115. Pieterse, *White on Black,* 171.

116. Eileen Bowser, "Racial/Racist Jokes in American Silent Slapstick Comedy," *Griffithiana* 53 (May 1995): 43.

3. Black Cinematic Ruptures and Ole Uncle Tom

1. Manthia Diawara, "Black Spectatorship: Problems of Identification and Resistance," in *Black American Cinema,* edited by Diawara (New York: Routledge, 1993), 211.

2. Judith Mayne, *Cinema and Spectatorship* (London: Routledge, 1993), 59.

3. bell hooks, "The Oppositional Gaze: Black Female Spectators," in *Black American Cinema,* edited by Manthia Diawara (New York: Routledge, 1993), 289.

4. Ibid.

5. For information on African-American participation in the Spanish-American War, see Hiram H. Thweatt, *What the Newspapers Say of the Negro Soldier in the Spanish American War* (Sanford, N.C.: Microfilming Corporation of America, 1982).

6. *Lubin Catalogue* (1907), 84. Positive portrayals of African-American soldiers were not always the norm. In *Colored Troops Disembarking* (Edison, 1898), black soldiers are mocked while they are coming down the steep gangplank of a ship. The catalog description says that their actions are "laughable" (*Edison Catalogue,* 1898, 6).

7. Ibid.

8. For example, the Edison Company produced *Rout of the Filipinos* in 1899.

9. *Lubin Catalogue* (1903), 76.

10. Kevin Gaines, *Uplifting the Race: Black Leadership, Politics, and Culture in the Twentieth Century* (Chapel Hill: University of North Carolina Press, 1996), 37.

11. Daniel Bernardi, "The Voice of Whiteness: D. W. Griffith's Biograph Films (1908–1913)," in *The Birth of Whiteness: Race and the Emergence of U.S. Cinema,* edited by Bernardi (New Brunswick, N.J.: Rutgers University Press, 1996), 108–109.

12. Finis Farr, *The Life and Times of Jack Johnson* (New York: Charles Scribner's Sons, 1964), 28.

13. Gail Bederman, *Manliness and Civilization* (Chicago: University of Chicago Press, 1995), 1–44.

14. Lerone Bennett, Jr., "Jack Johnson and the Great White Hope," *Ebony* (April 1994): 88.

15. Al-Tony Gilmore, *Bad Nigger! The National Impact of Jack Johnson* (Port Washington, N.Y.: Kennikut Press, 1975).

16. Charles Musser, *The Emergence of Cinema: The American Screen to 1907* (New York: Charles Scribner's Sons, 1990), 193–200.

17. Dan Streible, "Race and the Reception of Jack Johnson Fight Films," in *The Birth of Whiteness: Race and the Emergence of U.S. Cinema,* p. 174, edited by Daniel Bernardi (New Brunswick, N.J.: Rutgers University Press, 1996).

18. *Richmond Planet,* 9 February 1909, 4.

19. Henry T. Sampson, *Blacks in Black and White: A Source Book on Black Film* (New York: Scarecrow Press, 1995), 82.

20. *Variety* (30 October 1909).

21. Streible, "Race and the Reception of Jack Johnson Fight Films," 176.

22. Ibid., 177–178.

23. *Chicago Defender,* 2 July 1910, 1.

24. Sylvester Russell, "Musical and Dramatic," *Chicago Defender,* 30 April 1910, 4.

25. Streible, "Race and the Reception of Jack Johnson Fight Films," 175.

26. Ibid., 180–181.

27. "Cartoon," *Chicago Defender*, 4 February 1910, 1.

28. Farr, *The Life and Times of Jack Johnson*, 98.

29. Bennett, "Jack Johnson and the Great White Hope," 92.

30. *Chicago Defender*, 2 July 1910, 1.

31. Johnson was one of the first personalities to realize the economic and publicity potential of the motion picture medium. In 1910, shortly after the match, the American Cinephone Company made *Jack Johnson's Own Story of the Big Fight*. This was one of the first attempts to make a sound film. The reel was accompanied by two twelve-inch records of Johnson talking about the fight.

32. Streible, "Race and the Reception of Jack Johnson Fight Films," 182.

33. "Fight Pictures Prohibited Here by Mayor," *San Francisco Examiner*, 4 July 1910, 1.

34. Streible, "Race and the Reception of Jack Johnson Fight Films," 182–183.

35. Farr, *The Life and Times of Jack Johnson*, 133.

36. Streible, "Race and the Reception of Jack Johnson Fight Films," 185.

37. "John Arthur Johnson Still Holds the Championship Belt of the World," *Chicago Broad Axe*, 9 July 1910, 1.

38. Streible, "Race and the Reception of Jack Johnson Fight Films," 177.

39. Gilmore, *Bad Nigger*, 77.

40. "The Johnson-Jeffries Fight," *St. Paul Appeal*, 9 July 1910, 2.

41. Despite the fact that Johnson could no longer appear in the ring himself, cinematically his legend in motion pictures lived on. In Vitagraph's *The Night I Fought Jack Johnson*, the white challenger is looked upon as a buffoon. The Johnson character was a vigorous fighter as the white protagonist dreamed that he was actually fighting the champion.

42. Farr, *The Life and Times of Jack Johnson*, 127.

43. Ibid.

44. U.S. Congress, Senate Congressional Record, 62d Congress, 2d Session (19 July 1912), 9305.

45. *Selig Film Catalogue* (1903), 21.

46. Ibid.

47. Joan Mellen, *Big Bad Wolves: Masculinity in American Film* (New York: Pantheon Books, 1977), 3.

48. Ibid.

49. See Kenneth M. Cameron, *Africa on Film: Beyond Black and White* (New York: Continuum, 1994).

50. Sampson, *Blacks in Black and White*, 99–100.

51. Joel Williamson, *The Crucible of Race: Black-White Relations in the American South since Emancipation* (New York: Oxford University Press, 1984), 111, 115, 116–118, 121–122.

52. Michel Foucault, *History of Sexuality* (New York: Vintage Books, 1988), 97–102.

53. Jacquie Jones, "The Construction of Black Sexuality," in *Black American Cinema*, edited by Manthia Diawara (London: Routledge, 1993), 247.

54. See W. Fitzhugh Brundage, *Lynching in the New South* (Urbana: University of Illinois Press, 1993).

55. E. Ann Kaplan, *Looking for the Other: Feminism, Film, and the Imperial Gaze* (New York: Routledge, 1997), 70.

56. *Selig Film Catalogue* (1903), 86.

57. See Thomas F. Gossett, *Uncle Tom's Cabin and American Culture* (Dallas:

Southern Methodist University Press, 1985), and William Torbert Leonard, *Masquerade in Black* (London: Scarecrow Press, 1986).

58. Gossett, *Uncle Tom's Cabin and American Culture*, 383.

59. A review of a one-reel Thanhauser production of *Uncle Tom's Cabin* in *Moving Picture World* claimed, "It is needless to go over the story; everyone knows it, either by reading, or by hearing about it from others" (6 August 1910), 298.

60. Janet Staiger provides this comparison in *Interpreting Films: Studies in the Historical Reception of American Cinema* (Princeton, N.J.: Princeton University Press, 1992), 106–107.

61. This version of *Uncle Tom's Cabin* is in the Library of Congress.

62. Lubin also produced a version of the classic Stowe novel in 1903; unfortunately, a version of it no longer exists so it cannot be compared to the one produced by Edison. It was also made in tableaux style, demonstrating the slow progression to story-film by early directors. The novel was simply too long and complicated to tell in one reel, the industry norm in 1903.

63. Eileen Bowser, *The Transformation of Cinema, 1907–1915* (New York: Charles Scribner's Sons, 1990), 198.

64. *Moving Picture World* (13 August 1910), 350–351.

65. By 1909 the character of Uncle Tom was so well known that he was dramatized in films other than those based on the Stowe novel. One such example was the film *Uncle Tom Wins* (Edison, 1909). In this film, Tom wins the lottery.

66. Kalem produced a two-reel version of *Uncle Tom's Cabin* in 1913.

67. Leonard, *Masquerade in Black*, 185.

68. Ibid.

69. *Moving Picture World* (15 August 1914).

70. This film is available in the Library of Congress.

71. Bowser, *The Transformation of Cinema, 1907–1915*, 53–54. See also John Fell, *Film and the Narrative Tradition* (Norman: University of Oklahoma Press, 1974).

72. See Jack Spears, *The Civil War on the Screen and Other Essays* (New York: A. S. Barnes and Co., 1977). See also Edward D. C. Campbell, Jr., *The Celluloid South: Hollywood and the Southern Myth* (Knoxville: University of Tennessee Press, 1981).

73. Daniel Bernardi, "The Voice of Whiteness: D. W. Griffith's Biograph Films, 1908–1913," in *The Birth of Whiteness: Race and the Emergence of U.S. Cinema*, edited by Bernardi (New Brunswick, N.J.: Rutgers University Press, 1996), 104, 112.

74. Gerald R. Butters, Jr., "The Kansas Board of Review of Motion Pictures and Film Censorship, 1913–1924" (master's thesis: University of Missouri–Kansas City, 1989), 69–70.

75. Richard Schickel, *D. W. Griffith* (New York: Simon and Schuster, 1984), 91–92.

76. *The Honor of His Family* is available in the Library of Congress.

77. Bernardi, "The Voice of Whiteness," 112–113.

78. *The Guerilla* is available in the Library of Congress.

79. *In Old Kentucky* is available in the Library of Congress.

80. *Biograph Bulletin* (1911), 265. *His Trust* and *His Trust Fulfilled* are available in the Library of Congress.

81. Ibid.

82. Bernardi, "The Voice of Whiteness," 115.

83. *Moving Picture World* (29 January 1911), 194, 196.

84. Sampson, *Blacks in Black and White*, 50.

85. Ibid., 62.

86. In Thomas Cripps's beautifully crafted *Slow Fade to Black: The Negro in American Film, 1900–1942* (New York: Oxford University Press, 1977), the author argues that in the first ten years of commercial cinema, African Americans appeared in a more favorable light than they had in theater or fiction. In fact, Cripps argues that African Americans appeared in a wide range of screen roles. Regarding this thesis, I have to strongly disagree.

4. AFRICAN-AMERICAN CINEMA AND *THE BIRTH OF A NATION*

1. Kevin Gaines, *Uplifting the Race: Black Leadership, Politics, and Culture in the Twentieth Century* (Chapel Hill: University of North Carolina Press, 1996), xvi.

2. John Hope Franklin, "*The Birth of a Nation:* Propaganda As History," *Massachusetts Review* (July 1977): 418. See also Catherine Silk and John Silk, "*Birth of a Nation* and Silent Film," in *Racism and Antiracism in American Popular Culture,* edited by Silk and Silk (Manchester, N.Y.: Manchester University Press, 1990); R. E. Aitken, *The Birth of a Nation Story* (Middleburg, Va.: Denlinger, 1965); R. A. Armour, "History Written in Jagged Lightning: Realistic South vs. Romantic South in *The Birth of a Nation,*" in *The South on Film,* pp. 14–22, edited by W. French (Jackson: University Press of Mississippi, 1981); B. Gallagher, "Racist Ideology and Black Abnormality in *The Birth of a Nation,*" *Phylon* 43 (March 1982): 68–76; Michael Rogin, "The Sword Became a Flashing Vision: D. W. Griffith's *The Birth of a Nation,*" *Representations* 9 (winter 1985): 150–195.

3. Richard Schickel, *D. W. Griffith* (New York: Simon and Schuster, 1984), 78.

4. Gerald R. Butters, Jr., "The Kansas Board of Review of Motion Pictures and Film Censorship, 1913–1924" (master's thesis, University of Missouri–Kansas City, 1989), 66.

5. Ibid., 67–68.

6. Raymond Cook, *Thomas Dixon* (New York: Twayne Publishers, 1974), 58–64.

7. Ibid., 64–79.

8. Quoted in Thomas Cripps, *Slow Fade to Black: The Negro in American Film, 1900–1942* (New York: Oxford University Press, 1977), 44.

9. Raymond Allen Cook, *Fire from the Flint: The Amazing Careers of Thomas Dixon* (Winston-Salem, N.C.: John F. Blair Co., 1977), 126, 131.

10. Ibid., 101–108.

11. Robert A. Armour, "History Written in Jagged Lightning: Realistic South vs. Romantic South in *The Birth of a Nation,*" *Southern Quarterly* 19 (spring/summer 1981): 20.

12. Dixon quoted in Cook's *Fire from the Flint,* 181.

13. Jeffrey Martin, "Film Out of Theater: D. W. Griffith, *Birth of a Nation* and the Melodrama *The Clansman*" *Literature/Film Quarterly* 18, no. 2 (1990): 87–95.

14. Clyde Taylor, "The Re-Birth of the Aesthetic in Cinema," in *The Birth of Whiteness: Race and the Emergence of U.S. Cinema,* edited by Daniel Bernardi (New Brunswick, N.J.: Rutgers University Press, 1996), 33.

15. Manthia Diawara, "Black American Cinema: The New Realism," in *Black American Cinema,* edited by Diawara (New York: Routledge, 1993), 3.

16. Taylor, "The Re-Birth of the Aesthetic in Cinema," 16.

17. Martin, "Film Out of Theater," 87–95.

18. Taylor, "The Re-Birth of the Aesthetic in Cinema," 17.

19. Vincent F. Rocchio, *Reel Racism: Confronting Hollywood's Construction of Afro-American Culture* (Boulder, Colo.: Westview Press, 2000), 32.

20. This scene also implies that abolitionism was a white northern phenomenon, denying black involvement to free themselves and their brethern. The older female abolitionist may be a representative of Harriet Beecher Stowe, author of *Uncle Tom's Cabin* and a hated woman in the South.

21. Henry Stephen Gordon, "The Story of David Wark Griffith, Part Five," *Photoplay* (10 October 1916): 92.

22. Rocchio, *Reel Racism*, 37.

23. Gordon, "The Story of David Wark Griffith, Part Five," 91.

24. Rocchio, *Reel Racism*, 35.

25. The Reconstruction scenes can be "read" in a number of ways. Stuart Hall, in an influential essay, "Encoding, Decoding," proposes three decoding strategies when reading a text. First, one can accept the ideological stance of a film as given. Second, one can negotiate the text, accepting and rejecting parts of the product according to the specific social conditions of the spectator. Finally, one can oppose the text, totally rejecting the ideology of the film. (In *Cultural Studies Reader*, edited by Simon During [London: Routledge, 1993]: 90–103.)

26. Rocchio, *Reel Racism*, 50.

27. Philip Babcock, ed., *Webster's International Dictionary* (Springfield, Mass.: G. H. Merriam Company, 1981), 1,959.

28. In a contemporary *Photoplay* article, Griffith explained, "The decision was to have no black blood among the principals; it was only in the legislative scene that negroes were used." (Gordon, "The Story of David Wark Griffith, Part Five," 92.)

29. Jane Gaines, *Fire and Desire: Mixed-Race Movies in the Silent Era* (Chicago: University of Chicago Press, 2001), 239.

30. Whether this was intentionally planned as a rape scene is one of the most important controversies among scholars of Griffith. I have spoken with Thomas Cripps, who argues strongly that it was not intended as a rape scene. Whether it was or not, Griffith certainly knew how to appeal to the racial and sexualized fears of white Americans. The best article on the reception of *The Birth of a Nation* is Janet Staiger's "*The Birth of a Nation*: Reconsidering Its Reception," in *The Birth of a Nation*, edited by Robert Land (New Brunswick, N.J.: Rutgers University Press, 1994), 191–213.

31. Lillian Gish, who portrayed Elsie, described Lynch's actions as "gorilla-like." Kenneth S. Lynn, "The Torment of D. W. Griffith," *American Scholar* 59, no. 2 (spring 1990): 258.

32. Thomas Cripps, *Slow Fade to Black*, 51.

33. Richard Dyer, "Into the Light: The Whiteness of the South in *The Birth of a Nation*," in *Dixie Debates: Perspectives on Southern Cultures*, p. 165, edited by Richard H. King and Helen Taylor (Washington Square, N.Y.: New York University Press, 1996).

34. Thomas Cripps, "The Making of *The Birth of a Race*: The Emerging Politics of Identity in Silent Movies," in *The Birth of Whiteness: Race and the Emergence of U.S. Cinema*, p. 53, edited by Daniel Bernardi (New Brunswick, N.J.: Rutgers University Press, 1996).

35. Jesse Algeron Rhines, *Black Film/White Money* (New Brunswick, N.J.: Rutgers University Press, 1996), 17.

36. Cripps documents this in his prizewinning article "The Reaction of the Negro to the Motion Picture *Birth of a Nation*," *Historian* 25, no. 3 (May 1963): 244–262.

37. "Facts about *Birth of a Nation* Play at Colonial," *Chicago Defender,* 11 September 1915, 4.

38. "The Clansman," *Crisis* (May 1915): 33.

39. The National Board of Review was the unofficial censorship apparatus of Progressives and the motion picture industry.

40. *Crisis* (10 October 1915): 295–296.

41. *Crisis* (November 1915): 36.

42. Gaines, *Fire and Desire,* 223. Gaines argues that the campaign to ban the film has remained immune to the associations of censorship with intolerance and is an exception to the rule in the belief that constraint on cultural expression is dangerous.

43. "The Clansman," *Crisis* (May 1915): 33.

44. "The Birth of a Nation," *Crisis* (June 1915): 70.

45. W. Allison Sweeney, "W. Allison Sweeney Recites Facts about 'The Real Birth of a Nation,'" *Chicago Defender* (12 June 1915): 1.

46. *Crisis* (12 March 1916): 251.

47. Thomas Cripps, "The Reaction of the Negro to the Motion Picture 'Birth of a Nation,'" in *Focus on "The Birth of a Nation,"* edited by Fred Silva (Englewood Cliffs, N.J.: Prentice-Hall, 1971).

48. Janet Staiger, "The Birth of a Nation: Reconsidering Its Reception," in *The Birth of a Nation,* edited by Robert Lang (New Brunswick, N.J.: Rutgers University Press, 1984).

49. *Crisis* (11 December 1915): 86.

50. Taylor, "The Re-Birth of the Aesthetic in Cinema," 34.

51. Gaines, *Fire and Desire,* 232. Jane Gaines has an interesting discussion of the "desirability" of censorship regarding the film.

52. *Crisis* (12 March 1916): 251.

53. Manthia Diawara, "Black American Cinema: The New Realism," in *Black American Cinema,* edited by Diawara (New York: Routledge, 1993), 3.

54. Patricia Hanson King, ed., *American Film Institute Feature Films, 1911–1920* (Berkeley: University of California Press, 1988), 659.

55. May Childs Nerney to John E. Brent, 22 April 1915, in N.A.A.C.P. records, Library of Congress.

56. Gaines, *Fire and Desire,* 6.

57. May Childs Nerney to John E. Brent, 22 April 1915, in N.A.A.C.P. records, Library of Congress.

58. Rhines, *Black Film/White Money,* 19.

59. Ibid.

60. "Lincoln's Dream," *Crisis* (October 1915): 293.

61. Thomas Cripps, "The Birth of a Race Company: An Early Stride toward a Black Cinema," *Journal of Negro History* 59, no. 1 (January 1974): 33–34.

62. Ibid., 33–35.

63. Nickie Fleener, "Answering Film with Film: The Hampton Epilogue, a Positive Alternative to the Negative Black Stereotypes Presented in *The Birth of a Nation,*" *Journal of Popular Film and Television* 7 (1980): 410–411.

64. Ibid.

65. Oswald Garrison Villard to Alice P. Tapley, 29 November 1916, "The Birth of a Nation" file, Hampton Archives.

66. *The Birth of a Race* press material, *The Birth of a Race* file, George P. Johnson collection (hereafter referred to as GPJC), Special Collections, University of California, Los Angeles.

67. Ibid.

68. Cripps, "The Making of *The Birth of a Race,*" 48.

69. Henry T. Sampson, *Blacks in Black and White: A Source Book on Black Film* (New York: Scarecrow Press, 1995), 208–209. John W. Noble is designated as the "official" director in the credits.

70. *Variety* (22 November 1918): 50; *Moving Picture World* (10 May 1919).

71. *The Birth of a Race* is available in the Library of Congress. Apparently this film is only a portion of the completed work so my commentary is limited to the available footage.

72. Emmett J. Scott, *Variety* (6 December 1918).

5. The Defense of Black Manhood on the Screen

1. Mark A. Reid, "Early Black Independent Filmmakers," *Black Film Review* 12, no. 4 (1988): 21.

2. *Indianapolis Freeman,* 20 December 1913.

3. Ibid. Also see Manthia Diawara, "Black Spectatorship: Problems of Identification and Resistance," *Screen* 29, no. 1 (fall 1988): 66–76; Peter Biskind, "The Colour of Money," *Sight and Sound* 1 (August 1991): 6; Jacqueline Bobo, "The Subject Is Money: Reconsidering the Black Film Audience as a Theoretical Paradigm," *Black American Literature Forum* 25 (summer 1991): 421–432; Matthew Bernstein, "Black American Cinema: Aesthetics and Spectatorship," *Film Quarterly* 48 (summer 1995): 42–44.

4. Ibid.

5. *Indianapolis Freeman,* 13 March 1909, 5.

6. *Indianapolis Freeman,* 20 December 1913.

7. *New York Age,* 5 September 1913.

8. Zeinabu irene Davis's touching and poetic film *Compensation* (1998) recreates a scene in which an audience views *The Railroad Porter.* Davis not only replicates an early African-American moviegoing audience but also gives her version of the Foster film since it is now lost.

9. Reid, "Early Black Independent Filmmakers," 22.

10. Unfortunately, all we have are the titles of most of Foster's films. The actual films and promotional material regarding the films' synopses have been lost.

11. Juli Jones, Jr., "Moving Pictures Offers the Greatest Opportunity to the American Negro in History of Race from Every Point of View," *Chicago Defender* 9 (September 1915).

12. See Manthia Diawara, "Black Studies, Cultural Studies: Performative Acts," in *What Is Cultural Studies: A Reader,* edited by John Storey (London: Arnold Press, 1996), 300–306.

13. Richard Merelman, *Representing Black Culture* (New York: Routledge, 1995), 3.

14. Gladstone Yearwood, "Toward a Theory of Black Cinema Aesthetics," in *Black Cinema Aesthetics: Issues in Independent Black Filmmaking* (Athens, Ohio: Ohio University Press, 1982), 67.

15. Jane M. Gaines, *Fire and Desire: Mixed-Race Movies in the Silent Era* (Chicago: University of Chicago Press, 2001), 13. Gaines argues, "The significance of race movies would be the way in which they could be counterhegemonic without symmetrically 'countering' white culture on every point; for their oppositionality, if it could be called that, was in the circumvention in the way they produced images that didn't go *through* white culture."

16. Pearl Bowser and Louise Spence, *Writing Himself into History: Oscar Micheaux, His Silent Films, and His Audiences* (New Brunswick, N.J.: Rutgers University Press, 2000), 68. Bowser and Spence discuss the fact that there was never enough product for all-black films to be screened continuously through the year.

17. One such example is a review of the film *One Large Evening* (1917) in the black newspaper *New York Amsterdam News* (10 April 1914). The reviewer points out that the screenwriter Hunter C. Haynes "made a careful study of the methods of the various white scenario writers and directors and formulated his own ideas on the subject."

18. Bowser and Spence, *Writing Himself into History*, 59.

19. That is, according to the 14 March 1914 *Indianapolis Freeman* interview with Hunter Haynes, founder of the Afro-American Film Company. It can be assumed that this number increased slightly during the 1920s. Considering that there were about 32,000 white theater houses in the period, this means that theaters that catered exclusively to African-American spectators made up slightly less than 1 percent of all motion picture houses in the country.

20. In *Writing Himself into History*, 64, Bowser and Spence discuss the significance of black theaters in the African-American community.

21. Charlene Regester, "The Misreading and Rereading of African American Filmmaker Oscar Micheaux," *Film History* 7, no. 4 (winter 1995): 427.

22. Hunter Haynes pleaded in the 14 March 1914 edition of the *Indianapolis Freeman*, "Do you realize the fact that it costs the Afro-American Film Co. almost as much to make a 1000 foot picture as it does a white corporation. Then realize the fact of the limited territory as against theirs."

23. Gaines, *Fire and Desire*, 131.

24. Quoted in Gaines, *Fire and Desire*, 3.

25. The Western Film Producing Company of Kansas City was one of the rare examples where a woman played a pivotal role behind the camera. The first African-American female producer, Maria P. Williams, released a 1923 feature, *The Flames of Wrath*. The plot involved a group of robbers who steal a valuable diamond. The plot sharply contrasted "good" and "evil." What was unique about the film was the gendered professional roles played by the characters. The female characters included a black female prosecuting attorney (unknown in this period) and an amateur female detective. The majority of the male characterizations were thieves, crooked lawyers, or victims of circumstance. The film is no longer in existence.

26. Bowser and Spence, *Writing Himself into History*, 52.

27. David Levering Lewis, *When Harlem Was in Vogue* (New York: Vintage Books, 1982).

28. Yearwood, *Black Cinema Aesthetics*, 70–71.

29. Gaines, *Fire and Desire*, 10.

30. Madubuko Diakite, *Film Culture and the Black Filmmaker* (New York: Arno Press, 1980), 152.

31. Ibid., 153.

32. Steve Neale, "The Same Old Story: Stereotypes and Difference," *Screen Education* 32–33 (autumn/winter 1979–1980): 34. Neale has described the problems of dealing with criticism of stereotypes and counterartistic reactions to them. He claims that such criticisms are not based on the real world but the ideal.

33. The film did quite well at the famous Pekin Theatre in Chicago. According to Henry Sampson, large African-American crowds attended the film (Sampson, *Blacks in Black and White*, 183). Sampson has completed the most exhaustive research

concerning independent black film companies. Documentation on these companies will be taken from his book and from my research at the George P. Johnson collection (GPJC) at the University of California, Los Angeles.

34. Peter P. Jones Company file, GPJC.

35. For works on African-American participation in World War I, see Arthur E. Barbeau and Florette Henri, *Unknown Soldiers: Black American Troops in World War I* (Philadelphia: Temple University Press, 1974), and Arthur W. Little, *From Harlem to the Rhine: The Story of Negro Soldiers* (New York: Covici, 1936).

36. Ibid.

37. Downing Film Company file, GPJC. The Downing Film Company produced only one film in New York City in 1919.

38. Lester A. Walton, "Movies and War Photo Plays," *New York Age* (8 March 1917).

39. American Motion Picture Company file, GPJC. Little information is available regarding the American Motion Picture Company. The company produced at least one film in the Washington, D.C., area from 1919 to 1920.

40. Bowser and Spence, *Writing Himself into History*, 94.

41. Frederick Douglass Film Company file, GPJC. The Frederick Douglass Film Company was founded in Jersey City, New Jersey, in 1916. The company produced three films between 1917 and 1919—*The Colored American Winning His Suit* (1917), *The Scapegoat* (1917), and *Heroic Negro Soldiers of the World War* (1919).

42. Craig W. Campbell, *Reel America and World War I* (Jefferson, N.C.: McFarland and Company, 1985), 113. Leslie Midkiff DeBauche, *Reel Patriotism: The Movies and World War I* (Madison: University of Wisconsin Press, 1997), 165–166.

43. This idea of not forgetting the sacrifices of African-American participants in World War I is well documented by examining African-American newspapers between 1919 and 1921. There are a number of advertisements for books or artistic renderings of African-American military participation. Advertisements of the period include such works as *Negroes War for Human Rights* (*Chicago Defender*, 16 April 1919, 5), *History of the American Negro in the Great War*, and *History of the American Negro in the Great World War*, both in *Chicago Defender*, 26 April 1917.

44. "Two Reel Picture Makes a Big Hit," *New York Age*, 6 April 1918, 7. Little information is available regarding the Toussaint Film Company. The company was based in New York City and produced at least one film between 1918 and 1924.

45. See James R. Grossman, *Land of Hope: Chicago, Black Southerners and the Great Migration* (Chicago: University of Chicago Press, 1989); Joe William Trotter, ed., *The Great Migration in Historical Perspective* (Bloomington: Indiana University Press, 1991); Joe W. Trotter and Earl Lewis, eds., *African Americans in the Industrial Age: A Documentary History, 1915–1945* (Boston: Northeastern University Press, 1996).

46. Sampson, *Blacks in Black and White*, 344, 584, 621, 624. The Anderson-Walkins Film Company was founded in New York City in 1913 and produced at least one film. Crusader Films was founded in New York City in 1923 and also produced at least one film.

47. In 1913, the Afro-American Film Company developed a newsreel covering the National Negro Business League's annual meeting in Philadelphia, Pennsylvania (*New York Age*, 4 September 1913).

48. Sampson, *Blacks in Black and White*, 179, 593, 595, 607, 612.

49. Ibid., 605. Monumental Films was based in Washington, D.C., and produced several newsreels in the early 1920s. The Turpin Film Company was founded in

Kansas City during World War I and produced at least four newsreels between 1918 and 1922.

50. Ibid., 610.

51. Randy Roberts, *Papa Jack: Jack Johnson and the Era of White Hopes* (New York: Free Press, 1983), 138–155.

52. Johnson was paid $7,500 for eighteen and a half hours of work by the Andlauer Company, a handsome sum in 1921. The Andlauer Company, based in Kansas City, Missouri, produced only this one film in 1921 (Andlauer Company file, GPJC). The synopsis of the film is in the *As the World Rolls On* file, GPJC.

53. An excellent discussion of this phenomenon can be found in John Hoberman's *Darwin's Athletes: How Sport Has Damaged Black America and Preserved the Myth of Race* (Boston: Houghton Mifflin Co., 1997).

54. *Chicago Defender*, 26 January 1922, 7.

55. Advertisement for *For His Mother's Sake*, *Chicago Defender*, 15 February 1922, 7. The Blackburn-Velde Company was based in New York City and produced only this one film in 1921.

56. Synopsis, *For His Mother's Sake* file, GPJC.

57. Frederick Douglass Film Company Press Book, Frederick Douglass Film Company file, GPJC.

58. Ibid.

59. Synopsis of *The Colored American Winning His Suit*, Frederick Douglass Film Company file, GPJC.

60. Review of *The Colored American Winning His Suit*, *New York Age*, 20 July 1916.

61. Ibid.

62. *New York Age*, 17 May 1917.

63. Other examples include the *Indianapolis Freeman*'s criticism of the Afro-American Film Company's *Lovie Joe's Romance* (28 March 1914). The reviewer describes the film as "amateurish . . . disconnected . . . the camera is out of focus . . . and the general action of the piece is absolutely absurd." The *New York Age*'s review of the Afro-American Film Company's *National Negro Business League* (4 September 1914) describes the film as "mechanical" and "blurred."

64. Sampson, *Blacks in Black and White*, 270. The Unique Film Company was founded in Chicago in 1916 and produced only this one film.

65. *Chicago Defender*, 15 November 1920, 5. The Royal Garden Film Company was founded in Chicago in 1920 and produced only this one film.

66. Joan Mellen, *Big Bad Wolves*, 33.

67. *California Eagle*, 10 September 1921. The Bookertee Company was founded in Los Angeles in the early 1920s and produced two films.

68. Ibid.

69. *Kansas City Call*, 30 May 1924. Monarch Productions was founded in New York City in 1924.

70. *Los Angeles New Age Dispatch*, 29 August 1928. The Rosebud Film Corporation was founded in Los Angeles in 1928 and produced only this one film.

71. *Los Angeles Age*, 31 August 1928.

72. Sampson, *Blacks in Black and White*, 265; *Norfolk Journal and Guide*, 13 February 1921; *Norfolk Journal and Guide*, 19 February 1921.

73. *Chicago Defender*, 11 December 1920, 4.

74. This film is available in the Library of Congress.

75. *Indianapolis Freeman*, 26 November 1914. Hunter Haynes is the second

known African-American director and producer of films in the United States. His company was the Afro-American Film Company and was based in Chicago. The company produced at least two films in 1914.

76. Ibid.

77. Sampson, *Blacks in Black and White,* 145. Lone Star Motion Picture Producers was founded in San Antonio, Texas, in 1922. The company produced at least six films.

78. J. Ronald Green, *Straight Lick: The Cinema of Oscar Micheaux* (Bloomington: Indiana University Press, 2000), 130.

79. Oscar Micheaux is the preeminent figure in the history of black produced and directed silent film. He was not only the most prolific of all of the filmmakers but he was the most radical regarding the issues he addressed and the manner in which he chose to address them. He will be dealt with separately in the next chapter.

80. Sampson, *Blacks in Black and White,* 136.

81. His brother George claimed, "He gained the knowledge and experience in training and caring for horses far beyond his age which proved of great value later in his motion picture career" (Noble Johnson file, GPJC).

82. Jane M. Gaines, *Fire and Desire,* 99.

83. Bill Cappello, "Noble Johnson—Part 1," *Classic Images* 199 (January 1992): 42, 43, 63.

84. George Johnson's personal notes, Lincoln Motion Picture Company file, GPJC.

85. Mark A. Reid, *Redefining Black Film* (Berkeley: University of California Press, 1993): 47.

86. Letter from Clarence Brooks, Lincoln Motion Picture Company file, GPJC.

87. Ibid.

88. Ibid.

89. Lincoln Motion Picture Company file, GPJC.

90. *Realization of a Negroes Ambition* promotional material, Lincoln Motion Picture Company file, GPJC.

91. Kevin Gaines, *Uplifting the Race: Black Leadership, Politics, and Culture in the Twentieth Century* (Chapel Hill: University of North Carolina Press, 1996), 2.

92. Tony Langston, "Realization," *Chicago Defender,* 14 October 1916, 4.

93. "Photo-Play," *Chicago Defender,* 26 August 1916, 6.

94. Ibid.

95. Bowser and Spence, *Writing Himself into History,* 90.

96. Ibid.

97. Ibid.

98. Newspaper clipping, Lincoln Motion Picture Company file, GPJC.

99. Ibid.

100. Gaines, *Fire and Desire,* 107.

101. Advertisement for *Trooper of Troop K, Chicago Defender,* 7 October 1914, 4.

102. "Trooper of Troop K," *Chicago Defender,* 7 October 1916, 4.

103. Lincoln Motion Picture Company file, GPJC.

104. Ibid.

105. "Trooper of Troop K," *Chicago Defender,* 7 October 1916.

106. Reid, *Redefining Black Film,* 10.

107. C. H. Turpin to George Johnson, 21 November 1916, Lincoln Motion Picture Company file, GPJC.

108. Manager, Bryar Amusement Company, Nashville, Tennessee, to George Johnson, 21 April 1917, Lincoln Motion Picture Company file, GPJC.

109. Gaines, *Fire and Desire*, 140.

110. *The Law of Nature* synopsis, Lincoln Motion Picture Company file, GPJC.

111. Green, *Straight Lick*, 146.

112. Advertisement for *The Law of Nature*, *Chicago Defender*, 18 August 1917, 4.

113. Ibid.

114. Advertisement, *Chicago Defender*, 30 July 1917, 4.

115. Ibid.

116. Ibid.

117. Ibid.

118. Promotional material, Lincoln Motion Picture Company, GPJC.

119. Telegram from Noble Johnson to George Johnson, 31 July 1918, GPJC.

120. Unidentified clipping, *Chicago Defender*, GPJC.

121. W. H. Tamppert to George Johnson, 6 June 1918, Lincoln Motion Picture Company file, GPJC.

122. Bowser and Spence, *Writing Himself into History*, 70.

123. George Johnson's personal notes, Lincoln Motion Picture Company file, GPJC.

124. Ibid.

125. Clarence Brooks starred in the last two Lincoln features and made films throughout the 1930s. Clarence Brooks file, GPJC.

126. Film synopsis, Lincoln Motion Picture Company file, GPJC.

127. George Paul to Lincoln Motion Picture Company, 5 October 1919, Lincoln Motion Picture Company file, GPJC.

128. Ibid.

129. *Chicago Defender*, 27 September 1919, 9.

130. Lincoln Motion Picture Company file, GPJC.

131. This was an important motivation for African-American audiences. In "Colored Motion Pictures Are in Great Demand," published in the *New York Age*, Lester A. Walton argued, "Colored people throughout the country are clamoring for motion pictures dealing with Negro life. This piece of information is imparted by race promoters who have expended considerable money and energy in recent months to screen presentations which depict our men . . . in a favorable light and as they really are; not solely as hewers of wood and drawers of water" (6 March 1920).

132. Lincoln Motion Picture Company file, GPJC.

133. Gaines, *Fire and Desire*, 103.

134. Lincoln Motion Picture Company file, GPJC.

6. Oscar Micheaux: From Homestead to Lynch Mob

1. Pearl Bowser and Louise Spence, *Writing Himself into History: Oscar Micheaux, His Silent Films, and His Audiences* (New Brunswick, N.J.: Rutgers University Press, 2000), 14.

2. Bowser and Spence, *Writing Himself into History*; J. Ronald Green, *Straight Lick: The Cinema of Oscar Micheaux* (Bloomington: Indiana University Press, 2000); and Jane M. Gaines, *Fire and Desire: Mixed-Race Movies in the Silent Era* (Chicago: University of Chicago Press, 2001).

3. See Charlene Regester, "The Misreading and Rereading of African American

Filmmaker Oscar Micheaux" (*Film History* 7 [winter 1995]: 426–499), for an excellent analysis of the major waves of Micheaux scholarship. I have had to "re-create" many of Micheaux's silent productions through studio notes, advertisements, newspaper articles, and reviews.

4. Green, *Straight Lick*, xvi.

5. Regester, "Misreading," 433.

6. Richard Grupenhoff, *Black Valentino: The Stage and Screen Career of Lorenzo Tucker* (Metuchen, N.J.: Scarecrow Press, 1988), 66–67.

7. Daniel J. Leab, "A Pale Black Imitation: All-Colored Films, 1930–1960," *Journal of Popular Film* 4, no. 1 (1975): 4.

8. Gaines, *Fire and Desire*, 148.

9. Richard Gehr, "One-Man Show," *American Film* (May 1991): 38.

10. Green, *Straight Lick*, 61.

11. See Green, *Staight Lick*, 34, and Gaines, *Fire and Desire*, 17.

12. D. Ireland Thomas, *Chicago Defender*, 8 July 1922, 6.

13. Thomas Cripps, *Slow Fade to Black: The Negro in American Film, 1900–1942* (New York: Oxford University Press, 1977), 172.

14. Regester, "Misreading," 426–449.

15. Green, *Straight Lick*, 57.

16. Eileen Landay, *Black Film Stars* (New York: Drake Publishers, 1973), 45.

17. Oscar Micheaux, *The Conquest: The Story of a Pioneer* (Lincoln, Neb.: Woodruff Press, 1913), 145.

18. *Philadelphia Afro-American*, 24 January 1925.

19. Jesse Rhines, *Black Film/White Money* (New Brunswick, N.J.: Rutgers University Press, 1996), 23.

20. Gaines, *Fire and Desire*, 123.

21. Henry T. Sampson, *Blacks in Black and White: A Source Book on Black Film* (New York: Scarecrow Press, 1995), 142–143.

22. Ibid.

23. Ibid., 144.

24. Bowser and Spence, *Writing Himself into History*, 8.

25. Ibid., 8.

26. Apparently, McCracken's actions and character totally infuriated Micheaux. Despicable minister figures, apparently modeled after his father-in-law, would appear in a number of his films.

27. Sampson, *Blacks in Black and White*, 146.

28. Green, *Straight Lick*, xi.

29. Micheaux, *The Conquest*.

30. Bowser and Spence, *Writing Himself into History*, xix.

31. Ibid.

32. Joseph A. Young, *Black Novelist as White Racist* (New York: Greenwood Press, 1989), xi, 7–9.

33. Jane Gaines has recently questioned whether it was the Johnson brothers or Micheaux who actually backed out of the deal (*Fire and Desire*, 118).

34. Lincoln Motion Picture Company file, GPJC.

35. Young, *Black Novelist As White Racist*, 1–33.

36. Oscar Micheaux, *The Homesteader* (College Park, Md.: McGrath Publishing, 1969), 63–64.

37. Micheaux was certainly not oblivious to the problems that existed in the South for African Americans; this was a prevalent theme in his films and books.

38. In "One-Man Show," Richard Gehr explains that Micheaux had "considerable charm" and learned his salesmanship skills by selling his novels from door to door. Later, he used the same distribution strategy by selling his current product to finance his future film (36).

39. Sampson, *Blacks in Black and White*, 150–151.

40. Ibid., 252–254.

41. *Chicago Defender*, 22 February 1919, 6.

42. Ibid.

43. Promotional literature for *The Homesteader*, Micheaux file, GPJC.

44. *Chicago Defender*, 1 March 1919, 11.

45. Micheaux, *The Homesteader*, 22.

46. Ibid., 24.

47. *Chicago Defender*, 22 February 1919.

48. Micheaux, *The Homesteader*, 25.

49. Ibid.

50. *Chicago Defender*, 22 February 1919.

51. Micheaux, *The Homesteader*, 40.

52. Learthen Dorsey, Introduction to *The Homesteader* (Lincoln: University of Nebraska Press, 1994), 2.

53. Bowser and Spence, *Writing Himself into History*, 171.

54. Micheaux, *The Homesteader*, 59.

55. Ibid.

56. Ibid.

57. Ibid.

58. Ibid.

59. Ibid.

60. Bowser and Spence, *Writing Himself into History*, 26.

61. Micheaux, *The Homesteader*, 109.

62. Ibid.

63. Dorsey, Introduction to *The Homesteader*, 2.

64. Micheaux, *The Homesteader*, 209.

65. Ibid., 228.

66. Ibid., 268.

67. Ibid., 279.

68. Ibid., 228.

69. Green, *Straight Lick*, 16.

70. Micheaux, *The Homesteader*, 284.

71. *Chicago Defender*, 22 February 1919.

72. Bowser and Spence, *Writing Himself into History*, 25.

73. *Chicago Defender*, 22 February 1919.

74. In *The Afro-American and the Second World War*, Neil A. Wynn explains that California had half of all the shipbuilding and aircraft manufacturing plants in the nation in 1940 so migration to the West for employment was opportunistic during these years. The black population of San Francisco grew 560 percent between 1940 and 1946, and the black population of Los Angeles grew 109 percent in the same period (New York: Holmes and Meier Publishers, 1975), 60–62.

75. Bowser and Spence, *Writing Himself into History*, 156–157.

76. Green, *Straight Lick*, 153–154.

77. Most censorship boards would not allow negative portrayals of ministers, a frequent theme in Micheaux's films. The National Board of Review of Motion

Pictures, one of the first voluntary censorship boards in the nation, had eight prohibitive standards on which it based its judgment. The sixth standard stated, "The Board prohibits blasphemy, by which we understood the careless or wanton or unnecessary offense against religious susceptibilities of any large number of people of the country." Found in Edward De Grazia and Roger K. Newman's *Banned Films: Movies, Censorship and the First Amendment* (New York: R. R. Bowker Co., 1982), 12.

78. Advertisement for *The Homesteader, Chicago Defender,* 1 March 1919, 11.

79. *Chicago Defender,* 1 March 1919.

80. *Chicago Defender,* 31 May 1919, 9.

81. *Chicago Defender,* 30 April 1921, 6. For information on the Frank case, see Nancy Rosenbaum, *Jury Justice: A Look at the Scottsboro Case and the Leo Frank Trial* (Waltham, Mass.: Waltham Press, 1995), and the videotape *The Leo Frank Case* (Atlanta Jewish Federation, 1994). In *Blackface, White Noise: Jewish Immigrants in the Hollywood Melting Pot,* Michael Rogin discusses the interchangeability of anti-Semitism and racism in fictional Hollywood moviemaking (Berkeley: University of California Press, 1996).

82. *Gunsaulus Mystery* synopsis, Oscar Micheaux file, GPJC.

83. Sampson, *Blacks in Black and White,* 597.

84. In 1922 the Motion Picture Producers and Distributors of America (MPPDA) formed to keep the federal government from developing a system of national censorship of motion pictures. Will Hays, President Warren Harding's postmaster general, was hired to supervise the new organization. Hays developed a "gentleman's agreement" within the industry that consisted of thirteen points motion picture directors and producers agreed would not be contained in their motion pictures. Black independent film companies were not members of this organization but it was assumed by most censorship boards that they should uphold the same standards.

85. *Chicago Defender,* 3 January 1920, 6; 25 August 1920, 4; 4 September 1920, 4.

86. Ibid.

87. Gaines, *Fire and Desire,* 124.

88. *Chicago Defender,* 4 September 1920.

89. Charlene Regester, "Black Films, White Censors: Oscar Micheaux Confronts Censorship in New York, Virginia and Chicago," in *Movies, Censorship and American Culture,* p. 168, edited by Francis G. Couvares (Washington, D.C.: Smithsonian Institution Press, 1996).

90. *New York Age,* 11 September 1920.

91. Ibid.

92. *Chicago Defender,* 14 August 1920, 4.

93. Regester, "Black Films, White Censors," 176.

94. D. Ireland Thomas, *Chicago Defender,* 31 January 1925.

95. Regester, "Black Films, White Censors," 176–177.

96. Pearl Bowser's article "Oscar Micheaux's Body and Soul and the Burdens of Representation" is an excellent discussion of the filmmaker's discourse on racial identity (*Cinema Journal* 39, no. 3 [Spring 2000]).

97. Cripps, *Slow Fade to Black,* 191–192.

98. J. Ronald Green, "Twoness in the Style of Oscar Micheaux," in *Black American Cinema,* edited by Manthia Diawara (New York: Routledge, 1993), 38.

99. Gaines, *Fire and Desire,* 234.

100. Charles Musser discusses the problems of dealing with *Body and Soul* in "Re-

dream the Dreams of White Playwrights: Reappropriation and Resistance in Oscar Micheaux's Body and Soul," *Yale Journal of Criticism* 12, no. 2 (1999): 321–356. He argues that "a new analysis of *Body and Soul* has been greatly facilitated by the discovery and restoration of Micheaux's *Within Our Gates* (1920) and *The Symbol of the Unconquered* (1920)." He claims that the Eastman House version of *Body and Soul* is "reasonably complete and coherent" and that the film shares similar characteristics with Micheaux's other known films. Musser points out how the dream sequence is not that unusual in Micheaux or other black filmmakers' repertoires and that this forces a rethinking of Cripps's analysis of the film.

101. Bowser and Spence, *Writing Himself into History*, 187.

102. Cripps, *Slow Fade to Black*, 191–193. As Jane Gaines points out in *Fire and Desire*, this final "disjunctive" scene is later replicated in Micheaux's *God's Stepchildren* (1938). *Within Our Gates* also has a final disjunctive scene.

103. *New York Age*, 11 November 1925.

104. Green, *Straight Lick*, 208.

105. *Billboard*, 27 December 1924, 49.

106. Bowser and Spence, *Writing Himself into History*, 65.

107. *The Symbol of the Unconquered* synopsis, GPJC. This film is presently available on videotape.

108. *New York Age*, 25 December 1920.

109. *New York Age*, 1 January 1921.

110. See Bowser and Spence, *Writing Himself into History*, 158, 160.

111. Bernard L. Peterson, Jr., "The Films of Oscar Micheaux: America's First Fabulous Black Filmmaker," *Crisis* 86 (April 1979): 138.

112. Gaines, *Fire and Desire*, 217.

113. Ibid.

114. Ibid., 170.

115. Regester, "Black Films, White Censors," 170–171.

116. "Race Again Has Member on Censor Board," *Chicago Defender*, 8 May 1915, 1.

117. Ibid.

118. Sampson, *Blacks in Black and White*, 345. Bowling is not the only individual in Micheaux's real life to be attacked cinematically. His brother Swan Micheaux left the Film and Book Company in 1927 to take a job with a company that imported European films and then with the Dunbar Company, a distributor of black films. Swan left Micheaux's company in poor financial condition and his mishandling of his accounts was one of the major reasons for Micheaux's bankruptcy in 1929. Swan was roundly criticized in Micheaux's *Wages of Sin* (1927). In the film two brothers run a film production company. The younger brother spends money wildly on women and alcohol and eventually almost destroys his older brother financially.

119. *Chicago Defender*, 25 November 1922, 6.

120. Sampson, *Blacks in Black and White*, 322.

121. Censors' report, Virginia State Board of Motion Picture Censors, *The House Behind the Cedars* file.

122. Ibid.

123. Oscar Micheaux to Virginia State Board of Motion Picture Censors (13 March 1925).

124. Quoted in Bowser and Spence, *Writing Himself into History*, 18.

125. Ibid., 21.

126. Graeme Turner, *Film As Social Practice* (London: Routledge, 1988), 83.

127. Regester, "Black Films, White Censors," 171–172.
128. J. Ronald Green, "Micheaux v. Griffith," *Griffithiana* 60–61 (October 1997), 39.
129. Bowser and Spence, *Writing Himself into History*, 37.
130. Green, *Straight Lick*, 187.
131. Unfortunately, there is little information available regarding Micheaux's *Marcus Garland*, a film that was a thinly disguised replication of the life and ideas of Marcus Garvey. It would have been fascinating to have known Micheaux's "take" on the popular African-American leader.
132. *Billboard*, 26 January 1926.
133. Ibid.
134. *New York Age*, 19 January 1924.
135. Pearl Bowser has documented the tremendous censorship battles Micheaux underwent regarding the passage of the film. Both the Maryland State Board of Motion Picture Censors and the Virginia State Board of Motion Picture Censors demanded substantial cuts.
136. Sampson, *Blacks in Black and White*, 326.
137. Ibid.
138. Ibid.
139. Bowser and Spence, *Writing Himself into History*, 21.
140. bell hooks, "Micheaux: Celebrating Blackness," *Black American Literature Forum* 25, no. 2 (summer 1991): 351.
141. Green, *Straight Lick*, 123.
142. Jane M. Gaines, "*The Birth of a Nation* and *Within Our Gates:* Two Tales of the American South," in *Dixie Debates: Perspectives on Southern Culture*, edited by Richard King and Helen Taylor (New York: New York University Press, 1996), 179.
143. This is a beautiful quote from Jane Gaines in *Fire and Desire*, 8.
144. As Pearl Bowser and Louise Spence have commented, much more work needs to be done on this period in Micheaux's career.

7. *WITHIN OUR GATES*

1. The eight-reel film was produced in 1919 and released in Chicago and Detroit in January 1920.
2. Preface to restored version of *Within Our Gates*, Library of Congress.
3. Micheaux's film *The Gunsaulus Mystery* (1921) was another example of misplaced criminal blame and vigilante justice. *Jasper Landry's Will* (1923) was a sequel to *Within Our Gates* (Bernard L. Peterson, Jr., "The Films of Oscar Micheaux," *Crisis* 86 [April 1979]: 138).
4. Jane Gaines, "Race, Melodrama and Oscar Micheaux," in *Black American Cinema*, edited by Manthia Diawara (New York: Routledge, 1993), 51.
5. Ibid., 50.
6. J. Ronald Green, *Straight Lick: The Cinema of Oscar Micheaux* (Bloomington: Indiana University Press, 2000), 10.
7. Mark Reid, *Redefining Black Film* (Berkeley: University of California Press, 1993), 12.
8. Pearl Bowser and Louise Spence, *Writing Himself into History: Oscar Micheaux, His Silent Films, and His Audiences* (New Brunswick, N.J.: Rutgers University Press, 2000), 107.
9. Ibid., 129.

10. Jane M. Gaines, *Fire and Desire: Mixed-Race Movies in the Silent Era* (Chicago: University of Chicago Press, 2001), 132.

11. Green, *Straight Lick*, 111.

12. J. Ronald Green brilliantly points out the physical similarity between the Stratton character and that of the Lillian Gish/Elsie Stoneman character in *The Birth of a Nation*.

13. Vardaman was a leader of the southern Radicals. He claimed that "political equality for the colored race leads to social equality" (Joel Williamson, *The Crucible of Race: Black-White Relations in the American South since Emancipation* [New York: Oxford University Press, 1984], 379).

14. Lawrence Levine, *Black Culture and Black Consciousness* (Oxford: Oxford University Press, 1977), xiii.

15. As Pearl Bowser and Louise Spence point out, Micheaux makes it clear that the threat to white supremacy is not black sexuality but black autonomy and self-determination.

16. Gaines, "Race, Melodrama and Oscar Micheaux," 55.

17. One can only imagine the horror within an African-American moviegoing audience in 1920.

18. *Chicago Defender*, 10 January 1920, 6.

19. Grace Elizabeth Hale, *Making Whiteness: The Culture of Segregation in the South, 1890–1940* (New York: Pantheon Books, 1998), 204.

20. Bowser and Spence, *Writing Himself into History*, 133.

21. Gaines, "Race, Melodrama and Oscar Micheaux," 60.

22. Jane Gaines argues that in the original, uncensored version of the film, an African-American man comes to Sylvia's defense, breaking down the door and fighting Gridlestone. This interracial fight was apparently too much for the censors (Gaines, *Fire and Desire*, 243–244).

23. Gaines, "Race, Melodrama and Oscar Micheaux," 57.

24. Quoted in Bowser and Spence, *Writing Himself into History*, 125.

25. As J. Ronald Green argues in *Straight Lick*, Micheaux chose survival (210).

26. William Tuttle, *Race Riot: Chicago in the Red Summer of 1919* (New York: Antheum Press, 1970), 14–15.

27. *Omaha Nebraska Daily, Within Our Gates* file, GPJC.

28. *Chicago Defender*, 3 January 1920, 1.

29. Green, *Fire and Desire*, 151, 154–155.

30. Oscar Micheaux, *The Wind from Nowhere* (New York: Book Supply Company, 1944), 123.

8. THE LATE SILENT ERA

1. An examination of black newspapers between 1913 and 1929 demonstrates that mainstream studio productions were much more heavily advertised and critiqued than all-black features.

2. The best discussion of the end of blackface is Michael Rogin's *Blackface, White Noise: Jewish Immigrants in the Melting Pot* (Berkeley: University of California Press, 1996).

3. These films include: 1915—*A Colored Girl's Love, Colored Villainry, A Hot Time in Punkville, Moase Covington, Queen of the Jungle, Nedra, Troubles with Rufus;* 1916—*Around the World, The Jungle Outcasts, Mammy's Rose, Mixed Kids, Robinson Crusoe, Wurra Wurra, Shadows and Sunshine, Mixed Up in Black;* 1917—*Black*

Magic, Black Nine, Conning the Cannibal, His Cannibal Wife, Love Aflame, Minding the Baby, Mixed Color Scheme; 1918—*Free and Equal;* 1919—*Dark and Cloudy;* 1922—*Red Hot Romance;* 1924—*His Darker Self;* 1927—*Topsy and Eva.* This list was derived from the American Film Institute's catalog series on feature films.

4. Quoted in Michael Rogin's "Racial Masquerade in Motion Pictures," *Journal of American History* (December 1992): 1055.

5. Clyde Taylor, "The Re-Birth of the Aesthetic in Cinema," in *The Birth of Whiteness: Race and the Emergence of U.S. Cinema,* edited by Daniel Bernardi (New Brunswick, N.J.: Rutgers University Press, 1996), 32.

6. Literature on the violent reaction toward African Americans in the postwar era include William Tuttle, *Race Riot: Chicago in the Red Summer of 1919* (New York: Antheum Press, 1970); Lee E. Williams, *Anatomy of Four Race Riots: Racial Conflict in Knoxville, Elaine, Tulsa and Chicago, 1919–1921* (Hattiesburg: University and College Press of Mississippi, 1972); Mark Schneider, *Boston Confronts Jim Crow, 1890–1920* (Boston: Northeastern University Press, 1997); Herbert Shapiro, *White Violence and Black Response: From Reconstruction to Montgomery* (Amherst: University of Massachusetts Press, 1988).

7. Henry T. Sampson, *Blacks in Black and White: A Source Book on Black Film* (New York: Scarecrow Press, 1995), 54, 78–79, 91–92, 126, 284–285.

8. An example of this revival is the Christie comedies of the late 1920s. One promotional piece by the Christie Company claimed, "Negro comedies have been attempted before, but with Negro actors. Christie's innovation lies in the idea that white players, under careful direction, can bring out the comedy of the Negro with the skill of a trained white comedian." Christie Comedy files, GPJC.

9. See Robert L. Carringer, ed., *The Jazz Singer* (Madison: University of Wisconsin Press, 1979); Joseph Greenblum, "Does Hollywood Still Glorify Jewish Intermarriage? The Case of the Jazz Singer," *American Jewish History* 83 (December 1995): 445–469; Irv Saposnik, "Jolson, the Jazz Singer and the Jewish Mother," *Judaism* 43 (fall 1994): 432–442.

10. Michael Rogin, "Blackface, White Noise: The Jewish Jazz Singer Finds His Voice," *Critical Inquiry* 18 (spring 1992): 434.

11. Ibid., 420.

12. See Michael Rogin, *Blackface, White Noise.*

13. Daniel Bernardi, "The Voice of Whiteness," in *The Birth of Whiteness: Race and the Emergence of U.S. Cinema,* edited by Bernardi (New Brunswick, N.J.: Rutgers University Press, 1996), 125.

14. Kenneth Munden, ed., *American Film Institute Catalog of Feature Films, 1921–1930* (New York: R. R. Bowker, 1971), 895.

15. *The White Rose* is available in the Library of Congress.

16. Munden, *American Film Institute Catalog of Feature Films, 1921–1930,* 351.

17. *Picturegoer* (February 1927), GPJC.

18. Virginia Wright Wexman comments on the number of "Snowball" characters in films in "The Family on the Land: Race and Nationhood in Silent Westerns," in Daniel Bernardi's *The Birth of Whiteness,* 134.

19. Quoted in Thomas Cripps, *Slow Fade to Black: The Negro in American Film, 1900–1942* (New York: Oxford University Press, 1977), 140.

20. *Variety,* 22 June 1927.

21. Cripps, *Slow Fade to Black,* 153, 160, 162.

22. Edward D. C. Campbell, Jr., *The Celluloid South: Hollywood and the Southern Myth* (Knoxville: University of Tennessee Press, 1981), 67.

23. Quoted in William Torbert Leonard, *Masquerade in Black* (London: Scarecrow Press, 1986), 187.

24. An interesting review of *Uncle Tom's Cabin* exists in the clipping file of the film in the George P. Johnson collection (GPJC). African-American reviewer Floyd J. Calvin stated, "All through the story of the Negro is shown to splendid advantage, if a slave can be shown to advantage. The audience, almost all-white, generally applauded each time a slave scored a point. White people were used to play the parts of Eliza and her slave husband, but they did not wear makeup and were obviously white. It must be quite humiliating to some whites to see their own color treated as the blackest slave. James B. Lowe, as Uncle Tom, is of course the greatest attraction. His acting is superb. His humility makes you want to give him a swift kick at times but when you reflect that he is portraying a former condition, you forget it. *Uncle Tom's Cabin* has many lessons to teach the thoughtful person. It is humiliating for the colored spectator, but when you think of the $500 a week James B. Lowe was getting for the acting, you feel better."

25. A partial list of Noble Johnson's silent films include: 1916—*Intolerance, Kincaid Gambler, Western Governor's Humanity, The Lion's Ward, The Lady from the Sea*; 1917—*The Indian's Lament, Behind the Lines, Love Aflame, Noah's Ark*; 1918—*Bad Man from Cheyenne, The Law of Nature, Red Ace*; 1920—*Kismet, Under Crimson Skies*; 1922—*Adventures of Robinson Crusoe*; 1923—*The Ten Commandments, The Phantom Fortune*; 1924—*The Thief of Baghdad*; 1925—*Adventure*; 1926—*Manon Lecault*; 1927—*Topsy and Eva*; 1928—*Black Ace*; 1929—*Four Feathers, West of Zanzibar, The Apache*. This list is obtained from the Noble Johnson file in the GPJC.

26. A Pathepicture feature titled *Black Shadows* asked potential moviegoers, "Where are the most beautiful women in the world? And where are the ugliest? You see these dusky beauties in *Black Shadows*, you also see the grotesque and strange belles of the Solomon islands, black as coal." *Black Shadows* file, GPJC.

27. See David Fury, *Kings of the Jungle: An Illustrated Reference to "Tarzan" on Screen and Television* (Jefferson, N.C.: McFarland and Co., 1994), 13–19.

28. A title reads that Jane is "the first woman he had ever known." Underlying this title is the presumption that the black women Tarzan had encountered were of some other species; they were not true women.

29. Jan Nederveen Pieterse, *White on Black: Images of Africa and Blacks in Western Popular Culture* (New Haven, Conn.: Yale University Press, 1982), 110.

30. Terry Eagleton, *Literary Theory: An Introduction* (London: B. Blackwell, 1993), 80.

31. *Moving Picture World* (3 February 1917).

32. *West of Zanzibar* is available in the Library of Congress.

33. Tod Browning, director of the film, claimed, "The Negro as a race has the gift of pantomime in the highest degree. They feel keenly and respond to direction quickly being about the most plastic material I have ever worked with." *Big City* file, GPJC.

34. Sander Gilman, *Differences and Pathology: Stereotypes of Sexuality, Race and Madness* (Ithaca: Cornell University Press, 1985), 85.

35. In an MGM press release for *West of Zanzibar*, director Tod Browning claimed, "I believe that this 200 [African-American men] represents perhaps the most uniform collection of splendid physical development I have ever seen in any group of men" (*West of Zanzibar* file, GPJC).

36. Edward Said, "Racism, Colonialism and Cinema," *Screen* 24, no. 2 (1984): 328.

37. For example, see the earlier work of Thomas Cripps, Peter Noble, and Donald Bogle.

38. Mark Reid, *Redefining Black Film* (Berkeley: University of California Press, 1993), 2.

39. Gladstone Yearwood, *Black Cinema Aesthetics: Issues in Independent Black Filmmaking* (Athens: Ohio University Press, 1982), 27.

40. A great deal of the research conducted on these black independent film companies was conducted in the GPJC.

41. Sampson, *Blacks in Black and White*, 207.

42. Ibid., 239–240.

43. Ibid., 260–261.

44. *Two Knights of Vaudeville* is found in the Library of Congress.

45. Tony Langston, "Ebony Film Cancelled," *Chicago Defender*, 12 May 1917, 4.

46. Ibid.

47. Ibid.

48. Sampson, *Blacks in Black and White*, 204–207.

49. Quote found in Pearl Bowser and Louise Spence's *Writing Himself into History: Oscar Micheaux, His Silent Films, and His Audiences* (New Brunswick, N.J.: Rutgers University Press, 2000), 239.

50. Sampson, *Blacks in Black and White*, 207.

51. *A Reckless Rover* is found in the Library of Congress.

52. *Spying the Spy* is found in the Library of Congress.

53. *The Comeback of Barnacle Bill* is found in the Library of Congress.

54. *Exhibitors Herald*, 22 December 1917.

55. *Moving Picture World*, 8 December 1917.

56. Ibid.

57. Langston, "Ebony Film Cancelled," *Chicago Defender*, 12 May 1917, 4.

58. *Chicago Defender*, 1 July 1916.

59. *New York Age*, 29 October 1921.

60. *Atlanta Independent*, 3 December 1915.

61. Ibid.

62. Ibid.

63. Ibid.

64. Robert Levy file, GPJC.

65. *Chicago Defender*, 15 January 1921.

66. Ibid.

67. One can argue whether Levy could be considered "white" considering the level of anti-Semitism in American society in the 1920s. What cannot be dismissed, though, is Jewish participation in African-American entertainment forms.

68. Reol Company Pressbook, Robert Levy file, GPJC.

69. Ibid.

70. *Chicago Defender*, 31 December 1921, 6.

71. Ibid.

72. *Chicago Defender*, 19 February 1921.

73. *California Eagle*, 30 July 1921.

74. *Chicago Defender*, 7 May 1921.

75. Ibid.

76. *Easy Money* file, GPJC.

77. An advertisement for *The Secret Sorrow* argued that it "portrayed with dignity

and power the achievement of the colored race in the highest professional fields—
law and medicine." *Secret Sorrow* file, GPJC.

78. *Baltimore Afro-American*, 2 May 1924.

79. *Chicago Defender*, 18 November 1921.

80. Sampson, *Blacks in Black and White*, 310.

81. *Billboard* (1 October 1921).

82. *Billboard* (19 May 1922).

83. See Gloria J. Gibson-Hudson, "The Norman Film Manufacturing Company," *Black Film Review* 17, no. 4 (1993): 16–20. *The Scar of Shame* web site, *http://pantheon.cis.yale.edu/~catseye/interact/mscarbk.html*.

84. Black Film Center/Archive, Richard E. Norman collection, *http://www.indiana.edu/~bfca/norman.html*.

85. Promotional Advertising, Norman Film Manufacturing Corporation, Richard E. Norman Collection, Black Film Center/Archive, Department of Afro-American Studies, Indiana University, Bloomington, Indiana.

86. Black Film Center/Archive, Richard E. Norman Collection, *http://www.indiana.edu/~bfca/norman.html*.

87. Promotional literature for *The Bulldogger*, Norman Film Corporation, GPJC.

88. Norman Film Corporation Pressbook, Black Film Center/Archive, Indiana University, Bloomington, Indiana.

89. Gloria J. Gibson-Hudson, "The Norman Film Manufacturing Company," *Black Film Review* 7, no. 4 (1993): 16–20.

90. Ibid.

91. *Cleveland Gazette*, 12 February 1923.

92. *Billboard* (29 October 1921).

93. *Regeneration* synopsis, Norman Film Corporation collection, Black Film Center/ Archive, Indiana University, Bloomington, Indiana.

94. *The Flying Ace* is available at the Library of Congress.

95. Norman Film Corporation Pressbook, Black Film Center/Archive, Indiana University, Bloomington, Indiana.

96. Promotional material, *Injustice* file, GPJC.

97. *Los Angeles Leader*, 5 August 1919.

98. Quoted in Sampson, *Blacks in Black and White*, 209–211.

99. Promotional material for *Reformation*, Sidney Preston Dones file, GPJC.

100. *The Scar of Shame* website, *http://pantheon.cis.yale.edu/~catseye/interact/ mscarbk.html*.

101. *Philadelphia Bulletin*, 17 November 1927.

102. Thomas Cripps, *Hollywood's High Noon: Moviemaking and Society Before Television* (Baltimore: Johns Hopkins University Press, 1997), 133–135.

103. Thomas Elsaesser, "Tales of Sound and Fury: Observations on the Family Melodrama," *Monogram* 4 (1973): 3.

104. Chenault worked for a number of companies that produced all-black features. His films include *The Crimson Skull, The Brute, Symbol of the Unconquered, The Gunsaulus Mystery, The Devil's Disciple, The Call of His People, The Secret Sorrow, The Burden of Race*, and *Sport of the Gods*.

105. *Ten Nights in a Bar Room* is available in the Museum of Modern Art collection in New York City.

106. Tony Langston, "Ten Nights in a Bar Room," *Chicago Defender*, 15 January 1927.

107. Tony Langston, "Ten Nights in a Bar Room," *Chicago Defender,* 20 May 1927.

108. Ibid.

109. For a good analysis of the film, see Thomas Cripps, "The Scar of Shame," in *Black Film As Genre* (Bloomington: Indiana University Press, 1978).

110. Jesse Rhines, *Black Film / White Money* (New Brunswick, N.J.: Rutgers University Press, 1996), 1.

111. Alan Williams, "Historical and Theoretical Issues in the Coming of Recorded Sound to the Cinema," in *Sound Theory, Sound Practice,* edited by Rick Altman (London: Routledge, 1992), 136.

112. Jane Gaines, *Fire and Desire: Mixed-Race Movies in the Silent Era* (Chicago: University of Chicago Press, 2001), 278.

113. A good discussion of the transition from silent to sound film is Scott Eyman's *The Speed of Sound: Hollywood and the Talkie Revolution, 1926–1930* (New York: Simon and Schuster, 1997).

114. Reid, *Redefining Black Film,* 16.

115. Pearl Bowser and Louise Spence point out that Micheaux released *Daughter of the Congo* in 1930 and it was billed as "talking, singing [and] dancing." The reality was that there was only one short sound scene (*Writing Himself into History,* 212).

116. C. Eidsvik, "Perception and Convention in Acting for Theatre and Film," *Postscript* 19, no. 2 (1989): 21.

117. Michael Chion, *Audiovision: Sound on Screen* (New York: Columbia University Press, 1994), 5.

118. Richard Dyer, *The Matter of Images: Essays on Representation* (London: Routledge, 1993b), 2.

119. Quoted in Harry Geduld, *The Birth of the Talkies* (Bloomington: Indiana University Press, 1975), 270.

120. "Black Laughter," *Picturegoer* (February 1927), GPJC.

121. See films like *Old Time Songs* (Vitaphone, 1928) or *Kentucky Jubilee Singers* (Fox-Movietone, 1929).

122. "Hallelujah: An Epic of the Negro," *Hallelujah* clipping file, Museum of Modern Art, New York City.

123. *Hearts in Dixie* is available at the Museum of Modern Art.

124. Advertisement for *Hearts in Dixie, Motion Picture Herald,* 29 April 1929, 3.

125. *Chicago Whip,* 28 May 1929.

126. "Hearts in Dixie Film of Song and Pathos," *Chicago Defender,* 6 July 1929.

127. Robert Benchley, "Hearts in Dixie: The Real Talking Picture," *Opportunity* 7, no. 4 (1929).

128. *New York Times,* 10 March 1929, sect. 10, 6.

129. Ibid.

130. "Manhattan Critic Reviews New All-Colored Film," Christie file, GPJC.

131. *Chicago Defender,* 6 July 1929.

132. Miles Kreuger, "Roots of the American Musical Film, 1927–1932," program notes, *Hallelujah* file, Museum of Modern Art.

133. James Warnack, unknown newspaper, *Hallelujah* file, GPJC.

134. Donald Bogle, *Toms, Coons, Mulattoes, Mammies and Bucks: An Interpretive History of Blacks in American Films* (New York: Continuum, 1989), 31.

135. Cripps, *Slow Fade to Black,* 247.

136. Bogle, *Toms, Coons, Bucks,* 31.

137. Quoted in Edwin Bradley, *The First Hollywood Musicals: A Critical Filmography of 171 Features* (Jefferson, N.C.: McFarland and Co., 1996), 247.

138. Michel Foucault, *History of Sexuality* (New York: Vintage Books, 1992), 97–102.

139. "Screen Negro Melodies," *New York Times*, 24 February 1929, sect. 9, 8.

CONCLUSION

1. Richard Dyer, *White* (London: Routledge, 1997), 1.

2. Ibid., 20.

3. Michel Foucault, *Power/Knowledge: Selected Interviews*, edited by Colin Gordon (Brighton, Sussex: Harvester Press, 1980), 131.

BIBLIOGRAPHY

Addams, Jane. *The Spirit of Youth and the City Streets*. New York: Macmillan, 1912.

Aitken, R. E. *The Birth of a Nation Story*. Middleburg, Va.: Denlinger, 1965.

Allen, Richard. *Projecting Illusion: Film Spectatorship and the Impression of Reality*. New York: Cambridge University Press, 1995.

Allen, Robert C. *Vaudeville and Film, 1896–1915: A Study in Media Interaction*. New York: Arno Press Dissertation Series, 1980.

Anderson, Lisa. "From Blackface to 'Genuine Negroes': Nineteenth Century Minstrelsy and the Icon of the 'Negro.'" *Theatre Research International* 21 (spring 1996): 17–23.

Armour, R. A. "History Written in Jagged Lightning: Realistic South vs. Romantic South in *The Birth of a Nation*." In *The South on Film*, edited by W. French. Jackson: University Press of Mississippi, 1981.

Ayers, Edward. *The Promise of the New South*. New York: Oxford University Press, 1992.

———. *Southern Crossing: A History of the American South, 1877–1906*. New York: Oxford University Press, 1995.

———. *Vengeance and Justice: Crime and Punishment in the 19th Century American South*. New York: Oxford University Press, 1984.

Bannister, Robert C. *Social Darwinism: Science and Myth in Anglo American Social Thought*. Philadelphia: Temple University Press, 1995.

Barbeau, Arthur E., and Florette Henri. *Unknown Soldiers: Black American Troops in World War I*. Philadelphia: Temple University Press, 1974.

Bederman, Gail. *Manliness and Civilization*. Chicago: University of Chicago Press, 1995.

Bennett, Lerone, Jr. "Jack Johnson and the Great White Hope." *Ebony* (April 1994).

Bernardi, Daniel. *The Birth of Whiteness: Race and the Emergence of U.S. Cinema*. New Brunswick, N.J.: Rutgers University Press, 1996.

Bernstein, Matthew. "Black American Cinema: Aesthetics and Spectatorship." *Film Quarterly* 48 (summer 1995).

Biskind, Peter. "The Colour of Money." *Sight and Sound* 1 (August 1991).

Bobo, Jacqueline. "The Subject Is Money: Reconsidering the Black Film Audience As a Theoretical Paradigm." *Black American Literature Forum* 25 (summer 1991).

Bogle, Donald. *Toms, Coons, Mulattoes, Mammies, and Bucks: An Interpretive History of Blacks in American Films*. New York: Continuum, 1989.

249

Boskin, Joseph. *Sambo: The Rise and Demise of an American Jester*. New York: Oxford University Press, 1986.

Bowser, Eileen. "Racial/Racist Jokes in American Silent Slapstick Comedy." *Griffithiana* 53 (May 1995).

———. *The Transformation of Cinema, 1907–1915*. New York: Charles Scribner's Sons, 1990.

Bowser, Pearl. "Oscar Micheaux's Body and Soul and the Burdens of Representation." *Cinema Journal* 39, no. 3 (spring 2000).

Bowser, Pearl, and Louise Spence. *Writing Himself into History: Oscar Micheaux, His Silent Films and His Audiences*. New Brunswick, N.J.: Rutgers University Press, 2000.

Brown, Karl. *Adventures with D. W. Griffith*. New York: Farrar, Strauss and Giroux, 1973.

Brundage, W. Fitzhugh. *Lynching in the New South*. Urbana: University of Illinois Press, 1993.

Butler, Judith. *Gender Trouble*. New York: Routledge, 1990.

Butters, Gerald R., Jr. The Kansas Board of Review of Motion Pictures and Film Censorship, 1913–1924. Master's thesis, University of Missouri–Kansas City, 1989.

Cameron, Kenneth M. *Africa on Film: Beyond Black and White*. New York: Continuum, 1994.

Campbell, Craig W. *Reel America and World War I*. Jefferson, N.C.: McFarland and Company, 1985.

Campbell, Edward D. C., Jr. *The Celluloid South: Hollywood and the Southern Myth*. Knoxville: University of Tennessee Press, 1981.

Capeci, Dominic J., Jr., and Jack C. Knight. "Reckoning with Violence: W. E. B. DuBois and the 1906 Atlanta Race Riot." *Journal of Southern History* 62, no. 4 (November 1996).

Cappello, Bill. "Noble Johnson—Part 1." *Classic Images* 199 (January 1992).

Carringer, Robert L., ed. *The Jazz Singer*. Madison: University of Wisconsin Press, 1979.

Cashman, Sean Dennis. *African Americans and the Quest for Civil Rights, 1900–1990*. New York: New York University Press, 1991.

Chion, Michel. *Audiovision: Sound on Screen*. New York: Columbia University Press, 1994.

Cook, Raymond Allen. *Fire from the Flint: The Amazing Careers of Thomas Dixon*. Winston-Salem, N.C.: John F. Blair Co., 1977.

———. *Thomas Dixon*. New York: Twayne Publishers, 1974.

Cripps, Thomas. "The Birth of a Race Company: An Early Stride toward a Black Cinema." *Journal of Negro History* 59, no. 1 (January 1974).

———. *Black Film As Genre*. Bloomington: Indiana University Press, 1978.

———. *Making Movies Black: The Hollywood Message Movie from World War II to the Civil Rights Era*. New York: Oxford University Press, 1993.

———. "The Reaction of the Negro to the Motion Picture *Birth of a Nation*." *Historian* (May 1983): 244–262.

———. *Slow Fade to Black: The Negro in American Film, 1900–1942*. New York: Oxford University Press, 1977.

Damon, James. "Shaping the Popular Image of Post-Reconstruction American Blacks: The 'Coon Song' Phenomenon of the Gilded Age." *American Quarterly* 40 (December 1988).

David, F. James. *Who Is Black? One Nation's Definition*. University Park: Pennsylvania State University Press, 1991.

Dawson, Marion L. "The South and the Negro." *North American Review* 172, no. 81 (1901).

DeBauche, Leslie Midkiff. *Reel Patriotism: The Movies and World War I*. Madison: University of Wisconsin Press, 1997.

De Grazia, Edward, and Roger K. Newman. *Banned Films: Movies, Censorship and the First Amendment*. New York: R. R. Bowker Co., 1982.

Dennison, Sam. *Scandalize My Name: Black Imagery in American Popular Music*. New York: Garland Publishing, 1982.

Diakite, Madubuko. *Film Culture and the Black Filmmaker*. New York: Arno Press, 1980.

Diawara, Manthia, ed. *Black American Cinema*. New York: Routledge, 1993.

———. "Black Spectatorship: Problems of Identification and Resistance." *Screen* 29, no. 1 (fall 1988).

———. "Black Studies, Cultural Studies: Performative Acts." In *What Is Cultural Studies: A Reader*, edited by John Storey. London: Arnold Press, 1996.

Dittmer, John. *Black Georgia in the Progressive Era, 1900–1920*. Urbana: University of Illinois Press, 1977.

Dorsey, Learthen. Introduction to *The Homesteader*, by Oscar Micheaux. Lincoln: University of Nebraska Press, 1994.

Downmunt, Tony, Maris Clark, Rooney Martin, and Kobena Mercer. *Being White*. 55 min., Albany Video, 1991, videocassette.

DuBois, W. E. B. "Editorial." *Crisis* 3, no. 3 (January 1913).

Dyer, Richard. "Entertainment and Utopia." In *The Cultural Studies Reader*, edited by Simon During. London: Routledge, 1993.

———. "Into the Light: The Whiteness of the South in *The Birth of a Nation*." In *Dixie Debates: Perspectives on Southern Cultures*, edited by Richard H. King and Helen Taylor. New York: New York University Press, 1996.

———. *The Matter of Images: Essays on Representation*. London: Routledge, 1993.

———. *White*. London: Routledge, 1997.

Eagleton, Terry. *Literary Theory: An Introduction*. London: B. Blackwell, 1993.

Eidsvik, C. "Perception and Convention in Acting for Theatre and Film." *Postscript* 19, no. 2 (1989).

Ellsworth, Scott. *Death in a Promised Land: The Tulsa Race Riot of 1921*. Baton Rouge: Louisiana State University Press, 1982.

Elsaesser, Thomas, ed. *Early Cinema: Space, Frame, Narrative*. London: British Film Institute, 1990.

———. "Tales of Sound and Fury: Observations on the Family Melodrama." *Monogram* 4 (1973).

Emery, Lynn Fauley. *Black Dance: From 1619 to Today*. Salem, N.H.: Ayer Company Publishers, 1988.

Eyman, Scott. *The Speed of Sound: Hollywood and the Talkie Revolution, 1926–1930*. New York: Simon and Schuster, 1997.

Farr, Finis. *The Life and Times of Jack Johnson*. New York: Charles Scribner's Sons, 1964.

Fell, John. *Film and the Narrative Tradition*. Norman: University of Oklahoma Press, 1974.

Fleener, Nickie. "Answering Film with Film: The Hampton Epilogue, a Positive Alternative to the Negative Black Stereotypes Presented in 'The Birth of a Nation.'" *Journal of Popular Film and Television* 7 (1980).

Foucault, Michel. *History of Sexuality.* New York: Vintage Books, 1988.

———. *Language, Counter Memory, Practice: Selected Essays and Interviews.* Ithaca: Cornell University Press, 1977.

———. *Power/Knowledge: Selected Interviews.* Translated by Colin Gordon. Brighton, Sussex: Harvester Press, 1980.

Franklin, John Hope. "*The Birth of a Nation:* Propaganda As History." *Massachusetts Review* (July 1977).

———. *From Slavery to Freedom.* New York: Alfred A. Knopf, 1994.

Frazier, Thomas, ed. *Afro-American History: Primary Sources.* New York: Harcourt Brace, 1970.

Frederickson, George M. *The Black Image in the White Mind.* New York: Harper and Row, 1971.

Friedman, Lester D. *Unspeakable Images: Ethnicity and the American Cinema.* Urbana: University of Illinois Press, 1991.

Fury, David. *Kings of the Jungle: An Illustrated Reference to "Tarzan" on Screen and Television.* Jefferson, N.C.: McFarland and Co., 1994.

Gaines, Jane M. "*The Birth of a Nation* and *Within Our Gates:* Two Tales of the American South." In *Dixie Debates: Perspectives on Southern Cultures,* edited by Richard H. King and Helen Taylor. New York: New York University Press, 1996.

———. *Fire and Desire: Mixed-Race Movies in the Silent Era.* Chicago: University of Chicago Press, 2001.

———. "Race, Melodrama and Oscar Micheaux." In *Black American Cinema,* edited by Manthia Diawara. New York: Routledge, 1993.

Gaines, Kevin. *Uplifting the Race: Black Leadership, Politics, and Culture in the Twentieth Century.* Chapel Hill: University of North Carolina Press, 1996.

Gallagher, B. "Racist Ideology and Black Abnormality in *The Birth of a Nation.*" *Phylon* 43 (March 1982).

Garber, Marjorie. *Vested Interests: Cross-Dressing and Cultural Anxiety.* New York: Routledge, 1992.

Geduld, Harry. *The Birth of the Talkies.* Bloomington: Indiana University Press, 1975.

Gehr, Richard. "One-Man Show." *American Film* (May 1991).

Gibson-Hudson, Gloria J. "The Norman Film Manufacturing Company." *Black Film Review* 17, no. 4 (1993).

Gilman, Sander. *Differences and Pathology: Stereotypes of Sexuality, Race and Madness.* Ithaca, N.Y.: Cornell University Press, 1985.

Gilmore, Al-Tony. *Bad Nigger! The National Impact of Jack Johnson.* Port Washington, N.Y.: Kennikut Press, 1975.

Gomery, Douglas. *Shared Pleasures: A History of Movie Presentation in the United States.* Madison: University of Wisconsin Press, 1992.

Gordon, Henry Stephen. "The Story of David Wark Griffith, Part Five." *Photoplay* 10 (October 1916).

Gossett, Thomas F. *Race: The History of an Idea in America.* Dallas: Southern Methodist University Press, 1963.

———. *Uncle Tom's Cabin and American Culture.* Dallas: Southern Methodist University Press, 1985.

Grant, Madison. *Conquest of a Continent.* New York: Charles Scribner's Sons, 1934.

———. *The Passing of the Great Race.* New York: Charles Scribner's Sons, 1918.

Graves, John William. "Jim Crow in Arkansas: A Reconsideration of Urban Race Relations in the Post-Reconstruction South." *Journal of Southern History* 55, no. 3 (August 1989).

Green, J. Ronald. "Micheaux v. Griffith." *Griffithiana* 60–61 (October 1997).

——. *Straight Lick: The Cinema of Oscar Micheaux.* Bloomington: Indiana University Press, 2000.

——. "Twoness in the Style of Oscar Micheaux." In *Black American Cinema,* edited by Manthia Diawara. New York: Routledge, 1993.

Green, J. Ronald, and Horace Neal, Jr. "Oscar Micheaux and Racial Slur: A Response to 'The Rediscovery of Oscar Micheaux.'" *Journal of Film and Video* 40, no. 4 (fall 1990).

Greenblum, Joseph. "Does Hollywood Still Glorify Jewish Intermarriage? The Case of the Jazz Singer." *American Jewish History* 83 (December 1995).

Grossman, James R. *Land of Hope: Chicago, Black Southerners and the Great Migration.* Chicago: University of Chicago Press, 1989.

Grupenhoff, Richard. *Black Valentino: The Stage and Screen Career of Lorenzo Tucker.* Metuchen, N.J.: Scarecrow Press, 1988.

Gunning, Tom. *D. W. Griffith and the Origins of American Narrative Film: The Early Years at Biograph.* Urbana: University of Illinois Press, 1991.

Hale, Grace Elizabeth. *Making Whiteness: The Culture of Segregation in the South, 1890–1940.* New York: Pantheon Books, 1998.

Hall, Stuart. "Encoding, Decoding." In *Cultural Studies Reader,* edited by Simon During. London: Routledge, 1993.

Hansen, Miriam. *Babel and Babylon: Spectatorship in American Silent Film.* Cambridge, Mass.: Harvard University Press, 1991.

Hanson, Patricia King. *American Film Institute Feature Films, 1911–1920.* Berkeley: University of California Press, 1988.

Harlan, Louis R. *Booker T. Washington: The Wizard of Tuskegee, 1901–1915.* New York: Oxford University Press, 1983.

Harris, J. William. "Etiquette, Lynching, and Racial Boundaries in Southern History: A Mississippi Example." *American Historical Review* 100 (April 1995).

Haverly, Jack. *Negro Minstrels: A Complete Guide.* Upper Saddle, N.J.: New Jersey Literature House, 1969.

Haynes, Robert V. *A Night of Violence: The Houston Riot of 1917.* Baton Rouge: Louisiana State University Press, 1976.

Hazzard-Gordon, Katrina. *Jookin': The Rise of Social Dance Formations in African American Culture.* Philadelphia: Temple University Press, 1990.

Henri, Florette. *Black Migration: Movement North, 1900–1920.* Garden City, N.Y.: Anchor Books, 1976.

——. *Unknown Soldiers: Black American Troops in World War I.* Philadelphia: Temple University Press, 1974.

Hill, Geoffrey. *Illuminating Shadows: The Illuminating Power of Films.* New York: Shambhala, 1992.

Hoberman, John. *Darwin's Athletes: How Sport Has Damaged Black America and Preserved the Myth of Race.* Boston: Houghton Mifflin Co., 1997.

hooks, bell. *Art on My Mind: Visual Politics.* New York: Free Press, 1995.

——. "Micheaux: Celebrating Blackness." *Black American Literature Forum* 2 (summer 1991).

——. "The Oppositional Gaze: Black Female Spectators." In *Black American Cinema,* edited by Manthia Diawara. New York: Routledge, 1993.

Hoskins, James. *Black Dance in America: A History through Its People.* New York: Crowell, 1990.

Hughes, Langston. *Black Magic: A Pictorial History of the Negro in American Entertainment.* Englewood Cliffs, N.J.: Prentice-Hall, 1967.

Ingalls, Robert P. "Lynching and Establishment Violence in Tampa, 1858–1935." *Journal of Southern History* 53, no. 4 (November 1987).

Johnson, Albert. "Beige, Brown or Black." *Film Quarterly* 13 (fall 1959).

Jones, Jacqueline. *Labor of Love, Labor of Sorrow*. New York: Basic Books, 1985.

Jones, Jacquie. "The Construction of Black Sexuality." In *Black American Cinema,* edited by Manthia Diawara. London: Routledge, 1993.

Jones, Juli, Jr. "Moving Pictures Offers the Greatest Opportunity to the American Negro in History of Race from Every Point of View." *Chicago Defender* 9 (September 1915).

Jones, William G. *Black Cinema: Treasures Lost and Found*. Denton: University of North Texas Press, 1991.

Jordan, Winthrop. *White over Black*. Chapel Hill: University of North Carolina Press,1968.

Kaplan, E. Ann. *Looking for the Other: Feminism, Film, and the Imperial Gaze*. New York: Routledge, 1997.

Kellner, Douglas. "Television, Ideology, and Emancipatory Popular Culture." In *Television: The Critical View,* edited by Horace Newcomb. New York: Oxford University Press, 1987.

Kellogg, Charles Flint. *N.A.A.C.P.: A History of the National Association for the Advancement of Colored People*. Vol. 1, *1909–1920*. Baltimore: Johns Hopkins University Press, 1967.

King, Patricia Hanson, ed. *American Film Institute Feature Films, 1911–1920*. Berkeley: University of California Press, 1988.

Koszarski, Richard. *An Evening's Entertainment: The Age of the Silent Talking Picture, 1915–1928*. New York: Charles Scribner's Sons, 1990.

Kreuger, Miles. *Roots of the American Musical Film, 1927–1932*. Program notes, *Hallelujah* file, Museum of Modern Art, New York.

Landay, Eileen. *Black Film Stars*. New York: Drake Publishers, 1973.

Leab, Daniel J. "A Pale Black Imitation: All-Colored Films, 1930–1960." *Journal of Popular Film* 4, no. 1 (1975).

Leonard, William Torbert. *Masquerade in Black*. London: Scarecrow Press, 1986.

Levine, Lawrence. *Black Culture and Black Consciousness*. Oxford: Oxford University Press, 1977.

Levy, Leonard W., and Douglas L. Jones. *Jim Crow in Boston: The Origins of the Separate but Equal Doctrine*. New York: Da Capo Press, 1974.

Lewis, David Levering. *W. E. B. DuBois: Biography of a Race, 1869–1918*. New York: Hold, 1993.

———. *When Harlem Was in Vogue*. New York: Vintage Books, 1982.

Little, Arthur W. *From Harlem to the Rhine: The Story of Negro Soldiers*. New York: Covici, 1936.

Lofgren, Charles A. *The Plessy Case: A Legal-Historical Interpretation*. New York: Oxford University Press, 1987.

Lott, Eric. *Love and Theft: Blackface Minstrelsy and the American Working Class*. Oxford: Oxford University Press, 1993.

———. "The Seeming Counterfeit: Racial Politics and Early Blackface Minstrelsy." *American Quarterly* 42, no. 2 (June 1991).

Lynn, Kenneth S. "The Torment of D. W. Griffith." *American Scholar* 59, no. 2 (spring 1990).

Mahar, William J. "Black English in Early Blackface Minstrelsy: A New Interpretation of the Sources of Minstrel Show Dialect." *American Quarterly* 37 (summer 1985).

Malone, Jacqui. *Steppin' on the Blues: The Visible Rhythms of African American Dance*. Urbana: University of Illinois Press, 1996.

Martin, Jeffrey. "Film Out of Theater: D. W. Griffith, *Birth of a Nation* and the Melodrama *The Clansman*." *Literature/Film Quarterly* 18, no. 2 (1990).

Mast, Gerald. *A Short History of the Movies*. New York: Macmillan, 1986.

Mayne, Judith. *Cinema and Spectatorship*. London: Routledge, 1993.

McCrane, Bernard. *Beyond Anthropology: Society and the Other*. New York: Columbia University Press, 1989.

McMillen, Neil. *Dark Journey: Black Mississippians in the Age of Jim Crow*. Urbana: University of Illinois Press, 1989.

Meier, August. *Negro Thought in America, 1880–1915: Racial Ideologies in the Age of Booker T. Washington*. Ann Arbor: University of Michigan Press, 1969.

Mellen, Joan. *Big Bad Wolves: Masculinity in American Film*. New York: Pantheon Books, 1977.

Merelman, Richard. *Representing Black Culture*. New York: Routledge, 1995.

Merritt, Russell. "D. W. Griffith's *The Birth of a Nation*: Going after Little Sister." In *Close Viewings: An Anthology of New Film Criticism*, edited by Peter Lehman. Tallahassee: Florida State University Press, 1990.

Micheaux, Oscar. *The Conquest: The Story of a Pioneer*. Lincoln, Nebr.: Woodruff Press, 1913.

———. *The Homesteader*. College Park, Md.: McGrath Publishing, 1969.

———. *The Wind from Nowhere*. New York: Book Supply Company, 1944.

Mulvey, Laura. "Visual Pleasures and Narrative Cinema." *Screen* 16, no. 3 (autumn 1975).

Munden, Kenneth, ed. *American Film Institute Catalog of Feature Films, 1921–1930*. New York: R. R. Bowker, 1971.

Murray, James. *To Find an Image: Black Films from Uncle Tom to Super Fly*. Indianapolis: Bobbs-Merrill Co., 1973.

Musser, Charles. *Before the Nickelodeon: Edwin S. Porter and the Edison Manufacturing Company*. Berkeley: University of California Press, 1991.

———. *The Emergence of Cinema: The American Screen to 1907*. New York: Charles Scribner's Sons, 1990.

———. "Redream the Dreams of White Playwrights: Reappropriation and Resistance in Oscar Micheaux's *Body and Soul*." *Yale Journal of Criticism* 12, no. 2 (1999).

Nathan, Hans. *Dan Emmett and the Rise of Early Negro Minstrelsy*. Norman: University of Oklahoma Press, 1962.

Neale, Steve, and Frank Krutnik. *Popular Film and Television Comedy*. London: Routledge, 1990.

Nesteby, James. *Black Image in American Films, 1896–1954: The Interplay between Civil Rights and Film Culture*. Washington, D.C.: University Press of America, 1982.

Nichols, Bill. *Ideology and the Image: Social Representation in the Cinema and Other Media*. Bloomington: Indiana University Press, 1981.

———. "Sons on the Brink of Manhood." *East-West Film Journal* 4 (1989).

Noble, Peter. *The Negro in Films*. New York: Arno Press, 1948.

Null, Gary. *Black Hollywood: The Negro in Motion Pictures*. Secaucus, N.J.: Citadel Press, 1977.

Parks, Rita. *The Western Hero in Film and Television: Mass Media Mythology*. Ann Arbor, Mich.: UMI Research Press, 1982.

Peterson, Bernard L., Jr. "The Films of Oscar Micheaux: America's First Fabulous Black Filmmaker." *Crisis* 86 (April 1979).

Pieterse, Jan Nederveen. *White on Black: Images of Africa and Blacks in Western Popular Culture*. New Haven, Conn.: Yale University Press, 1992.

Pines, Jim. *Blacks in Films: A Survey of Racial Themes and Images in the American Film*. London: Studio Vista, 1975.

Prather, H. Leon. *We Have Taken a City: Wilmington Racial Massacre and Coup of 1898*. Rutherford, N.J.: Fairleigh Dickinson University Press, 1984.

Ray, Robert. *A Certain Tendency of the Studio System, 1930–1980*. Princeton, N.J.: Princeton University Press, 1985.

Regester, Charlene. "Black Films, White Censors: Oscar Micheaux Confronts Censorship in New York, Virginia and Chicago." In *Movies, Censorship and American Culture*, edited by Francis G. Couvares. Washington, D.C.: Smithsonian Institution Press, 1996.

———. "Lynched, Assaulted, Intimidated: Oscar Micheaux's Most Controversial Films." *Popular Culture Review* 5, no. 1 (February 1994).

———. "The Misreading and Rereading of African American Filmmaker Oscar Micheaux." *Film History* 7, no. 4 (winter 1995).

Reid, Mark A. "Early Black Independent Filmmakers." *Black Film Review* 12, no. 4 (1988).

———. *Redefining Black Film*. Berkeley: University of California Press, 1993.

Rhines, Jesse Algernon. *Black Film/White Money*. New Brunswick, N.J.: Rutgers University Press, 1996.

Roberts, Randy. *Papa Jack: Jack Johnson and the Era of White Hopes*. New York: Free Press, 1983.

Rocchio, Vincent F. *Reel Racism: Confronting Hollywood's Construction of Afro-American Culture*. Boulder, Colo.: Westview Press, 2000.

Roediger, David. *The Wages of Whiteness*. London: Verso, 1991.

Rogin, Michael. *Blackface, White Noise: Jewish Immigrants in the Melting Pot*. Berkeley: University of California Press, 1996.

———. "Blackface, White Noise: The Jewish Jazz Singer Finds His Voice." *Critical Inquiry* 18 (spring 1992).

———. "Racial Masquerade in Motion Pictures." *Journal of American History* (December 1992).

———. "The Sword Became a Flashing Vision: D. W. Griffith's *The Birth of a Nation*." *Representations* (winter 1985).

Rosenbaum, Nancy. *Jury Justice: A Look at the Scottsboro Case and the Leo Frank Trial*. Waltham, Mass.: Waltham Press, 1995.

Said, Edward. "Racism, Colonialism and Cinema." *Screen* 24, no. 2 (1984).

Sampson, Henry T. *Blacks in Black and White: A Source Book on Black Film*. New York: Scarecrow Press, 1995.

———. *Blacks in Blackface: A Source Book on Early Black Minstrel Shows*. Metuchen, N.J.: Scarecrow Press, 1980.

Saposnik, Irv. "Jolson, the Jazz Singer and the Jewish Mother." *Judaism* 43 (fall 1994).

Savada, Eric, ed. *American Film Institute Catalog: Film Beginnings, 1893– 1910*. Metuchen, N.J.: Scarecrow Press, 1995.

Schickel, Richard. *D. W. Griffith*. New York: Simon and Schuster, 1984.

Schmidt, Benno C., Jr. "Principle and Prejudice: The Supreme Court and Race in the Progressive Era: Part 1: The Heydey of Jim Crow." *Columbia Law Review* 82 (1982).

Schneider, Mark. *Boston Confronts Jim Crow, 1890–1920*. Boston: Northeastern University Press, 1997.

Semonche, John E. *Charting the Future: The Supreme Court Responds to a Changing Society, 1890–1920*. Westport, Conn.: Greenwood Press, 1978.

Senechal, Roberta. *The Sociogenesis of a Race Riot: Springfield, Illinois, in 1908.* Urbana: University of Illinois Press, 1990.

Shapiro, Herbert. *White Violence and Black Response: From Reconstruction to Montgomery.* Amherst: University of Massachusetts Press, 1988.

Silk, Catherine, and John Silk. "*Birth of a Nation* and Silent Film." In *Racism and Antiracism in American Popular Culture.* Manchester, N.Y.: Manchester University Press, 1990.

Sklar, Robert. *Film: An International History of the Medium.* New York: Harry N. Abrams, 1993.

Slide, Anthony. *Early American Cinema.* Metuchen, N.J.: Scarecrow Press, 1994.

Smith, William Benjamen. *The Color Line.* New York: McClure, Philip and Co., 1905.

Spears, Jack. *The Civil War on the Screen and Other Essays.* New York: A. S. Barnes and Co., 1977.

Staiger, Janet. "*The Birth of a Nation:* Reconsidering Its Reception." In *The Birth of a Nation,* edited by Robert Land. New Brunswick, N.J.: Rutgers University Press, 1994.

———. *Interpreting Films: Studies in the Historical Reception of American Cinema.* Princeton, N.J.: Princeton University Press, 1992.

Streible, Dan. "Race and the Reception of Jack Johnson Fight Films." In *The Birth of Whiteness: Race and the Emergence of U.S. Cinema,* edited by Daniel Bernardi. New Brunswick, N.J.: Rutgers University Press, 1996.

Taylor, Clyde. "The Re-Birth of the Aesthetic in Cinema." In *The Birth of Whiteness: Race and the Emergence of U.S. Cinema,* edited by Daniel Bernardi. New Brunswick, N.J.: Rutgers University Press, 1996.

Thorpe, Edward. *Black Dance.* New York: Woodstock, 1990.

Thweatt, Hiram H. *What the Newspapers Say of the Negro Soldier in the Spanish American War.* Sanford, N.C.: Microfilming Corporation of America, 1983.

Toll, Robert. *Blacking Up: The Minstrel in Nineteenth Century America.* New York: Oxford University Press, 1974.

Townsend, Charles. *Negro Minstrels.* Upper Saddle, N.J.: New Jersey Literature House, 1969.

Trotter, Joe William, ed. *The Great Migration in Historical Perspective.* Bloomington: Indiana University Press, 1991.

Trotter, Joe N., and Earl Lewis, eds. *African Americans in the Industrial Age: A Documentary History, 1915–1945.* Boston: Northeastern University Press, 1996.

Turner, Graeme. *Film As Social Practice.* London: Routledge, 1988.

Tuttle, William. *Race Riot: Chicago in the Red Summer of 1919.* New York: Antheum Press, 1970.

Tyler, Parker. *Magic and the Myth of the Movies.* New York: Simon and Schuster, 1970.

Weiss, Nancy. *The National Urban League, 1910–1940.* New York: Oxford University Press, 1974.

Wells-Barnett, Ida. *On Lynchings: Southern Horrors.* New York: Arno Press, 1969.

Williams, Alan. "Historical and Theoretical Issues in the Coming of Recorded Sound to the Cinema." In *Sound Theory, Sound Practice,* edited by Rick Altman. London: Routledge, 1992.

Williams, Lee E. *Anatomy of Four Race Riots: Racial Conflict in Knoxville, Elaine, Tulsa, and Chicago, 1919–1921.* Hattiesburg: University and College Press of Mississippi, 1972.

Williamson, Joel. *The Crucible of Race: Black-White Relations in the American South since Emancipation.* New York: Oxford University Press, 1984.
———. *The Origins of Segregation.* Boston: D. C. Heath, 1968.
Woodward, C. Vann. *The Strange Career of Jim Crow.* New York: Oxford University Press, 1966.
———. *Tom Watson: Agrarian Rebel.* New York: Oxford University Press, 1963.
Wynn, Neil A. *The Afro-American and the Second World War.* New York: Holmes and Meier Publishers, 1975.
Yearwood, Gladstone. *Black Cinema Aesthetics: Issues in Independent Black Film-making.* Athens: Ohio University Press, 1982.
Young, Joseph. *Black Novelist as White Racist.* New York: Greenwood Press, 1989.

SPECIAL COLLECTIONS

The Birth of a Nation File, Hampton Archives.
George P. Johnson Collection, Special Collections, University of California, Los Angeles.
John E. Bruce Collection, Schomburg Collection, New York Public Library.
NAACP Records, Library of Congress.

INDEX

FILMOGRAPHY